CANADA'S
favourite recipes

CANADA'S
favourite recipes

ROSE MURRAY & ELIZABETH BAIRD

whitecap

Whitecap Books is known for its expertise in the cookbook market, and has produced some of the most innovative and familiar titles found in kitchens across North America. Visit our website at www.whitecap.ca.

PUBLISHER: Michael Burch
EDITOR: Theresa Best
DESIGNER: Mauve Pagé (mauvepage.com)
FOOD PHOTOGRAPHY AND STYLING: Tracey Kusiewicz
PHOTO ASSISTANT: Mark Gardiner
AUTHORS' PHOTOGRAPH ON BACK COVER: Stan Switalski
ADDITIONAL PHOTOGRAPHY: Michelle Furbacher (pages 8–9; page 42, bottom; page 87, top; page 103, bottom; page 149, bottom); ©Habman_18/Veer (page 13); Chris Cheadle (page 24); ©iStockphoto.com/Dougall_Photography (page 42, top); ©iStockphoto.com/sprokop (page 43); ©iStockphoto.com/ImagineGolf (page 51; pages 54–55; page 309, top); ©iStockphoto.com/Murphy_Shewchuk (page 69); Barrett & MacKay (pages 90–91); ©iStockphoto.com/laughingmango (page 102); ©stevemc/Veer (page 103, top); ©iStockphoto.com/GMVozd (page 104); ©hoch2wo/Veer (page 107); ©iStockphoto.com/liquidfog (page 126); ©onepony/Veer (pages 134–135; page 137, bottom; page 168); ©Natalia Bratslavsky/Veer (page 137, top); ©tarasov/Veer (page 148); ©iStockphoto.com/wwing (page 149, top); ©iStockphoto.com/mysticenergy (pages 196–197); ©iStockphoto.com/kongxinzhu (pages 214–215); ©iStockphoto.com/Phil Augustavo (pages 234–235); ©iStockphoto.com/digi_guru (page 247); ©iStockphoto.com/dmathies (pages 282–283); ©iStockphoto.com/JoeBiafore (page 296); ©iStockphoto.com/kichkine (page 308); ©iStockphoto.com/drmarkg (page 309, bottom)

PRINTED IN CHINA

Library and Archives Canada Cataloguing in Publication

Murray, Rose, 1941–

Canada's favourite recipes / Rose Murray, Elizabeth Baird.

Includes index.

ISBN 978-1-77050-098-3

1. Cooking, Canadian. 2. Cookbooks. I. Baird, Elizabeth, 1939– II. Title.

TX715.6.M855 2012   641.5971   C2011-908313-2

The publisher acknowledges the financial support of the Government of Canada through the Canada Book Fund (CBF) and the Province of British Columbia through the Book Publishing Tax Credit.

12 13 14 15 16   5 4 3 2 1

The following recipes have appeared in other publications and are used with permission: "All the Best" Macaroni and Cheese (from *All the Best Recipes*, Jane Rodmell, Robert Rose Inc., 2009); Edna Staebler's "Schnippled Bean Salad" (from *Food That Really Schmecks*, Edna Staebler Estate, Wilfrid Laurier University Press, 2007); Maple Walnut Fudge (from *Canadian Living Cooks*, Elizabeth Baird, Daphna Rabinovitch and Emily Richards, Random House Canada, 2003); Old-Fashioned Pea Soup with Smoked Ham (from *500 Best Comfort Food Recipes*, Johanna Burkhard, Robert Rose Inc., 2010); Pad Thai (from *Complete Book of Thai Cooking*, Linda Stephen, Robert Rose Inc., 2007); Salmon Cream Cheese Spread (from *Tin Fish Gourmet*, Barbara-Jo McIntosh, West Winds Press, 1998).

For cooks across Canada who keep
the flame of home-cooking alive
and welcome family and friends
to share their best-loved dishes.
Cooks like our mothers,
Josephine Varty and Olive Davis.

Contents

Introduction

WHAT'S YOUR FAVOURITE RECIPE? That's the question we asked food-passionate friends and colleagues of all ages across the country. Sometimes we posed it by email, phone or letter, sometimes over a cup of tea or a glass of wine or often after sharing a meal. Enjoying food together just naturally brings out how we value good food and its preparation. We wanted to put together a book of not only tried-and-true recipes others love and wish to keep and share, but recipes that readers would seek out as typical, good, simple Canadian fare they could easily cook in their own kitchens. We wanted to hear echoes of "I haven't had that lasagna in ages; my mother used to make one just like it." And yes, most of the recipes came with childhood or lifetime memories or attachments to significant occasions or people.

We have included the wonderful stories (of varying lengths—memories are hard to measure) that came with the recipes. We kept reading and rereading the stories, enjoying the way food memories opened doors to other lives, other places, other times. We think you will enjoy reading about these recipes as much as we have—they're recipes that are favourites because they are best loved.

The recipe ideas were plentiful, and we know you will find pleasure in cooking any of the dishes. You will note that the recipes are all things you can make in your own kitchen. We have not included any for those popular dishes you usually order in restaurants. It was interesting that even our chef friends gave us recipes they remembered from home—perhaps from a father, an aunt, a grandmother or a mother-in-law— rather than recipes for the fancy (and impressive!) things they create in their restaurant kitchens and that we indulge in when dining out. We believe that food lovingly prepared at home is the ultimate in cooking.

And if any of you doubted that Canadians have a collective sweet tooth, doubt no longer. We do—cookies, candies, pudding, cakes and pies topped the number of recipes when we began collecting. Fortunately for us, and our waistlines, we were able to balance the selection of sweet things with great soups, succulent roasts and seasonal vegetables. And we've included recipes for those among us who yearn for a jar of preserves, whether that jar contains sweet and sour pickles or a strictly luscious toast topper.

It took us years to seek out Canada's favourite recipes, but it was fun to connect with people who shared our passion for this country's amazing food resources, including the indigenous ingredients we love so much, as well as those signature dishes that immigrant kitchens have contributed over the decades to the country's palate. In *Canada's Favourite Recipes*, you will discover not only such predictable ingredients as maple syrup, corn and the intriguing fiddlehead introduced to us by the First Nations, but also dishes such as pad Thai, chicken souvlaki and potstickers, introduced here over the years and adopted lovingly as our own.

After collecting and selecting the recipes, it was a delight to cook all the dishes ourselves, to savour the results and realize why these dishes are so beloved and prominent on many of our tables. We hope the vignettes and recipes will inspire you to start asking your parents and grandparents for family dishes and their history, but most of all, make you want to head to the kitchen to cook these absolutely delicious best-loved recipes. May they be your favourites too.

Appetizers

Grilled Cheese Sandwiches

Makes 2 servings

. . . .

YOU KNOW THAT a dish has reached its zenith when big-time chefs start serving it as cocktail-party finger food. The lowly grilled cheese sandwich is definitely there, albeit with its crusts trimmed, neatly quartered and with ingredients like lobster and truffles slid between the slices. Popular as the lobster version may be, it needs to be taken, not down, but to a more affordable and yet still-enticing and satisfying level. In line with this new temperance is this recipe, for two people—multiply amounts if there are others who crave a nice, crusty, oozy, nippy (or mild) grilled cheese sandwich. Serve with things tangy like Must-Make Tomato Salsa (page 311), Fruit Chili Sauce (page 306), ketchup or pickles.

. . . .

4 slices whole-grain, country white or rye bread

2 tsp (10 mL) Dijon or honey mustard

2 to 4 oz (60 to 125 g) old Cheddar cheese, Gouda or Gruyère, thinly sliced

2 tsp (10 mL) butter, softened and divided

SET OUT THE bread on a cutting board. Spread mustard over 2 of the slices. Cover the mustard with the cheese, opting for the higher amount if you're aiming for a full grilled cheese experience, and cover each with the other slice of bread. Press lightly; butter the top of each sandwich with half of the butter.

Place the sandwich buttered-side down in a griddle or skillet heated over medium heat. Butter what's now the top of the sandwich with the remaining butter. An offset spatula (a tool with a rounded, blunt metal blade angled from the handle) is handy.

Cook, turning once, until the bread is crusty brown, top and bottom, and the cheese is oozing seductively out the sides, about 6 minutes.

VARIATION: Fillings, Spreads, Breads

The variations to grilled cheese sandwiches are limitless. Try the following, cooking the sandwiches as described in the main recipe.

› Skip the mustard and layer the cheese with thinly sliced Crunchy Bread-and-Butter Pickles (page 315), dill pickles, apple chutney or pesto, basil on its own or basil and sundried tomato.

› Change the cheeses suggested to your personal favourites, to mild cheeses such as havarti or Muenster cheese or to firm cheeses such as aged goat cheese or sheep cheese. For an explosion of flavour, there are smoked or flavoured cheeses such as jalapeño cheese or Colby cheese.

› Go mild and unctuous with sliced Brie and a generous spoonful of cranberry sauce instead of the mustard.

› Layer rye bread with cream cheese, smoked salmon, thinly sliced red onion and capers.

› Lean to the Italian—use mozzarella cheese or provolone with slices of prosciutto or salami, and strips of roasted peppers between slices of thick focaccia. Layer in fresh basil leaves, or a sprinkle of dried basil or oregano.

› Use other breads such as sourdough, challah (egg bread), pumpernickel or country-style or whole-grain breads.

› Make a filling to complement the cheese, such as a layer of Caramelized Onions or Sautéed Mushrooms (recipes follow). Make the cheese a thick slice of Gruyère or fontina.

CARAMELIZED ONIONS:
Makes enough for 4 sandwiches

In a skillet, melt 2 tbsp (30 mL) butter over medium heat. Add 2 thinly sliced onions, a speck of sugar and salt and a sprinkle of thyme. Fry, stirring, as the onions soften, reduce in volume and become golden, about 30 minutes. Keep the cooked onions in the refrigerator in an airtight container for up to 1 week to have on hand when you need something special to add to a grilled cheese.

SAUTÉED MUSHROOMS:
Makes enough for 4 sandwiches

In a skillet, melt 2 tbsp (30 mL) butter over medium heat. Add 1 onion, diced, 1 clove garlic, minced, and 3 cups (750 mL) sliced mushrooms (8 oz/250 g), a generous pinch of salt, pepper and dried thyme. Fry, stirring, as the mushrooms soften, reduce in volume and develop a deep woodsy aroma, about 20 minutes.

Sherry Potted Cheese

Makes about 2 cups (500 mL)

....

ROSE: Potted cheese is a traditional English cheese spread. It should be prepared at least a week in advance so that the flavours will meld. Potted cheese can in fact be kept for weeks in the refrigerator, but allow it to come to room temperature before serving, for better spreading and taste. Serve it with crackers that have no strong flavours in themselves—melba toast, for example—or a thinly sliced fresh baguette. I included a version of potted cheese in my very first book (*The Christmas Cookbook*, 1979) and have demonstrated it at many talks to enthusiastic response.

....

8 oz (250 g) old Cheddar cheese

4 oz (125 g) cream cheese, cubed

¼ cup (60 mL) freshly grated
   Parmesan cheese

1 tsp (5 mL) dry mustard

½ tsp (2 mL) freshly ground black pepper

¼ tsp (1 mL) ground mace
   or a pinch of nutmeg

¼ cup (60 mL) dry sherry

½ tsp (2 mL) hot pepper sauce
   (or to taste since these vary in strength)

USING A FOOD processor fitted with the shredding blade, shred the Cheddar cheese. Replace the shredding blade with the metal blade. Add the cream cheese and process until well combined. (If you do not have a food processor, shred the Cheddar cheese by hand and use a wooden spoon to mix.) Add the Parmesan cheese and the mustard, pepper and mace; process until well mixed. Add the sherry and pepper sauce; process until the mixture is smooth and creamy. Taste and adjust the seasoning if necessary.

   Pack into a little crock or bowl, cover and refrigerate for at least a week before using.

Salmon Cream Cheese Spread

Makes about 2 cups (500 mL)

BARBARA-JO MCINTOSH, of Barbara-Jo's Books to Cooks in Vancouver: This is my variation of a recipe that I picked up on my travels in Lunenburg, Nova Scotia. I have used this versatile recipe on numerous occasions, both for myself and for events that I have catered. People never seem to tire of the tantalizing results of its simple preparation.

WE ALSO LIKE the simple preparation involved, especially with ingredients a cook would probably have on hand. Although Barbara-Jo suggested fashioning the mixture into a roll and coating it with pecans and parsley, we simply packed it into a pretty bowl and served it as a spread with a sliced baguette or crackers.

1 pkg (8 oz/250 g) cream cheese, cubed
  and softened
2 tbsp (30 mL) goat cheese (optional)
1 tbsp (15 mL) fresh lemon juice
1 green onion, finely chopped

1 tbsp (15 mL) horseradish
pinch cayenne, or more to taste
1 can (15 oz/425 g) salmon, drained
1 tbsp (15 mL) finely chopped parsley
  or snipped dill

IN A MEDIUM bowl, blend together the cream cheese, goat cheese (if using), lemon juice, green onion, horseradish and cayenne.

Remove any skin from the salmon and mash it, removing the bones if desired. Stir into the cheese mixture until evenly mixed and pack into a serving bowl. Sprinkle a border of parsley around the edge of the bowl. (MAKE-AHEAD: Cover and refrigerate for up to 6 hours. Bring out to slightly warm a few minutes before serving.)

Cretons (Spiced Pork Pâté)

Makes about 2 cups (500 mL)

....

COLETTE RICHARD: For the annual Murray family Canada Day party, I bring everyone's favourite appetizer—a lovely dish of cretons along with tiny toasts and cornichons to serve with the pâté. We had cretons often when I was growing up in Quebec, mostly for breakfast, on warm toasted white bread, but it was store-bought. I remember that cretons for me was always Cretons Taillefer, a quality brand name then. I started making cretons from scratch when I moved out to my first apartment because I thought it would be foolproof for a new cook, and the ratio of ingredients was all one to one to one . . . impossible to mess up! I make it for July First get-togethers because it seems so traditionally Québecois.

....

1 lb (500 g) ground pork (not lean)

1½ cups (375 mL) fresh bread crumbs from crusty white bread (see Note)

1 onion, shredded

1 cup (250 mL) whole milk

½ tsp (2 mL) salt

¼ tsp (1 mL) each cinnamon and freshly ground black pepper

⅛ tsp (.05 mL) each cloves, ginger and nutmeg

IN A MEDIUM saucepan, stir together the pork, bread crumbs, onion and milk, breaking up the pork with a wooden spoon. Bring to a simmer and cook for 30 minutes.

Stir in the salt, cinnamon, pepper, cloves, ginger and nutmeg; cook for 30 minutes longer. Give the mixture a few pulses with a hand blender to make it spreadable and smooth. Transfer cretons to a serving dish or dishes (non-metallic) to cool, and then refrigerate. (MAKE-AHEAD: Cover and refrigerate for up to 3 days or freeze for longer storage.) Bring out to room temperature to serve on toast or crackers.

> **NOTE**
> A large kaiser roll, ripped open and left on the counter to dry a bit makes great bread crumbs.

Black Bean Hummus

Makes about 2 cups (500 mL)

THE CLASSIC MEDITERRANEAN dip is usually made with chickpeas and often appears alongside raw vegetables or tortilla chips as well as slathered onto bread to perk up sandwiches. This Caribbean take on it has lots of flavour and is super-easy to make.

1 can (19 oz/540 mL) black beans, drained and rinsed
½ cup (125 mL) tahini (ground sesame paste)
¼ cup (60 mL) fresh lime juice
3 tbsp (45 mL) canola oil
½ tsp (2 mL) each ground coriander and cumin

¼ tsp (1 mL) cayenne
2 large cloves garlic
salt and freshly ground black pepper
2 tbsp (30 mL) chopped fresh coriander (cilantro)

IN A FOOD processor, purée the beans, tahini, lime juice, oil, ground coriander, cumin and cayenne until smooth, dropping the garlic through the feed tube with the motor running. Transfer to a bowl and stir in salt and pepper to taste and the fresh coriander. (MAKE-AHEAD: Cover the hummus and refrigerate for up to 2 days.) The dip will thicken upon standing; if you want a thinner dip, stir in 2 to 4 tbsp (30 to 60 mL) water.

VARIATION: Traditional Sixties-Style Hummus
Substitute a can of chickpeas for the black beans, lemon juice for the lime juice and olive oil for the canola oil.

Sesame Cheese Crisps

Makes about 50 crisps

CHEESE CRISPS ARE a very civilized item to keep on hand for entertaining. Bake them ahead and store them in a tin ready to serve or, even better, shape the dough into logs and keep in the freezer, ready to "slice and bake" at a moment's notice. An excellent savoury accompaniment to a glass of wine.

¼ cup (60 mL) sesame seeds
½ cup (125 mL) butter, softened
4 tsp (20 mL) sesame oil
1 cup (250 mL) freshly grated
   Parmesan cheese

1 cup (250 mL) all-purpose flour
¼ cup (60 mL) fine cornmeal
¼ tsp (1 mL) each cayenne and
   dry mustard

LINE 2 RIMLESS baking sheets with parchment paper.

In a shallow, dry skillet, toast the sesame seeds over medium heat, stirring often, until golden and fragrant, about 5 minutes. Set aside to cool.

In a large bowl, beat the butter, sesame oil and Parmesan cheese until smooth. In a separate bowl, whisk together the flour, cornmeal, cayenne and mustard. Whisk in the sesame seeds.

A third at a time, stir the dry ingredients into the Parmesan cheese mixture to make a smooth dough. Divide the dough in half. Shape each half into an evenly shaped log about 6 inches (15 cm) long (see Note). Wrap in waxed paper and chill until firm, about 1 hour. (MAKE-AHEAD: Enclose the logs in freezer bags and freeze for up to 1 month. Let soften for 5 minutes before cutting and baking.)

Cut the chilled logs into ¼-inch (5 mm) slices. Arrange about 1 inch (2.5 cm) apart on the prepared baking sheets. Bake in the centre of a 350°F (180°C) oven until the crisps are golden around the edge and on the bottom, about 12 to 15 minutes. Let the crisps firm up for a couple of minutes on the sheets on a cooling rack. Transfer the crisps to the rack to cool completely. (MAKE-AHEAD: Layer the crisps with waxed paper in airtight containers and store at room temperature for up to 3 days.)

NOTE
For perfectly round crisps, roll the chilled dough a few times to round out any flat sides that may have developed. For square crisps (and easy slicing), form the dough into a square log before chilling.

Cake au Jambon (Ham Loaf)

Makes about 10 slices

NIGEL DIDCOCK, executive chef, Toronto Granite Club: When I arrived in Canada with my fiancée, Catherine, we were planning our wedding, which was to take place back in France—well, most of the planning was done by Catherine's parents. The wedding was to be spread over four days, the kind of memorable occasion the French do so well, I discovered.

After getting through all the technicalities and logistics of pulling off an event overseas, I was left with menu planning—that's where mothers-in-law step in! Catherine's mother, Jeannine, insisted on her *cake au jambon* (a savoury cake—really a loaf) being served during the aperitif hour.

It is traditional in France that after the church ceremony the father of the bride pays tribute to all his guests during *le vin d'honneur* (a special reception in which all the friends and family are offered an aperitif). There would be over 200 in attendance at my wedding, and for those who have experienced an aperitif in France, *le vin d'honneur* is not an occasion to be missed.

A month prior to the wedding, Jeannine was busy preparing the cakes and freezing them, and we received weekly updates on her progress, until she had filled a whole freezer chest. The wedding day arrived—a very hot summer's day—and slice after slice of *cake au jambon* was consumed. I had been ribbing Jeannine for months, as she cooked away and made so many cakes. But she knew best—there wasn't a crumb left in sight and I concluded that *le cake au jambon* had served its purpose—as a sponge for soaking up the alcohol of an extended aperitif that seemed to last for hours.

THIS RECIPE BROUGHT back fond memories of France to Nigel and is a favourite at Nigel and Catherine's dinner parties in Canada. It is delicious but has a coarser texture than an ordinary quick bread, probably to better soak up the alcohol it's served with.

1¼ cups (300 mL) all-purpose flour
1½ cups (375 mL) shredded Gruyère
  (4 oz/125 g)
1 tsp (5 mL) salt
1 envelope (8 g) active dry yeast
  (2¼ tsp/11 mL)

1 cup (250 mL) diced ham (½-inch/
  1.25 cm pieces)
4 large eggs
⅓ cup (75 mL) olive oil

LINE A 9- × 5-inch (2 L) loaf pan with parchment paper.

In a large bowl, stir together the flour, Gruyère, salt and yeast. Stir in the ham to combine well.

In a separate bowl, whisk together the eggs and oil and then stir into the dry ingredients. Spoon the mixture into the prepared pan and bake in the centre of a 375°F (190°C) oven until a tester comes out clean, 40 to 45 minutes. Remove the cake from the pan, carefully remove the paper and let cool on a rack. When the loaf is at room temperature, slice and serve. (MAKE-AHEAD: Cool, wrap in plastic wrap and store in the refrigerator up to 1 day, or wrap in plastic wrap as well as in foil and freeze for up to 1 month.)

Mini Scotch Eggs

Makes 32 pieces

ROSE: Scotch eggs (a classic treat from our Scottish heritage) have always been a favourite picnic food for the Murray family. Here, I make them into company fare as an appetizer using tiny quail eggs (available in Asian grocery stores and some markets). You could of course use the same recipe for the meat wrapping on four regular hens' eggs for a picnic.

16 quail eggs
1 lb (500 g) good-quality pork sausage meat
1 tbsp (15 mL) each Dijon mustard and
  snipped fresh chives
2 tsp (10 mL) chopped fresh thyme
  (or ½ tsp/2 mL dried)
1 tsp (5 mL) chopped fresh sage
  (or ¼ tsp/1 mL crumbled dried)

½ tsp (2 mL) salt
¼ tsp (1 mL) freshly ground black pepper
⅓ cup (75 mL) all-purpose flour
¾ cup (175 mL) fine dry bread crumbs
1 hen's egg
2 tbsp (30 mL) milk
2 tbsp (30 mL) canola oil (approx)

SET ASIDE A bowl of water and ice. Place the eggs in a medium saucepan and cover them with several inches of cold water. Cover the pan and bring almost to a boil over high heat, stirring occasionally. Uncover, reduce the heat to a brisk simmer and cook for 2 minutes, stirring occasionally. With a slotted spoon, immediately transfer the eggs to the ice water and cool well.

Pat each egg dry and lightly tap all over on a hard surface, then roll gently before peeling by pulling away the membrane with the shell attached. (The secret is to get under the membrane.)

Meanwhile, in a large bowl, combine the sausage meat, mustard, chives, thyme, sage, salt and pepper. Divide into 16 portions. Wrap each portion of pork mixture around an egg. Spread the flour and bread crumbs on 2 separate plates. In a small bowl, beat the hen's egg with the milk. Roll the sausage-encased eggs first in the flour, then in the milk mixture, then in the bread crumbs to coat well. Set aside on a platter in the refrigerator for 15 minutes.

In a large skillet over medium-high heat, heat the oil; in batches, fry the coated eggs, turning often, until the sausage is browned on all sides, adding more oil if needed. Transfer the browned eggs to a baking sheet with a slotted spoon. Bake in a 350°F (180°C) oven until the pork is cooked through, about 12 minutes. Refrigerate until cold. (MAKE-AHEAD: Cool, cover and refrigerate for up to 1 day.) With a sharp knife, cut in half to serve cold.

Devilled Eggs

Makes 12 devilled eggs

....

ELIZABETH: No summer reunion of the Morris family (Morris was my mother's side) was ever complete without a Tupperware container of Aunt Marjorie's devilled eggs. Aunt Marjorie did have an advantage—the eggs came from her own hens on the farm she and Uncle Ray worked. And she was a very fine cook. While her devilled eggs recipe is pretty classic, you can fuss up the mounded yolks with a small spoonful of whitefish caviar, a twirl of smoked salmon, a sprig of fresh herbs (dill, tarragon or chives are excellent), a slice of anchovy or a sprinkle of smoked paprika.

....

6 large eggs, cold from the refrigerator
4 tsp (20 mL) sour cream (approx)
1 tbsp (15 mL) Salad Dressing, Old and New (recipe, page 174) or mayonnaise

¼ tsp (1 mL) each salt and Dijon mustard
dash hot pepper sauce
2 tsp (10 mL) minced chives or green onion tops, divided

PLACE THE EGGS in a single layer in a medium saucepan and add cold water to come 1 inch (2.5 cm) above the eggs. Cover and bring to a boil over medium-high heat. Immediately remove from the heat and let stand for 13 minutes.

Drain the eggs and scoop into a large bowl of ice water to chill. (MAKE-AHEAD: Refrigerate the drained eggs for up to 5 days.) Peel the eggs (see Note).

Slice the eggs in half lengthwise. To create a flat bottom for the devilled eggs to lie on, trim a narrow slice off the bottom of each half, being careful not to tear the whites. Gently scoop the yolks out and put into a bowl.

With a fork, mash the egg yolks until smooth. Mix in the sour cream, Salad Dressing, salt, mustard and hot pepper sauce. (Add another teaspoon [5 mL] sour cream for a softer filling if desired.) Mix in half the chives. Spoon or pipe the mixture back into the egg whites and sprinkle with the remaining chives. (MAKE-AHEAD: Refrigerate in an airtight container for up to 1 day.)

NOTE
The easiest way to peel hard-cooked eggs is to roll them on the counter first to crack the shell. Then peel them under water, starting at the big end.

Crab Cakes

Makes about 24 crab cakes

....

JAMES LORIMER, cookbook publisher and avid cook: As a special Christmas present one year, I received a gift certificate for a day in the kitchen with Craig Flinn, the chef and owner of the very well regarded Chives Restaurant in Halifax. On the day's menu and lesson plan: Atlantic Snow Crab Cakes. I spent a small part of the day cracking crabs and picking the meat out of their shells. I thought the process was hugely tedious—you have to feel through all the meat with your fingers to get rid of all the bits of shell. But the results? Worth every minute! Since that day, these virtually-all-crab cakes have become my sit-down appetizer of choice for entertaining. The cakes are also great as a pass-around cocktail nibble if you accompany the platter with small plates and forks for easy eating.

....

CRAB CAKES

2 large eggs

2 shallots, finely diced

¼ tsp (1 mL) each salt and freshly ground black pepper

1 lb (500 g) shelled, picked over and drained crabmeat (see Note)

1 cup (250 mL) panko bread crumbs*

2 tbsp (30 mL) each butter and canola oil

*Panko, a very crisp bread crumb coating, coarser than other commercial dry bread crumbs, is quite widely available in major supermarkets and in Asian and specialty food shops.

SAUCE

½ cup (125 mL) light mayonnaise

1 tsp (5 mL) wasabi powder

2 tbsp (30 mL) thinly sliced chives or green onion

1 tbsp (15 mL) fresh lemon juice

CRAB CAKES → Whisk the eggs with the shallots, salt and pepper in a bowl. With a fork, mix in the crabmeat; cover and let stand in the refrigerator for 30 minutes.

Spread the bread crumbs on a plate. Scoop out a heaping tablespoon (15 mL) of the crab mixture for each cake. Flatten each tablespoon into a patty, about 1¾ inches (4 cm) in diameter. Press the patty into the bread crumbs, keeping its shape and coating it all around. (MAKE-AHEAD: Arrange the patties in a single layer on a small tray and refrigerate, uncovered, for up to 30 minutes.)

SAUCE → In a small bowl, combine the mayonnaise with the wasabi powder. Mix in the chives and lemon juice and refrigerate for 30 minutes. (MAKE-AHEAD: Refrigerate for up to 8 hours.)

Heat a large skillet over medium heat. Add half each of the butter and oil. Working with half a batch of cakes at a time, arrange the crab cakes in the pan. Fry until golden brown on the bottom, about 6 minutes. Supporting the cakes from below, turn the cakes carefully. Fry until golden brown, about 6 minutes. Lift onto warmed serving plates and keep warm. Wipe out the pan, add the remaining butter and oil and fry the remaining cakes. Serve hot, with the sauce.

NOTE

Choose frozen or refrigerated shelled and picked crabmeat. If the crab is frozen, thaw it in the refrigerator. Although already-shelled crabmeat is easier to deal with than whole steamed crabs, it still needs to be checked over very carefully. Feel your way through the meat, picking out and discarding any bits of shell. To drain crabmeat, place it in a sieve and press down firmly, to extract as much of the juice as you can. The crabmeat should feel light and just moist.

To speed up the measuring out of the crab mixture, you can use a #40 ice cream scoop, often called a disher.

Spiced Shrimp
with Lime-Ginger Sauce

Makes about 30 pieces

EVERYONE LOVES TRADITIONAL cold cooked shrimp around a spicy seafood sauce. This version is just the reverse . . . spicy shrimp, served hot with a cooling dip on the side.

SAUCE

⅔ cup (150 mL) mayonnaise
2 tbsp (30 mL) grated fresh ginger
1 tbsp (15 mL) grated lime zest
2 tbsp (30 mL) fresh lime juice

SHRIMP

1 tbsp (15 mL) canola oil, divided
2 tsp (10 mL) fresh lime juice

1 tsp (5 mL) each ground coriander, paprika, ground cumin and brown sugar
½ tsp (2 mL) each sea salt and dried oregano
¼ tsp (1 mL) cayenne
1 lb (500 g) large shrimp, peeled, with tail portion left intact
lime wedges

SAUCE → In a small bowl, combine the mayonnaise, fresh ginger, lime zest and lime juice. (MAKE-AHEAD: Cover and refrigerate for up to 6 hours.)

SHRIMP → In a small bowl, combine 1 tsp (5 mL) of the oil, the lime juice, coriander, paprika, cumin, brown sugar, salt, oregano and cayenne. In a large bowl, evenly coat the shrimp with the mixture. Cover and marinate at room temperature for 20 minutes. (MAKE-AHEAD: Cover and refrigerate for up to 3 hours.)

In a large skillet, heat the remaining 2 tsp (10 mL) of canola oil over medium-high heat. Stir-fry the marinated shrimp until bright pink (no longer opaque) and just cooked through, 1 to 2 minutes. Serve hot. Arrange on a platter with the sauce for dipping; garnish with lime wedges.

VARIATION: Barbecued Shrimp
Prepare the shrimp as in the main recipe. Soak wooden or bamboo skewers in cold water for at least 1 hour. Thread one marinated shrimp on a soaked skewer by putting the skewer through the shrimp twice. Repeat for all the shrimp pieces. Brush the remaining 2 tsp (10 mL) of oil over the grill on medium-high heat and cook the shrimp until bright pink (no longer opaque) and just cooked through, about 2 minutes a side.

Cod and Potato Fritters with Spicy Lemon Mayonnaise

Makes about 60 pieces

THIS RECIPE GOES full circle. Portuguese fishermen who came to Canada's Grand Banks in the 1500s took salt cod back home with them. This recipe for salt cod appetizers was shared by Portuguese immigrants who set up a family grocery business in Cambridge, Ontario.

MAYONNAISE
1 cup (250 mL) mayonnaise
2 tsp (10 mL) finely grated lemon zest
2 tbsp (30 mL) fresh lemon juice
1½ tsp (7 mL) hot pepper sauce
¼ tsp (1 mL) salt

FRITTERS
1¼ lb (625 g) salt cod, preferably fillets
5 cups (1.25 L) riced or finely mashed
   russet potatoes cooked without salt
½ cup (125 mL) finely chopped onion
⅓ cup (75 mL) finely chopped fresh parsley
4 tsp (20 mL) fresh lemon juice
¼ tsp (1 mL) each nutmeg and freshly
   ground black pepper
3 large eggs, beaten
canola oil for deep-frying

MAYONNAISE → In a small bowl, whisk together the mayonnaise, lemon zest and juice, hot pepper sauce and salt until smooth. (MAKE-AHEAD: Cover and refrigerate for up to 1 day.)

FRITTERS → Rinse the cod and soak for 12 hours or overnight in several changes of cold water in the refrigerator.

Drain and place in a large saucepan. Cover with cold water; bring to a boil. Reduce the heat and simmer until the fish flakes easily when tested, about 15 minutes. Drain and let cool; remove the skin and all bones if not using fillets. In a food processor or by hand, chop the cod very finely until no chunks remain.

In a large bowl, combine the cod, potatoes, onion, parsley, lemon juice, nutmeg and pepper; stir in the eggs to form a firm but malleable mixture. Using a dessertspoon, scoop out a heaping spoonful of the cod mixture. Using a second dessertspoon cupped over the first, press and form the mixture into a rounded oval, letting any excess fall back into the bowl. Place the oval on a large parchment or waxed paper–lined baking sheet. Repeat with the remaining mixture.

In a deep-fryer, heat 3 inches (8 cm) of oil to 375°F (190°C); fry ovals about 8 at a time, until golden and crisp, about 2 minutes. Drain on paper towels. Serve immediately or keep warm until serving. Accompany with the spicy lemon mayonnaise.

Lettuce Wraps

Makes 4 to 6 main-course lunch servings or 12 appetizers

WAYSON CHOY, author of *The Jade Peony:* I fondly remember holidays with my Vancouver aunt, Mary Low. As Aunt Mary worked her seamless way through preparing the 10-course Chinese meal for the delight of her family and guests, cleaning up even as the last stir-fry hotly sizzled, she inspired her kids Jim, Jeff and Janet to "help Mom." With no gender bias, the three were given tasks to do, whether separating lettuce leaves or scouring pots. They helped so much that they all became excellent cooks—a loving tribute to my equal-rights Aunt Mary. And I am, happily, their spoiled family guest. This dish is one of the many that Mary makes every year for Chinese New Year. It contains dried oysters (which symbolize "all good things") and is a family favourite.

4 to 5 large dried oysters (or 2 tbsp/
  30 mL small)
4 whole dried shitake mushrooms
  (or ½ cup/125 mL sliced)

MARINADE
1 tbsp (15 mL) each soy sauce
  (preferably dark) and dry sherry
1 tbsp (15 mL) minced fresh ginger
1 tsp (5 mL) each granulated sugar and
  canola oil
1 large clove garlic, minced
½ lb (250 g) lean ground pork

WRAPS
1 oz (25 g) fine rice vermicelli noodles
½ cup (125 mL) peanut or canola oil
  (approx)
1 or 2 heads butterhead lettuce,
  such as Boston or Bibb
3 carrots, finely diced
2 stalks celery, finely diced
1 onion, finely diced
2 tbsp (30 mL) minced fresh ginger
2 cloves garlic, minced
1 can (227 mL) water chestnuts, finely diced
1 tbsp (15 mL) oyster sauce
1 tbsp (15 mL) each soy sauce and
  cornstarch
½ cup (125 mL) hoisin sauce

SOAK THE DRIED oysters in warm water until softened, about 30 minutes. Drain well, dice and set aside. Soak the mushrooms in warm water until softened, 30 minutes to 1 hour. Drain well, squeeze dry, remove stems and finely dice. Set aside.

MARINADE → In a small bowl, stir together the soy sauce, sherry, ginger, sugar, oil and garlic. Add the pork and mix well. Set aside.

WRAPS → Place the noodles in a bag and break into 4-inch (10 cm) lengths. In a wok or large skillet, heat the oil until very hot. Working in batches, add a handful of noodles and cook until they turn white but not brown, a few seconds. Immediately transfer to drain on paper towels. Cool and arrange on a serving platter. Set aside.

Separate the lettuce into leaves, about all the same size (put small leaves aside for another use). Wash, dry and stack the leaves on top of each other on another serving platter. Set aside.

To the same wok used to fry the noodles, add the carrots, celery, onion, ginger and garlic and cook over high heat until tender, about 5 minutes. Add the diced mushrooms; cook for 2 minutes. Remove from the wok and set aside.

If necessary, add 1 tbsp (15 mL) oil to the wok. Stir in the pork and marinade; brown the meat, breaking it up with the back of a spoon to ensure a nice, even texture. Stir in the diced oysters; cook with the meat for 3 minutes. Stir in the water chestnuts and cook for 2 minutes. Add back the vegetable mixture and stir in the oyster sauce.

In a separate bowl, combine the soy sauce, cornstarch and 2 tsp (10 mL) water. Stir into the wok and cook for 1 or 2 minutes, stirring.

Spoon onto the platter of noodles, leaving a border of noodles around the edge. Serve with the platter of lettuce and a small bowl of the hoisin sauce.

Each person takes a lettuce leaf and places a spoonful of hoisin on it, followed by a scoop of the meat-vegetable-noodle mixture, then rolls the lettuce to enclose everything and eats the wrap with his or her hands. (Supply lots of serviettes.)

Potstickers with Chili-Soy Dipping Sauce

Makes 45 potstickers

....

VANESSA YEUNG, chef and teacher: How do traditions start? Sometimes they start out as necessity—learning to eat starts out as a basic of life. Other times, traditions are born by accident—my tradition of making pork potstickers was part necessity and part accident.

I was 19 when I was invited to my first potluck party. With few dishes to my credit and my future cooking career not yet decided, I didn't know what to take. My mother kindly offered to make my favourite Chinese dumplings, pork potstickers. Little did I know that her generous offer would make me the belle of the potluck party—my Canadian friends liked this Chinese dish! When many of the guests at the party asked how I had made them, I very quietly replied that my mother had made them for me. I was embarrassed by my lack of knowledge about my culinary heritage. I left the party with an empty dish and a desire to learn more.

That day, I realized that my culture could and would be embraced by other cultures if I had passion about sharing it. I asked my mother to teach me how to make the potstickers and started to forge ahead with a culinary career. I think of these potstickers as a bridge between East and West, and I look forward to the day when I can teach my little girl about her Chinese heritage through them. That is how traditions survive.

....

SAUCE

¼ cup (60 mL) soy sauce

1 tbsp (15 mL) granulated sugar

2 tsp (10 mL) rice vinegar

1 tsp (5 mL) chili oil or Asian hot chili sauce (or to taste)

1 clove garlic, minced

POTSTICKERS

5 leaves napa cabbage

½ lb (250 g) ground pork

1 tbsp (15 mL) soy sauce, preferably dark

1 tbsp (15 mL) hoisin sauce

1 tbsp (15 mL) minced fresh ginger

2 tbsp (30 mL) cornstarch

¼ cup (60 mL) warm water

45 round dumpling wrappers

1½ tbsp (22 mL) canola oil (approx)

SAUCE → In a small bowl, stir together the soy sauce, sugar, vinegar, chili oil and garlic until the sugar is dissolved. Let sit while you make the potstickers to allow the flavours to meld.

POTSTICKERS → Remove any big ribs from the cabbage and cut the leaves into thin strips. You should have about 1½ cups (375 mL) strips. Place the strips in a pot with ¼ cup (60 mL) water and steam until just limp, 5 to 10 minutes. Drain well and set aside to cool.

In a medium bowl, mix together the pork, soy sauce, hoisin sauce and ginger. Add the cooled cabbage and set aside for 1 hour for flavours to meld.

In a small bowl, dissolve the cornstarch in the water.

Taking one dumpling wrapper at a time, place 1 tsp (5 mL) of the pork mixture in the centre of each wrapper. Dip a finger in the cornstarch mixture and rub it around the inside edge of half the wrapper. Fold the wrapper in half and pinch firmly to enclose the pork mixture. (If you wish, make 3 or 4 decorative pleats and stand pleated-side up.) As you work, place the potstickers (without touching each other) on a parchment paper–lined tray and cover with a clean dry tea towel.

Into a large nonstick skillet over medium-high heat, pour enough oil to just coat the bottom, about 1½ tsp (7 mL). When hot, add the potstickers in batches, being careful not to crowd them. Allow them to brown on one side, 2 to 3 minutes; flip them over and brown them on the other side. Add water to the pan to just thinly cover the bottom and quickly cover the pan to prevent splattering. Allow the potstickers to steam until the filling is firm and the water has evaporated, 3 to 4 minutes. Serve hot with the dipping sauce.

Soups

Roasted Squash Soup

Makes 8 to 10 servings

WHEN FALL ARRIVES, we are delighted to see that every good restaurant takes advantage of the sweetness of squash to make a velvety soup. Roasting the squash enhances its own natural sugars. Pancetta, an Italian bacon that is salt-cured but not smoked, is now available in the deli counters of most supermarkets. *Pictured with Down East Oatmeal Bread (page 178).*

1 butternut squash (about 2¾ lb/1.25 kg)

4 oz (125 g) pancetta, coarsely chopped

2 onions, coarsely chopped

2 cloves garlic, minced

1½ tbsp (22 mL) chopped fresh sage
  (or 1½ tsp/7 mL crumbled dried)

¼ tsp (1 mL) hot pepper flakes

6 cups (1.5 L) chicken broth

salt and freshly ground black pepper

sour cream

1 large ripe tomato, diced

8 to 10 sage leaves, fresh or dried (optional)

CUT THE SQUASH in half, remove the seeds and roast, cut-side down and covered with foil, in a greased or parchment paper–lined baking pan in a 400°F (200°C) oven until tender, about 45 minutes. When cool enough to handle, scrape the flesh from the rind.

Meanwhile, in a large saucepan, cook the pancetta over medium heat until crisp, about 5 minutes. With a slotted spoon, transfer to paper towels to drain. Refrigerate.

In the pan drippings, over medium-low heat, cook the onions, garlic, sage and hot pepper flakes until the onions are very soft, about 10 minutes, stirring occasionally. Add the roasted squash, broth, and salt and pepper to taste. Bring to a boil, reduce the heat, cover and simmer, stirring often, for 20 minutes for flavours to blend.

Purée in a blender (holding down the lid) in batches or with an immersion blender until smooth. (MAKE-AHEAD: Cool, cover and refrigerate for up to 3 days.)

Return to a clean saucepan and gently reheat. Taste and adjust the seasoning.

Serve in heated bowls, garnishing each serving with a dollop of sour cream, a sprinkle of diced tomato and pancetta and a sage leaf (if using).

Hot and Sour Soup

Makes 6 servings

ROSE: The Cantonese think of soup not only as a delicious food but also as essential therapy for rehydrating the body and skin. Many wonderful soups were offered for sampling at the Magnificent Soup Carnival I attended as part of the Hong Kong Food Festival one year. This version of the popular hot and sour soup is thick and full flavoured . . . and just the thing to warm chilled Canadians during winter months.

1 cup (250 mL) Chinese dried mushrooms

12 oz (375 g) extra-firm tofu

8 cups (2 L) chicken broth

½ lb (250 g) lean pork shoulder butt, slivered

1½ cups (375 mL) julienne (matchstick-cut) bamboo shoots (fresh or canned, rinsed)

2 tbsp (30 mL) rice vinegar (approx)

1 tbsp (15 mL) Chinese black vinegar or Worcestershire sauce

1 tbsp (15 mL) rice wine or dry sherry

1 tbsp (15 mL) minced fresh ginger

½ tsp (2 mL) each salt and freshly ground black pepper

2 tbsp (30 mL) cornstarch

¼ cup (60 mL) cold water

1 cup (250 mL) frozen peas

1 large egg, lightly beaten

2 tsp (10 mL) sesame oil

1 tsp (5 mL) chili oil (or to taste)

2 green onions, finely chopped

IN A SMALL bowl, cover the mushrooms with ¾ cup (175 mL) warm water; let soak for 30 minutes. Drain and discard the water. Trim off any tough stems; slice the caps into thin julienne strips.

Cut the tofu into thin julienne strips.

In a large pot, bring the chicken broth to a boil. Add the mushrooms, pork and bamboo shoots; return to a boil, reduce the heat, cover and simmer for 3 minutes.

Add the tofu, rice vinegar, black vinegar, rice wine, ginger, salt and pepper. (MAKE-AHEAD: Cool, cover and refrigerate for up to 1 day ahead.)

Heat to boiling; taste and adjust the seasoning, adding more vinegar if necessary. In a small bowl, dissolve the cornstarch in the water. Slowly add the cornstarch mixture to the hot soup, stirring constantly; simmer until thickened. Stir in the peas and heat through.

Remove from the heat and slowly add the egg, pouring it in a thin stream around the edge and carefully stirring once or twice to have the egg form streamers. Transfer to a heated tureen or serving bowl. Carefully stir in the sesame oil and chili oil. Sprinkle with the green onions and serve immediately.

Vichyssoise with Oysters

Makes 6 servings

JONATHAN GUSHUE, executive chef, Langdon Hall Country Inn, Cambridge, Ontario: My father was born and raised in Newfoundland. In 1957, at the age of 24, he received a Rhodes scholarship to Oxford. After Oxford, he worked in Rome for several years before moving home to St. John's and becoming a Supreme Court judge.

During his time abroad, he gained a great respect for food and its sources. As a child, I benefited hugely from this. Usually on Saturdays Dad would cook a soup in the morning, then go off with me to Belbin's, a small, locally inspired grocery store, and decide what he would cook for my mother and me for dinner. It was those Saturdays and my father's holiday specials that I believe started me on my road to food obsession.

Dad adored all soup, but I think his vichyssoise was without question his best work. It was so comforting, I found myself helplessly going back to the refrigerator again and again when it was there. This soup he would make every Saturday without fail, except in the fall, when he would make his version of a Mediterranean fish soup.

Oysters were only served at Christmas in our house (I have no idea why) and they were a big deal. Friends from up and down the street would come and share Dad's leek and potato soup—to which, on this day, he had added oysters.

My father was truly my first teacher, showing me everything. I never really participated, just watched, learned and ate.

1 tbsp (15 mL) unsalted butter
¼ cup (60 mL) extra virgin olive oil, divided
2 large leeks, white part only, thinly sliced
3 medium russet potatoes, peeled and cubed
½ tsp (2 mL) salt

4 cups (1 L) chicken or vegetable broth or water
1 cup (250 mL) whipping cream
6 oysters, shucked, with their liquor (optional)
snipped fresh chives

IN A LARGE saucepan over medium heat, melt the butter in half the oil; add the leeks and cook until very soft but not coloured, about 10 minutes, stirring often. Add the potatoes, salt and broth. Bring to a boil, reduce the heat, cover and simmer for 20 minutes. Cool slightly, and then blend briefly with an immersion or regular blender. (Do not overblend or use a food processor, as this will make the soup gluey.) Pass the soup through a fine sieve, cool, cover and refrigerate, preferably overnight.

Just before serving, whisk in the cream. Taste and adjust the seasoning if necessary. Serve in large cool bowls topped with the oysters and their liquor (if using). Drizzle each with some of the remaining olive oil and a few chives.

French Onion Soup

Makes 4 servings

INSTEAD OF THE usual Gruyère, we've added a taste of Canadian smoked Cheddar cheese to a simple French classic we've been making for years. The toast should just fit inside the soup bowl. If using a skinny baguette, allow two slices per bowl.

2 large Spanish onions
2 tbsp (30 mL) unsalted butter
1 tsp (5 mL) granulated sugar
4 cups (1 L) beef broth
1 clove garlic, minced
½ tsp (2 mL) dried thyme

¼ tsp (1 mL) freshly ground black pepper
pinch salt
4 slices French bread
1¼ cups (300 mL) shredded smoked
    Cheddar cheese (about 4 oz/125 g)

CUT THE ONIONS in half lengthwise; thinly slice crosswise (you should have about 8 cups/2 L). In a large heavy saucepan, melt the butter over medium heat. Add the onions and sugar; cook, stirring often, until very soft and coloured, about 30 minutes.

Pour in ½ cup (125 mL) of the broth and bring to a boil. Cook, stirring up any brown bits from the bottom of the pan, until the broth has evaporated. Repeat with another ½ cup (125 mL) of the broth. Stir in the remaining broth, the garlic, thyme, pepper and salt. Bring to a boil, reduce the heat and simmer gently for 15 minutes, stirring occasionally. (MAKE-AHEAD: Cool, cover and refrigerate for up to 3 days. Gently reheat.)

Toast the bread slices until golden. Place four ovenproof soup bowls on a baking sheet; ladle the soup into them. Sprinkle half the cheese over the soup and place a piece of toast in each bowl. Sprinkle with the remaining cheese. Broil until the cheese melts and is golden, about 3 minutes.

All-Canadian Chowder

Makes 6 servings

A PERENNIAL ITEM on fish restaurant menus, chowder is also a satisfying supper. It is so quick and easy to cook, and you can make it as proverbially "chock full" of seafood tidbits as you like. An added bonus: Your own house chowder need never be glutinous, like the versions in so many restaurants. What's particularly appealing about chowder is how it changes depending on the local fish—Arctic char for friends in Yukon kitchens, lobster, cod and mussels for Atlantic Canada and, on the West Coast, halibut. Fresh, sustainable fish is what counts. Feel free to choose the best seafood available, on the dock if you're that lucky, or in a good fishmonger's if you're landlocked.

2 tbsp (30 mL) butter
1 large onion, diced
1 tender stalk celery, diced
1 tsp (5 mL) dried thyme or savory
¼ cup (60 mL) all-purpose flour
4 cups (1 L) fish or chicken broth
2 large potatoes, peeled and diced
1 carrot, diced

1 to 1¼ lb (500 to 625 g) fresh seafood
　(all one kind or a mix, see Note)
½ cup (125 mL) fresh or frozen corn kernels
　(optional)
1 cup (250 mL) 18% cream
2 tbsp (30 mL) minced fresh parsley
2 tbsp (30 mL) diced sweet red pepper
2 tbsp (30 mL) thinly sliced chives or green
　onion tops

IN A LARGE heavy-bottomed saucepan, melt the butter over medium heat. Stir in the onion, celery and thyme; sweat (cook gently), stirring a few times until slightly softened, about 5 minutes. Stir in the flour; cook, stirring, for 1 minute.

Gradually stir in the broth, then the potatoes and carrot. Bring to a boil, stirring occasionally. Reduce the heat, cover and simmer until the potatoes and carrot are tender but not mushy, about 10 to 15 minutes.

Add the seafood and corn (if using). Bring back to a simmer. Cook gently until the seafood is opaque, about 3 minutes. Stir in the cream and parsley; heat through until steaming.

Serve in warm bowls garnished with red pepper and chives.

NOTE
A tasty mix of seafood is a generous ¼ lb (125 g) each of cubed salmon and any white fish, plus the same amount of small shelled, raw shrimp and lobster or scallops. Or try 1 lb (500 g) diced white fish plus ¼ lb (125 g) small shelled, raw shrimp.

Real Cream of Tomato Soup

Makes 4 to 6 servings

LIZ DRIVER, author of *Culinary Landmarks: A Bibliography of Canadian Cookbooks, 1825 to 1949*, and curator of Campbell House Museum in Toronto, knows her way around historic cookbooks. When researching for her extraordinary book, she came across a recipe for mock bisque soup (cream of tomato soup) in the *Royal Victoria Cook Book* (compiled by the Women's Auxiliary to Royal Victoria Hospital, in Barrie, in 1900). To her amazement, the recipe was by a relative of Liz's on her mother's side, a Miss Shortreed of Toronto. This recipe is inspired by that early version of cream of tomato soup.

2 tbsp (30 mL) butter
1 onion, chopped
2 tbsp (30 mL) all-purpose flour
3 cups (750 mL) chopped tomatoes,
   fresh or canned
2 tbsp (30 mL) chopped parsley
2 tsp (10 mL) granulated sugar

½ tsp (2 mL) salt
¼ tsp (1 mL) freshly ground black pepper
pinch cayenne
2 bay leaves
3 cups (750 mL) chicken or vegetable broth
1 cup (250 mL) light cream or milk

IN A HEAVY-BOTTOMED saucepan, melt the butter over medium heat. Add the onion; cook, stirring until softened, about 3 minutes. Stir in the flour; cook, stirring, for 2 minutes. Add the tomatoes, parsley, sugar, salt, pepper, cayenne and bay leaves; cook, stirring, until the tomatoes start to soften, about 5 minutes.

Add the broth; bring to a boil. Cover and reduce the heat to simmer the soup until fresh tomatoes are completely soft and, for both fresh and canned, the flavours have blended, about 30 minutes. Remove the bay leaves.

Press the soup through a food mill or fine sieve to smooth it and eliminate tomato seeds and skins. Stir in the cream and heat through.

NOTE
A swirl of cream or sour cream added to the top of the soup gives the soup a *soupçon* of glamour, as does a sprinkle of minced parsley.

Minestrone

Makes 8 servings

THIS ITALIAN VEGETABLE soup with its many variations has long been a crowd-pleaser in Canada since it is thick, hearty and full of easy-to-find ingredients. If you have a wedge of real Parmesan cheese (Parmigiano Reggiano) on hand, save a bit of the rind—it gives lots of flavour to the soup when added with the broth.

2 tbsp (30 mL) each butter and olive oil
2 leeks (white parts only), chopped
1 onion, chopped
1 cup (250 mL) each diced celery and carrots
2 cups (500 mL) peeled diced potatoes
1 cup (250 mL) shredded cabbage
3 cloves garlic, minced
1 tsp (5 mL) each dried basil and oregano
½ tsp (2 mL) freshly ground black pepper

6 cups (1.5 L) chicken or vegetable broth
1 cup (250 mL) diced canned tomatoes, undrained
1 can (19 oz/540 mL) white kidney beans, drained and rinsed
½ cup (125 mL) orzo or other small pasta, such as tubetti
1 cup (250 mL) chopped spinach
freshly grated Parmesan cheese

IN A LARGE saucepan over medium-low heat, melt the butter in the oil. Cook the leeks and onion until golden in colour but not brown, about 10 minutes. Add the celery and carrots; cook for 3 minutes over medium heat. Add the potatoes, cabbage and garlic; cook for 3 minutes. Stir in the basil, oregano and pepper. Add the broth and tomatoes; bring to a simmer and cook, stirring often, until the vegetables are tender, 10 to 15 minutes.

Purée half the beans in a food processor or blender. Add the purée and the whole beans to the soup with the pasta. Simmer until the pasta is tender, 5 to 8 minutes, according to the instructions on the box. Stir in the spinach and cook for 1 minute (see Note). Serve with lots of Parmesan cheese sprinkled overtop.

NOTE
If making ahead, leave out the pasta and spinach. Bring the soup to a simmer. Add the pasta and cook for 5 minutes; add the spinach and cook for 1 minute.

Old-Fashioned Pea Soup with Smoked Ham

Makes 8 servings

JOHANNA BURKHARD, author of *300 Best Comfort Food Recipes:* My family came from the Netherlands to Southern Ontario in the 1950s and we were raised on this warming Dutch soup. When I lived in Quebec for several years, I discovered pea soup was also a key staple in that province's food heritage and I felt right at home.

Most hams sold today in supermarkets are boneless, so this recipe calls for chopped smoked ham as well as chicken broth; these make a good substitute for a ham bone. If you do have a meaty ham bone for the soup, use water instead of broth. Remove the ham bone at the end of cooking, scrape off any meat and stir it into the soup. A smoked pork hock is another alternative if a ham bone is not available.

2 tbsp (30 mL) butter
1 medium leek, white and light green part
  only, chopped
1 large onion, chopped
2 large cloves garlic, finely chopped
3 carrots, peeled and chopped
1 large stalk celery including leaves,
  chopped
1½ tsp (7 mL) dried marjoram

1 bay leaf
¼ tsp (1 mL) freshly ground black pepper
  (approx)
8 cups (2 L) chicken broth (approx)
2 cups (500 mL) chopped smoked ham
1½ cups (375 mL) dried green or yellow
  split peas, picked over and rinsed
salt and freshly ground black pepper
¼ cup (60 mL) chopped fresh parsley

IN A STOCKPOT or Dutch oven over medium heat, melt the butter. Add the leek, onion, garlic, carrots, celery, marjoram, bay leaf and pepper; cook, stirring often, until softened, about 8 minutes.

Stir in the broth, ham and split peas. Bring to a boil; reduce the heat, cover and simmer, stirring occasionally, until the split peas are tender, about 1½ hours.

Remove the bay leaf. Adjust the seasoning with salt and pepper to taste. Stir in the parsley. The soup thickens as it cools; thin with additional broth or water to desired consistency.

Caldo Verde

Makes 8 servings

ELIZABETH: Rosa Carvalho brought her own chouriço when she came to show me how to make *caldo verde*. This is a potato soup with paper-thin slices of collards and smoky chouriço. Caldo verde ("green soup") is a specialty of Minho, the region near Porto, Portugal, where Rosa and her husband, Antonio, grew up, and a soup Rosa often makes for his hot lunches.

8 cups (2 L) cubed potatoes (about
   3 lb/1.5 kg)
1 onion, coarsely chopped
4 cups (1 L) each water and chicken broth

1 link smoked chouriço (about 6 oz/175 g)
15 collard leaves
½ tsp (2 mL) salt
extra virgin olive oil

IN A LARGE saucepan, combine the potatoes, onion, water, broth and the whole chouriço link. Cover and bring to a boil over medium heat. Reduce the heat and simmer, stirring occasionally, until the potatoes are fork tender, about 30 minutes. Remove the chouriço; slice thinly. With an immersion or regular blender, in batches, buzz the soup until smooth.

Meanwhile, cut the stems and coarse veins from the collards and cut each leaf in half lengthwise. Tightly roll the leaves, about 5 at a time. Holding the roll firmly, cut crosswise into paper-thin slices. (You will have about 4 cups/1 L packed.) Stir into the soup with the salt and bring it to a boil uncovered.

Divide the chouriço slices among the warmed bowls. Ladle in the soup and give each portion a nice drizzle of olive oil.

Ukrainian Borscht

Makes 8 to 10 servings

....

SHARON BOYD: My aunt Stella Chomut grew up in Fort William, Ontario (now part of Thunder Bay). She lived in the West End, which was known as West Fort, where there was a very large Ukrainian population. In fact, many youngsters didn't hear or speak much English until they went to school. My aunt recalls that, although they did live in the city, they and most of their neighbours kept chickens and even a dairy cow in their yards. A neighbour came by each morning to take the cows to a nearby pasture where they could graze all day and then he returned them in the evening. The frugal residents grew most of the vegetables they ate in their large vegetable gardens. What went into the traditional Ukrainian borscht depended on what was ready in the garden at the time.

....

2 tbsp (30 mL) canola oil
1 lb (500 g) pork spareribs
8 cups (2 L) chicken or vegetable broth
   or water
1 tsp (5 mL) salt
2 tbsp (30 mL) butter
3 cups (750 mL) peeled, shredded beets
   (about 4 medium)
1 carrot, shredded
1 onion, diced
1 stalk celery, diced
salt and freshly ground black pepper

1 can (14 oz/398 mL) stewed tomatoes,
   undrained
1 clove garlic, minced
2 tbsp (30 mL) red wine vinegar
1 tbsp (15 mL) chopped parsley
1 tsp (5 mL) granulated sugar
2 bay leaves
2 cups (500 mL) shredded cabbage
1 can (19 oz/540 mL) navy beans, drained
   and rinsed
1 tbsp (15 mL) snipped fresh dill (approx)
sour cream

IN A LARGE saucepan, heat oil over medium-high heat. Brown the spareribs. Stir in the broth and salt and bring to a boil, skimming off any foam. Reduce the heat, and cover and simmer until the meat is tender, about 1 hour.

Meanwhile, in another large saucepan, melt the butter over medium heat. Cook the beets, carrot, onion and celery, sprinkling with salt and pepper and stirring often, for 5 minutes. Stir in the tomatoes, garlic, vinegar, parsley, sugar and bay leaves. Bring to a simmer and cook, covered, for 10 minutes. Add the cabbage and beans and cook for 10 minutes.

Remove the spareribs. Cut and dice any meat from the bones, discard the bones and return meat to the broth with the vegetable mixture. Bring to a simmer and cook for 10 minutes. Taste and adjust the vinegar and sugar if necessary. Discard the bay leaves; stir in the dill to serve. Garnish with a dollop of sour cream and sprinkle more fresh dill overtop.

Double-Mushroom, Beef and Barley Soup

Makes about 8 servings

....

ROSE: My husband, Kent, is a serious soup connoisseur and rates this soup among my best. Now that so many exotic mushrooms are available in supermarkets, we tend to overlook the dried version, which can lend a delightful nuttiness to a dish. Look for good-quality dried mushrooms that have a pleasing fragrance. For the fresh mushrooms needed, buy either common or exotic mushrooms.

....

½ cup (125 mL) dried mushrooms, such as porcini, morel or other (about ½ oz/15 g)

2 tbsp (30 mL) canola oil

1 beef shank (about 1½ lb/750 g)

3 cups (750 mL) sliced fresh mushrooms (slightly over ½ lb/250 g)

2 carrots, finely diced

2 onions, chopped

1 stalk celery with leaves, chopped

2 cloves garlic, minced

½ tsp (2 mL) each dried thyme and marjoram

1 bay leaf

½ cup (125 mL) Madeira, Marsala or medium sherry (or additional beef broth)

5 cups (1.25 L) beef broth

½ tsp (2 mL) each salt and freshly ground black pepper

½ cup (125 mL) pot or pearl barley*

½ cup (125 mL) chopped fresh parsley

*Barley is a grain that is widely available. Both pot and pearl barley are polished (pearl more so) and can be used interchangeably.

COMBINE THE DRIED mushrooms with 1 cup (250 mL) boiling water; let stand for 30 minutes. Drain in a sieve set over a bowl. Slice the mushrooms and strain the liquid to remove any grit; set aside mushrooms and liquid.

In a large heavy saucepan or Dutch oven, heat the oil over medium-high heat. Brown the beef well and remove to a plate.

Add the fresh mushrooms, carrots, onions and celery to the pan; cook, stirring, for 5 minutes. Add the garlic, thyme, marjoram and bay leaf; cook, stirring, for 2 minutes. Stir in the Madeira and bring to a boil, scraping up any brown bits from the bottom of the pan. Add the browned beef shank, broth, salt and pepper. Bring to a boil, reduce the heat and simmer, covered, for 1½ hours or until the beef is very tender.

Remove the beef shank, discard the bone and dice the beef. Stir in the reserved mushrooms and their liquid, the diced beef and the barley. Cover and simmer for 30 minutes or until the barley is tender.

Discard the bay leaf; taste and adjust the seasoning. Stir in the parsley and serve. Any leftover soup will thicken upon cooling; thin with broth or water.

Chunky Beef Goulash Soup

Makes 8 generous servings

....

ROSE: A Hungarian chef taught me how to make this soup years ago. It remains high on the list of favourite soup choices for the Baird and Murray families.

....

2 tbsp (30 mL) lard or canola oil
1½ lb (750 g) lean beef, cubed (¾ inch/ 2 cm pieces)
2 onions, sliced
2 tbsp (30 mL) caraway seeds, crushed*
1 tbsp (15 mL) sweet paprika
½ tsp (2 mL) salt (approx)
1 can (19 oz/540 mL) tomatoes, undrained and chopped
1¼ tsp (6 mL) dried basil
2 sweet peppers (green, red or yellow), diced

¼ cup (60 mL) water
4 potatoes, peeled and diced
7 cups (1.75 L) beef broth
1¼ tsp (6 mL) dried marjoram
¾ tsp (4 mL) freshly ground black pepper
¼ lb (125 g) egg noodles

*Crush caraway seeds with a mortar and pestle or place in a sturdy plastic bag and roll firmly with a rolling pin.

IN A LARGE heavy-bottomed saucepan, melt the lard over medium-high heat; add the meat and cook until browned all over. Add the onions and cook until softened, about 5 minutes.

Remove from the heat; stir in the caraway seeds, paprika and salt. Return to low heat; cover and cook for 20 minutes, stirring occasionally.

Stir in the tomatoes, basil, sweet peppers and water; bring to a boil. Reduce the heat, cover and simmer for about 1 hour or until meat is almost tender, adding a little water if necessary to prevent sticking.

Add the potatoes and broth; bring to a boil. Reduce the heat, cover and cook until the potatoes and meat are tender, about 30 minutes. Taste and add more salt if necessary. Stir in the marjoram and pepper; cook for 2 minutes. (MAKE-AHEAD: Cool, cover and refrigerate for up to 1 day. Reheat slowly, stirring often.)

Stir in the noodles; cook for about 7 minutes or until the noodles are tender but firm. Ladle into heated bowls.

Grilled Party Sirloin

Makes 6 to 8 servings

. . . .

ALFRESCO ENTERTAINING IS a way of life in our Canadian summers. For this easy party main dish, choose a nice thick steak that you can slice, and then spoon a flavourful make-ahead blue cheese sauce over the juicy slices.

. . . .

2 tbsp (30 mL) white vermouth
2 tsp (10 mL) olive oil
1 tsp (5 mL) Worcestershire sauce
½ tsp (2 mL) finely minced fresh rosemary
 (or ¼ tsp/1 mL dried)
½ tsp (2 mL) freshly ground black
 pepper, divided

2 lb (1 kg) top sirloin grilling steak
 (at least 1½ inches/4 cm thick)
4 oz (125 g) crumbled Stilton or other
 mild blue cheese, divided
⅓ cup (75 mL) sour cream
1 tsp (5 mL) Dijon mustard
pinch cayenne

IN A FLAT, glass baking dish, stir together the vermouth, oil, Worcestershire sauce, rosemary and half the pepper. Add the steak and turn to coat all over. Cover and marinate in the refrigerator for at least 4 hours or up to 8 hours, turning once or twice.

In a small bowl, mash three-quarters of the cheese; stir in the sour cream, mustard, remaining pepper and cayenne until smooth. (MAKE-AHEAD: Cover and refrigerate for up to 8 hours.)

Remove the steak from the refrigerator 30 minutes before grilling. Place on a greased grill over medium-high heat, close the lid and grill for 7 minutes. Reduce the heat to medium, turn the steak over and grill on the second side until desired doneness, about 7 to 10 minutes for medium rare (see Note). Transfer to a cutting board, tent with foil and let stand for 5 minutes. Slice thinly on an angle across the grain and divide the slices among warm plates. Spoon the smooth cheese mixture over the slices and sprinkle with the remaining crumbled blue cheese.

NOTE
For winter parties, if you are not a brave all-year barbecue expert, use a grill pan indoors. Spray the grill pan with nonstick spray or brush with oil, and cook the steak over medium-high heat for 2 minutes a side until well browned. Transfer to a 400°F (200°C) oven until desired doneness, about 10 minutes for medium rare.

Best Burgers

Makes 4 servings

THERE IS NO doubt—hamburgers have not lost their charm, whether you find them in a neighbourhood mom and pop joint or the fanciest upscale restaurant. There are even mini burgers called sliders that pass as appetizers. We still love burgers, whether we dress them with the usual condiments—mustard, ketchup and relish—or adorn them with olive spread and arugula. They're usually made with ground beef, but you shouldn't neglect other ground meats, such as lamb, chicken and pork. Stuffed with chèvre and accompanied by a mint relish, lamb burgers are extraordinary. A famous diner, Harmony Lunch, in Waterloo, Ontario, makes nothing but ground pork burgers.

However, there is nothing like a homemade beef burger cooked either on an outdoor grill or in a skillet. Use this base recipe for your best burgers and serve on your bun of choice with your preferred toppings. The whipping cream keeps the patties moist regardless of which type of ground beef you use. The secret is not to mix too much, and to resist pressing down on the patties with a spatula as they cook because this toughens them.

⅓ cup (75 mL) whipping cream
¼ cup (60 mL) each dry bread crumbs and
   minced onion
1 tbsp (15 mL) Worcestershire sauce

1 tsp (5 mL) salt
½ tsp (2 mL) freshly ground black pepper
1 lb (500 g) medium ground beef
1 tbsp (15 mL) canola oil (if skillet cooking)

IN A LARGE bowl, mix together the cream, bread crumbs, onion, Worcestershire sauce, salt and pepper. Add the beef and with moist hands, mix well and gently form into four ¾-inch (2 cm) patties. Cover and refrigerate at least 1 hour or up to 4 hours before cooking.

To barbecue, place patties on a lightly oiled grill over medium-high heat. Cook until no longer pink inside and a thermometer inserted sideways into the centre of each patty registers 160°F (70°C), 5 to 7 minutes a side, turning only once.

To cook indoors, heat oil in a large heavy skillet over medium-high heat and cook patties until no longer pink inside (test with the tip of a sharp knife) and the temperature of each patty is 160°F (70°C), 5 to 7 minutes a side, turning only once.

Place the patties on buns of your choice, such as ciabatta or sesame buns, toasted French bread, grilled naan bread, grilled flour tortillas or toasted pita-bread pockets. Homemade hamburger buns make a sensational treat (see Refrigerator Rolls, page 183).

Top the burgers with the condiments of your choice, such as mustard, ketchup, Hot Dog Relish (page 313), sliced onion, tomato, avocado, sweet peppers (fresh or pickled), Crunchy Bread-and-Butter Pickles (page 315), bacon, lettuce, pesto, guacamole and any kind of good melting cheese.

VARIATION: Chili Cheeseburgers

Stir together 1 tbsp (15 mL) ketchup, 2 tsp (10 mL) chili powder and ¼ tsp (1 mL) dried oregano and add it to the beef mixture as made in the main recipe. Shape into 8 thin patties. Stir together 1 cup (250 mL) shredded cheese and 1 tbsp (15 mL) diced jalapeño pepper; divide this mixture into 4 parts and mound each part into the centre of 4 patties. Top with the remaining 4 patties, pressing the meat around the edges to seal well. Cover and refrigerate as in the main recipe; then cook as in the main recipe. Serve the patties open-face style on top of crispy fried tortillas. Sprinkle with slivers of hot pepper, chopped lettuce and a dollop of sour cream and guacamole or taco sauce.

VARIATION: Cheese-Stuffed Burgers

Use 2 oz (50 g) fresh, mild goat cheese, formed into 4 rounds, or 2 oz (50 g) blue cheese, crumbled. Make a pocket in the centre of each patty, as made in the main recipe, fill with the cheese and bring the meat around to cover it.

Polpettone (Veal Meatloaf)

Makes 8 servings

DONNA PARIS, section editor at *Canadian Living* magazine: This Italian meatloaf comes from my mother, Rosa Altobello, who is originally from the Puglia region of Italy. When we four kids, all born in Canada, were growing up, she made it once a week for our family, and we complained about having to eat it so often. The tables have turned in our family, and my mother has the last word: "Now the children are all adults, and when they come for dinner, I always ask them what they would like to eat. Inevitably, it's this meatloaf!"

2 large eggs

1½ lb (750 g) lean ground veal

⅓ cup (75 mL) freshly grated Parmesan cheese

1 tbsp (15 mL) minced fresh parsley

4 cloves garlic, minced, divided

¾ tsp (4 mL) each salt and freshly ground black pepper, divided

4 to 8 small leaves Swiss chard, blanched and trimmed (see Note)

4 very thin slices cooked ham

4 thin slices provolone

4 sprigs fresh parsley

⅔ cup (150 mL) dry bread crumbs

2 tbsp (30 mL) extra virgin olive oil

1 onion, finely diced

2 stalks celery, finely diced

1 can (28 oz/796 mL) tomatoes, undrained

¼ cup (60 mL) tomato paste

½ tsp (2 mL) dried oregano

IN A LARGE bowl, beat the eggs; mix in the veal, Parmesan, minced parsley, one-quarter of the garlic and ½ tsp (2 mL) each salt and pepper. Divide the mixture in half.

On a sheet of plastic wrap, pat half of the veal mixture into an 8- × 7-inch (20 × 18 cm) rectangle. Lay half of the Swiss chard leaves, 2 ham slices, 2 provolone slices and 2 parsley sprigs lengthwise down the centre of the rectangle. Lift up the long side of plastic wrap to the centre, pressing the veal mixture into a cylinder that encloses the filling; press the edges to seal. Using another sheet of plastic wrap, repeat with the remaining veal, Swiss chard, ham, provolone and parsley.

Place the bread crumbs in a small tray or baking pan. Using the plastic wrap and hands, unroll the loaves, one at a time, onto the bread crumbs, and roll to coat all around, removing the plastic wrap as you roll.

Heat the olive oil in a large skillet over medium-high heat; brown the loaves, one at a time, on one side; using two spatulas, loosen the bottom of the loaf and turn over to brown the second side, reducing the heat if necessary to prevent bread crumbs from burning. Supporting the loaf with two spatulas, lift out of the skillet and place in a 13- × 9-inch (3.5 L) glass baking dish or similar-sized pan; repeat with second loaf and bread crumbs. Set aside.

In the same skillet over medium heat, fry the onion, celery and the remaining garlic, salt and pepper until softened, about 5 minutes. Add the tomatoes, tomato paste and oregano. Break up the tomatoes with a potato masher or fork until almost smooth; bring to a boil. Reduce the heat and simmer, stirring often, until saucy and thickened, about 15 minutes; spoon over the loaves and bake in a 350°F (180°C) oven until the sauce has thickened appetizingly over and around the loaves and a meat thermometer registers 170°F (77°C), about 45 to 55 minutes. Let stand for 5 minutes before cutting into 1-inch (2.5 cm) slices. Arrange on a platter and spoon the sauce overtop.

NOTE

To blanch Swiss chard leaves, remove the stems. Lower the leaves into a large saucepan with about 2 inches (5 cm) boiling water in the bottom. Cook until the leaves are limp, about 1 minute. Remove and arrange in a single layer on towels. With a knife held horizontally, trim off the coarse veins to create evenly thin leaves. The number of leaves that you can roll easily at one time will depend on the size of the leaves—4 may be the limit.

Nana Ortenzia's Meatballs with Emily's Pasta Sauce

Makes about 30 meatballs, 4 to 6 servings

EMILY RICHARDS, home economist, food writer, broadcaster, teacher and author of *Get in the Kitchen and COOK!:* I relish the flavourful dishes of my Italian heritage. My grandmother and mother make some pretty mean meatballs, and I felt I had to follow suit. These are moist and tasty, just like Nana's (my grandmother's). I've made them for friends and family and they just love them!

½ cup (125 mL) fresh bread crumbs (see Note)

1 large egg

2 tbsp (30 mL) finely chopped flat-leaf parsley

2 tbsp (30 mL) freshly grated Parmesan cheese

1 clove garlic, minced

½ tsp (2 mL) salt

pinch hot pepper flakes

8 oz (250 g) each ground veal and pork

3 cups (750 mL) Emily's Pasta Sauce (recipe follows) or store-bought pasta sauce

IN A LARGE bowl, mix together the bread crumbs, egg, parsley, Parmesan cheese, garlic, salt and hot pepper flakes. Gently mix in the veal and pork until well combined. Using wet hands, roll a rounded 1 tbsp (15 mL) of the meat mixture into 1-inch (2.5 cm) balls. Place on a foil-lined baking sheet. Bake in a 350°F (180°C) oven until no longer pink inside but not browned outside, about 12 minutes.

Heat gently in the sauce to serve.

NOTE
If you don't have fresh bread crumbs, soak some stale bread in milk or water and break up into small pieces.

EMILY'S PASTA SAUCE
Makes about 4½ cups (1.25 L)

THIS IS AN easy sauce to make on the weekend for use through the week. The recipe makes a bit more than you need for the meatballs, but you will appreciate having it on hand for quick pasta dishes or to spoon over chicken or pork chops. It also freezes well. Leaving the onions and garlic in large pieces adds a soft flavour; they themselves become very soft and great tasting.

2 cans (28 oz/796 mL each) tomatoes, undrained
8 sprigs flat-leaf parsley
4 sprigs or large leaves fresh basil
2 cloves garlic

1 onion, halved
¼ cup (60 mL) extra virgin olive oil
1 tbsp (15 mL) dried oregano
1 tsp (5 mL) salt
½ tsp (2 mL) hot pepper flakes

IN A BLENDER, purée the tomatoes until smooth; pour into a large saucepan. Stir in the parsley, basil, garlic, onion, oil, oregano, salt and hot pepper flakes; bring to a boil. Cover partially and simmer until thickened, about 2 hours, stirring occasionally. (The garlic should melt into the sauce.) Remove the onion and herb sprigs if desired.

Lasagna Bolognese

Makes 6 to 8 servings

....

DONNA BARTOLINI, chef, food writer and food stylist: At the very centre-point of the Bartolini family's Christmas dinner — an epic sit-down of nine courses — is this traditional lasagna. Yes, a lasagna, and you're still only halfway through the meal. But even with cutlets, the turkey and several desserts to come, no one ever passes this by.

This is a classic Bolognese lasagna, with a béchamel instead of cheesy layers folded into the sauce. But if you can't imagine a lasagna without ricotta, you can whisk together 2 cups (500 mL) of it, 2 eggs and ¼ tsp (1 mL) salt; then spread the mixture over a couple of the layers before the sauce. Glazing the bottom of the pan is crucial to developing the best flavour for this sauce. It's great on pasta and freezes beautifully.

....

BOLOGNESE SAUCE

2 tbsp (30 mL) butter
¼ cup (60 mL) olive oil
½ cup (125 mL) each diced celery,
   carrot and onion
4 oz (125 g) prosciutto, diced
2 lb (1 kg) lean ground beef
1 cup (250 mL) dry red wine
¾ cup (175 mL) tomato paste
3 cups (750 mL) chicken broth
1 cup (250 mL) water
½ tsp (2 mL) freshly ground black pepper
1 cup (250 mL) whole milk

BÉCHAMEL SAUCE

1½ cups (375 mL) whole milk
3 tbsp (45 mL) butter
3 tbsp (45 mL) all-purpose flour
pinch salt

LASAGNA

15 lasagna noodles
½ cup (125 mL) freshly grated
   Parmesan cheese

BOLOGNESE SAUCE → In a heavy-bottomed saucepan or Dutch oven over medium-high heat, melt the butter in the oil. Add the celery, carrot, onion and prosciutto; cook, stirring often, until golden, about 8 minutes.

Break up the ground beef and add it to the pan. Cook, stirring occasionally, until the beef is browned and the bottom of the pan is glazed and golden brown.

Stir in the wine and cook until evaporated. Add the tomato paste, broth and water, stirring as you do so until well combined. Bring to a boil, reduce the heat to low, partly cover and simmer, stirring often, until thick and deeply coloured but still saucy, 1½ to 2 hours. Stir in the pepper and milk; simmer for 15 minutes longer. (MAKE-AHEAD: Cool and refrigerate in an airtight container for up to 2 days or freeze for up to 1 month.)

BÉCHAMEL SAUCE → In a small saucepan on the stovetop or in a measuring cup in the microwave oven, heat the milk until steaming, but do not boil.

In a medium saucepan, melt the butter over low heat. Stir in the flour and cook, stirring, for 2 minutes. Remove from the heat.

Whisk half the milk in a thin, steady stream into the flour mixture until it is smooth. Stir in the remaining milk and the salt. Return to the heat and cook, stirring with a wooden spoon until the sauce is thickened. Cover the surface directly with plastic wrap if not using right away.

LASAGNA AND ASSEMBLY → Cook the lasagna noodles in a large pot of boiling salted water according to the package directions, until *al dente*.

Stir the béchamel sauce into the Bolognese sauce. Spread 1 cup (250 mL) over the bottom of a 13- × 9-inch (3.5 L) ceramic or glass baking dish. Layer 3 noodles on top and top with a layer of sauce. Sprinkle the sauce with some of the Parmesan cheese and continue layering noodles, sauce and cheese, ending with sauce and Parmesan. The dish will be quite full; cover with foil. (MAKE-AHEAD: Cool, cover and refrigerate for up to 1 day.)

Bake, covered, in a 350°F (180°) oven for 40 minutes; uncover and bake until bubbly and heated through, about another 20 minutes, adding more time if baking from refrigerated. Let stand for 5 minutes before serving.

Quebec Tourtière

Makes 2 deep-dish 9-inch (23 cm) or 10-inch (25 cm) pies

JULIAN ARMSTRONG, author of *A Taste of Quebec* and columnist for the Montreal *Gazette:* The meat pie known as tourtière is a four-century favourite in Quebec. Its name can be traced back to the cast-iron pan of the same name brought to New France by settlers in the 17th century. Originally made with leftovers of roasted meat, usually pork, it has as many variations as there are Quebec cooks. Beef is often used, as is veal. The basic vegetable is the onion, but some recipes include potatoes, carrots, garlic or leeks. Bread crumbs are the usual thickener. My pie uses rolled oats, a tradition that developed after the arrival of the Scots on the Quebec culinary scene. Using cloves and cinnamon together is a tradition dating from medieval cooking in Europe. Savory, Quebec's favourite herb, and celery leaves are tourtière regulars.

Tourtière is the most popular ready-made meal sold in Quebec. As a Toronto-born journalist who has been making and enjoying Quebec tourtières for 50 years, I mourn the closing (in 2010) of a Montreal headquarters for these pies—the modest East End restaurant called Chez Clo. I was never able to coax the recipe from owner Claudette Massé or her chef, Isabelle Ruel, but developed this recipe, which I think is a dead ringer for the pie I enjoyed so often at that restaurant. Helping me test the recipe, my daughter, Claire O'Brien, modelled the pastry on a recipe belonging to my longtime friend, Jehane Benoît, the late, celebrated Quebec chef. Jehane would have approved of using lard—she always said it made the flakiest pastry. *Pictured with Pickled Baby Beets (page 316).*

PASTRY

5 cups (1.25 L) all-purpose flour

4 tsp (20 mL) baking powder

2 tsp (10 mL) salt

1 package (1 lb/454 g) lard, cubed

1 large egg

4 tsp (20 mL) fresh lemon juice
  or white vinegar

ice water

FILLING

2 lb (1 kg) medium ground beef

1 lb (500 g) lean ground pork

2 large onions, chopped

1 cup (250 mL) chopped celery, with leaves

1 cup (250 mL) chopped flat-leaf parsley

1½ cups (375 mL) water

2 tsp (10 mL) dried savory

1 tsp (5 mL) each ground cinnamon
  and cloves

1 tsp (5 mL) each salt and freshly
  ground black pepper

½ tsp (2 mL) nutmeg

¾ cup (175 mL) large-flake rolled oats

1 large egg yolk

1 tbsp (15 mL) milk

continued . . .

PASTRY → In a large mixing bowl, whisk together the flour, baking powder and salt. Using a pastry blender, cut in the lard until the mixture resembles fine crumbs. In a liquid measuring cup, use a small whisk or fork to combine the egg and lemon juice. Add enough ice water to make 1 cup (250 mL). Drizzle the egg mixture slowly over the dry ingredients, tossing them with a fork to make a ragged dough that clumps together. Press the dough into 4 equal discs, wrap individually with plastic wrap and refrigerate until chilled, about 30 minutes. (MAKE-AHEAD: Refrigerate for up to 3 days. Let come to room temperature before rolling.)

FILLING → In a large heavy pot, combine the beef, pork, onions, celery, parsley, water, savory, cinnamon, cloves, salt, pepper and nutmeg. Bring to a boil over medium-high heat, constantly breaking up the meat and stirring until the meat has lost its pinkness and is crumbly, about 15 minutes. Reduce the heat to medium-low and simmer, covered, stirring occasionally, until the liquid has almost evaporated, about 1 hour. Remove from the heat; stir in the rolled oats. Let cool. (MAKE-AHEAD: Let cool for 30 minutes; refrigerate uncovered until cold. Cover and refrigerate for up to 1 day.)

On a floured work surface, using a floured rolling pin, roll out 1 of the pastry discs to a scant ¼-inch (5 mm) thickness. Line a deep 9-inch (23 cm) or 10-inch (25 cm) pie plate with pastry, leaving the edge untrimmed. Fill with half of the meat mixture. Moisten the pastry on the rim of the pie plate with water. Roll out a second disc of pastry and unroll over the filling. Trim and flute edges to seal. Repeat for the second pie (see Note 1). (MAKE-AHEAD: Double-wrap with heavy-duty foil. Freeze for up to 2 months. Let thaw in refrigerator; add about 10 minutes to baking time.)

Cut steam vents in the centre of each pie. In a cup, mix the egg yolk with the milk and brush over the surface of both pies. Bake in the bottom third of a 400°F (200°C) oven until the pastry is golden and the filling piping hot, about 40 to 50 minutes (see Note 2).

Serve Quebec Tourtière with Fruit Chili Sauce (page 306), known in Quebec as *ketchup aux fruits*, or Pickled Baby Beets (page 316).

NOTE 1
There will be leftover pastry scraps. Reroll and cut out decorations, *fleurs de lys*, for example, and press onto the top of the glazed pies. Brush the cutouts with glaze. Or make *pets de soeur* (nun's farts), pinwheels that are a traditional children's treat. Roll out pastry, sprinkle generously with brown sugar and dust with cinnamon. Roll up like a jellyroll. Cut into generous ¼-inch (5 mm) slices and bake at 400°F (200°C) until browned and crisp.

NOTE 2
To test the hotness of the filling, insert a pointy knife through one of the steam vents. Let it stay for 15 seconds; remove and feel. If the knife is piping hot and the crust is golden brown, the tourtière is ready.

Ginger Beef Pot Roast

Makes 6 to 8 servings

....

THIS HOMEY WINTER standby is great on its own with lovely crusty bread, or with silky mashed potatoes and parsnips. Cook together equal numbers of potatoes and parsnips with a healthy handful of peeled garlic. Drain the vegetables and mash them to a velvety purée, adding a generous dollop of butter along with salt, pepper and ground ginger to taste. If you wish, garnish the meat platter with slivers of green onion.

....

1 beef pot roast, boneless crossrib or blade
   (about 4 lb/2 kg)
salt and freshly ground black pepper
¼ cup (60 mL) all-purpose flour
2 tbsp (30 mL) canola oil
2 onions, quartered
1 stalk celery, quartered
1-inch (2.5 cm) piece peeled fresh ginger
4 cloves garlic
¼ cup (60 mL) dry sherry
¼ cup (60 mL) soy sauce
1 tbsp (15 mL) brown sugar
4 cups (1 L) beef broth

2 cinnamon sticks
2 whole star anise*
2 large sweet potatoes, in 2-inch (5 cm)
   chunks
24 baby carrots
12 shallots

*Star anise, an eight-podded star-shaped spice with a strong licorice flavour, is always available in Asian grocery stores, but it is appearing more and more often in supermarkets.

DRY THE MEAT with paper towels, sprinkle with salt and pepper and dredge well with the flour.

In a large Dutch oven or flameproof casserole, heat the oil over medium-high heat and brown the meat on all sides. Remove to a plate and reduce the heat to medium.

Add the onions, celery and ginger to a food processor and chop finely, dropping the garlic through the feed tube with the motor running. Stir the mixture into the drippings in the pan and cook until softened, about 5 minutes. Stir in any remaining flour and cook, stirring, 1 minute. Gradually stir in the sherry, scraping up any brown bits in the bottom of the pan. Gradually add the soy sauce and brown sugar and cook until the sugar is dissolved. Gradually stir in the broth, cinnamon sticks and star anise; bring to a boil. Add back the meat, cover tightly and place in a 325°F (160°F) oven for 1½ hours.

Add the sweet potatoes, carrots and shallots; cover and roast until the meat and vegetables are very tender, about 1 hour. (MAKE-AHEAD: Cool, cover and refrigerate for up to 2 days. Reheat gently to proceed.) Remove the meat and vegetables to a heated platter; cover and set aside to keep warm.

Remove the cinnamon and star anise. Boil the liquid in the pan until desired consistency for sauce, 5 to 10 minutes. Slice the beef and arrange with the vegetables on the platter. Pass the sauce in a warmed gravy boat.

Glorious Roast Beef with Gravy and Yorkshire Pudding

Makes 12 servings

....

ELIZABETH: In my husband's (George Baird's) family, roast beef was the bedrock of Sunday dinner. While this meal has faded as an institution as families shrink and settle farther than a short ride from their home kitchen, roast beef as a special-occasion centrepiece has endured. In fact it has increased in popularity, not just for family get-togethers but also for dinner and holiday parties. When it comes to roast beef, prime rib is the king of cuts and epitomizes the whole roast beef experience—from discussions with the butcher to seasoning, roasting and finally eating—its crusty bones and beautiful eye of lean rare meat surrounded by a juicier, crispier and fattier covering (to eat if you dare, or not). Then there's the gravy, Yorkshire Pudding (page 68) and horseradish you will serve alongside. Choose a chef's cut, in which the bones have been removed and tied back on for easy carving.

....

ROAST

6 to 8 lb (2.7 to 3.5 kg) prime rib roast,
    4 to 5 bones

⅓ cup (75 mL) Dijon mustard

2 tbsp (30 mL) cracked or very coarsely
    ground black pepper

1 tbsp (15 mL) chopped fresh thyme
    (or 1 tsp/5 mL dried)

2 tsp (10 mL) chopped fresh oregano
    (or ½ tsp/2 mL dried)

1 tbsp (15 mL) Worcestershire sauce

2 tsp (10 mL) anchovy paste

1 tsp (5 mL) coarse sea salt

GRAVY

⅓ cup (75 mL) all-purpose flour

3 cups (750 mL) beef broth or water
    (approx), divided

2 tbsp (30 mL) brandy (optional)

1 tsp (5 mL) fresh or dried thyme

salt and freshly ground black pepper

ROAST → Wipe the meat dry if needed; place bone-side down in a roasting pan large enough to hold it comfortably.

In a small bowl, whisk together the mustard, pepper, thyme, oregano, Worcestershire sauce and anchovy paste. Brush all over the meat. If there's time, lightly cover and refrigerate for at least 2 hours or up to 1 day. Let stand at room temperature for 1 hour before roasting.

Sprinkle with the salt. Roast in a 350°F (180°C) oven for about 2 to 2½ hours or to desired doneness, using an ovenproof meat thermometer to monitor the interior temperature in the centre of the roast:

RARE: 130°F (55°C)
MEDIUM-RARE: 140°F (60°C)
MEDIUM: 150°F (65°C)

MEDIUM-WELL: 155°F (69°C)
WELL DONE: 160°F (70°C)

You will find that if the very centre of the roast is registering medium-rare (140°F/60°C), meat at both ends will be hotter, into the medium range, thus providing slices for the variety of tastes you find around a dinner table.

Transfer the roast to a cutting board and tent with foil. Let the roast rest for up to 30 minutes before slicing off and separating the ribs and carving the meat across the grain into slices, the thickness of which we leave in your hands.

GRAVY → While the roast is resting, tip the roasting pan up and skim off the fat to use for Yorkshire Pudding (page 68). Use a flat whisk or wooden spoon to work the flour into the pan drippings. Whisk in half of the broth. Set the pan over medium heat and bring to a boil, whisking and stirring up all the delicious brown bits from the bottom of the pan. Whisk in the remaining broth, brandy (if using), and thyme. Bring back to a boil, reduce the heat and simmer, whisking to smoothness, a few minutes longer. Add more broth if desired. Taste, adding salt and pepper as needed.

Strain the gravy through a sieve into a large measuring cup or a saucepan. Reheat in the microwave oven or on the stovetop, and pour it piping hot into a warmed gravy boat.

VARIATION: Glorious Barbecued Beef

Looking for a stand-out item for a barbecue? Choose the same prime rib cut as in the main recipe, seasoned with the same ingredients, and cook the meat to succulence on the barbecue. So that the meat cooks evenly without the outside burning, set the meat on a greased grill over indirect medium heat (see Indirect Heat Grilling, page 84). With the lid down, cook to desired doneness.

See the main recipe for temperatures (you'll need about 2½ hours for medium-rare doneness).

CONTINUED . . .

YORKSHIRE PUDDING

Makes 12 servings

ANNE LINDSAY, author of many cookbooks, including her most recent, *Lighthearted at Home (The Very Best of Anne Lindsay):* When I was growing up in Vancouver, we had roast beef and Yorkshire pudding for dinner most Sunday nights in the winter. Potatoes were cooked in the pan with the roast. We usually had broccoli and a green salad with tomatoes (rock-hard ones that came in a package of four or five), cucumber and green onion or chives from the garden. Salad dressing was made of white vinegar and oil shaken up in the nearly empty ketchup bottle. Apple pie, made with apples from our trees, was dessert.

Most nights we ate in the dining room, table set with a tablecloth, bread and butter side plates and dessert ready on the sideboard, but on Sunday nights we carried the whole dinner in serving bowls and a platter down to the rec room, placed it on the bar and served it from the bar while we watched television, ending with *The Ed Sullivan Show.*

Sometimes we had a prime rib roast, but more often it was a rump roast. Mum would get an extra piece of fat from the butcher if it were a rump roast and put it on top of the beef while it was roasting, as we needed the drippings to make gravy and the Yorkshires. My mother always mixed up the batter a couple of hours before she baked the puddings and left it at room temperature; she said this was important.

2 large eggs	½ tsp (2 mL) salt
1 cup (250 mL) milk	pan drippings
1 cup (250 mL) all-purpose flour	

IN A SMALL mixing bowl, beat the eggs until frothy; stir in the milk, then the flour and salt. Don't worry about a few small lumps. Let stand at room temperature for 2 hours.

Pour about 1½ tsp (7 mL) pan drippings into the bottom of each cup of a 12-cup medium muffin pan (enough to cover the bottom of each cup). Place the pan in the centre of a 425°F (220°C) oven until the drippings are very hot, 1 to 2 minutes. Remove the pan from the oven and pour the batter into the hot drippings. (The cups will be only one-half to two-thirds full.) Return the pan to the oven and bake until the Yorkshires have risen and are golden brown, 20 to 25 minutes. Serve immediately.

Brisket, Old and New

Makes 8 to 10 servings

....

DAPHNA RABINOVITCH WALTERS, chef, cookbook author and consultant: I didn't really grow up with brisket. For Jewish holidays, my mom, an adventurous cook, mixed traditional dishes with new ethnic ones, but never got around to brisket. When I got married I discovered that New Year's, Hannukah or Passover were just not the same for my husband without his favourite cranberry and onion brisket. So I have become somewhat of an expert on brisket. Although I'm inclined to try new things, hence this pomegranate brisket, the one constant at our festive dinner tables is Cranberry Brisket (recipe follows). *Pictured with Latkes (Potato Pancakes) (page 159).*

....

POMEGRANATE BRISKET

1 double brisket* (5 lb/2.5 kg)

2 tsp (10 mL) dried thyme

1 tsp (5 mL) dried rosemary, crushed

¾ tsp (4 mL) salt

½ tsp (2 mL) freshly ground black pepper

¼ tsp (1 mL) cayenne

1 tbsp (15 mL) olive oil

2 leeks, mostly white part, sliced (see Note)

3 large onions, coarsely chopped

6 cloves garlic, minced

2 large carrots, coarsely chopped

2 cups (500 mL) pomegranate juice, divided

2 cups (500 mL) chicken broth (approx)

½ cup (125 mL) dry white wine

2 bay leaves

*Brisket is the cut of meat from the lower breast of beef; a double brisket includes the point and some of the flat part.

TRIM THE BRISKET of excess fat, leaving a thin layer of fat remaining. In a small bowl, combine the thyme, rosemary, salt, pepper and cayenne; rub over the brisket. Place the brisket in a large roasting pan, fat-side up.

In a large skillet, heat the oil over medium heat. Add the leeks, onions, garlic and carrots. Cook, stirring, until softened, about 10 minutes. Stir in 1 cup (250 mL) of the pomegranate juice, scraping up any browned bits from the bottom. Bring to a boil; boil gently for 5 minutes. Add the remaining juice and the broth, wine and bay leaves. Bring just to a boil.

CONTINUED . . .

Pour the juice mixture over the brisket. Cover the pan tightly with foil. Roast in a 325°F (160°C) oven, basting every 30 minutes, until the meat is very tender, 3½ to 4 hours. Remove the brisket to a cutting board. Pour the juice mixture and vegetables into a blender or food processor; purée until smooth. Thin with ½ cup (125 mL) more chicken broth if necessary to have gravy consistency. Return this puréed gravy and the brisket to the pan. Let cool at room temperature for 30 minutes. Refrigerate until cold, then cover and refrigerate for at least 8 hours or up to 24 hours.

Spoon off any solidified fat. Remove the brisket to a cutting board; slice thinly across the grain. Return the slices to the pan, spooning some of the gravy over the slices. Cover and reheat in 325°F (160°C) oven until steaming hot, about 1 hour.

NOTE
To clean leeks, trim off the root end and any coarse green leaves. Cut crosswise into ½-inch (1.25 cm) slices; place in sieve. Swish the sieve in a bowl of cold water, pushing the slices apart to separate them and dislodge the sand that hides between the leaves. Rinse well, and shake off the water.

CRANBERRY BRISKET

TRIM THE BRISKET of excess fat, leaving a thin layer of fat remaining. Combine 2 packages (1½ oz/40 g each) onion soup mix with 2 cans (348 mL each) jellied cranberry sauce; whisk together well, adding up to ½ cup (125 mL) water to help liquefy. Sprinkle both sides of 1 double brisket (5 lb/2.5 kg) with hot pepper flakes, dried garlic powder, dried thyme and pepper. Place fat-side up in a deep roasting pan. Pour the cranberry sauce mixture overtop, letting it slide under the brisket as well. Cover with foil and marinate overnight. Roast, slice and reheat as in the Pomegranate Brisket recipe.

Braised Short Rib Supper

Makes 4 to 6 servings

DIANE SLIMMON: I grew up in the Fifties in Stratford, Ontario, where my father, Oliver Strahm, owned Dufferin Market butcher shop. Over his career, he also worked in a meat packing plant, sold meat wholesale and was a government meat inspector. Needless to say, we didn't eat many tuna sandwiches in our house. In fact, I used to trade cold roast beef sandwiches for peanut butter and jam ones in the high school cafeteria.

I started cooking when I was in grade seven or eight—that's when my parents ran their butcher shop (I remember that short ribs were 30 cents a pound). My mother never planned meals much in advance because we ate what wasn't selling. One of the first meat dishes that I remember liking to make was braised short ribs, possibly because the long cooking time gave me lots of time to read and the entire meal cooked in one pot, making cleanup easier. It was a meal that I made for company, as a new bride, in my wedding-gift electric frying pan.

3 lb (1.5 kg) beef short ribs

¼ cup (60 mL) all-purpose flour

½ tsp (2 mL) each salt and freshly ground black pepper

1 tbsp (15 mL) butter

1 tbsp (15 mL) canola oil

2 cups (500 mL) beef broth, wine or water (or a combination)

½ cup (125 mL) red wine vinegar

½ cup (125 mL) chopped fresh parsley

3 tbsp (45 mL) tomato paste

2 tbsp (30 mL) brown sugar

6 whole cloves

1 bay leaf

4 to 6 small onions

3 cloves garlic, minced

4 potatoes, peeled and quartered

3 each carrots and parsnips, or 6 carrots, quartered

4 to 6 wedges cabbage

chopped fresh parsley

CUT THE RIBS into serving pieces. In a large sturdy plastic bag, combine the flour, salt and pepper; toss the ribs in the mixture to coat well. In a Dutch oven or deep frying pan with a lid, over medium heat, melt the butter in the oil; brown the ribs in batches, removing them to a plate as they brown. Add any remaining flour mixture to the pan; cook, stirring, for 2 minutes. Very gradually stir in the broth and bring to a boil, stirring until thickened and smooth.

In a small bowl, stir together the vinegar, parsley, tomato paste, brown sugar, cloves, and bay leaf. Stir into the broth along with the onions and garlic. Return the ribs to the pan and bring to a boil. Reduce the heat and simmer, covered, for 1 hour on the stovetop. Or transfer the pan to a 350°F (180°C) oven for 1 hour.

Add the potatoes, carrots and parsnips; simmer for 1 hour. Add the cabbage and simmer until the vegetables are tender and the meat is falling off the bones, 30 minutes longer. Remove the cloves and bay leaf. Garnish with fresh parsley to serve.

Pork

Slow-Roast Pork with Gravy and Cider-Baked Applesauce

Makes 8 generous servings

ON A WINTERY Saturday morning, Rob Firing, food shopper extraordinaire, shared his tastiest destinations in Toronto's Kensington Market with a group of friends. One, Sanagan's Meat Locker, is where he buys a shoulder of pork to roast with masses of garlic and herbs. He loves the idea of slow-roasting the pork to fill the kitchen with come-hither aromas and bring the "crispy" on the outside meat to the point of almost-falling-apart succulence. His enthusiasm inspired this roast, to serve with Cider-Baked Applesauce (recipe follows) and, if there are leftovers, to make Hachis Parmentier (page 92).

ROAST

4 lb (2 kg) trimmed boneless pork
   shoulder blade roast
10 peeled garlic cloves, divided
2 tbsp (30 mL) herbes de Provence
¾ tsp (4 mL) coarse salt
¾ tsp (4 mL) coarsely ground black pepper
2 large onions
1½ cups (375 mL) dry white wine

GRAVY

⅓ cup (75 mL) all-purpose flour
3½ cups (875 mL) chicken broth (approx)
salt and freshly ground black pepper

ROAST → Cut 16 slits in the roast. Cut 4 of the garlic cloves in quarters; press into the slits.

In a small bowl, stir together the herbes de Provence with the salt and pepper. Rub all over the roast, reserving any remaining. Tie the roast thrice crosswise, twice lengthwise.

Cut each onion into 6 wedges; arrange in the bottom of a shallow roasting pan that holds the roast comfortably. Add the remaining whole garlic cloves and any remaining herb mixture. Set the roast on this bed of deliciousness. Pour the wine around the onions. Cover and roast at 450°F (230°C) for 15 minutes. Reduce the heat to 300°F (150°C) and roast, basting every 30 minutes or so, until the pork is almost pull-apart tender, about 3 hours.

Transfer the roast to a cutting board and tent with foil. Let it rest for about 15 minutes.

GRAVY → Meanwhile, skim the excess fat off the pan juices. With a flat whisk or wooden spoon, work the flour into the pan juices. Place the roasting pan over medium heat; whisk in the chicken broth. Cook until boiling, whisking up any brown bits from the bottom of the pan. Reduce the heat and simmer until the gravy is thickened and smooth, about 5 minutes. Pour the gravy through a sieve into a saucepan, pressing the onions and garlic through the sieve. Reheat; taste, adding salt and pepper and more broth if needed.

To serve, remove the string and slice the roast across the grain. Spoon some of the gravy over the slices, passing the remainder in a warmed gravy boat.

CIDER-BAKED APPLESAUCE
Makes about 2 cups (500 mL)

USE EMPIRE OR McIntosh apples that cook to a nice purée for this easy sauce. Substitute cranberry juice for apple cider or apple juice to give the applesauce a lovely pinkness. If you want unsweetened applesauce, leave out the sugar.

5 apples
1 tbsp (15 mL) fresh lemon juice
¼ cup (60 mL) packed brown sugar

pinch each cinnamon and nutmeg
¼ cup (60 mL) apple cider, apple juice
   or cranberry juice

PEEL, CORE AND cut the apples into eighths; place in an 8-inch (2 L) square baking dish. Toss with the lemon juice; sprinkle with the brown sugar, cinnamon and nutmeg. Drizzle with the cider; stir gently until the sugar is dissolved. Cover and bake in a 350°F (180°C) oven until the apples are soft, 35 to 45 minutes. Mash with a potato masher.

Chili Pulled Pork

Makes 8 generous servings

....

IF CANADIANS HAD been asked five years ago for their favourite dishes, chances are pulled pork would not have made the list. But trust our taste buds to seek new thrills. Pulled pork piled on a crusty kaiser roll with a load of Creamy Coleslaw (page 170) has become a must-make dish for casual parties and potlucks. There is a connection between pulled pork made from bargain-priced pork shoulder and slow cooking. This cut bubbles into blissful eating on slow, steady heat, which you can achieve with stovetop braising or a slow cooker.

....

4 lb (2 kg) trimmed boneless pork
   shoulder blade roast
½ tsp (2 mL) each salt and freshly
   ground black pepper
1 tbsp (15 mL) canola oil
2 onions, diced
3 large cloves garlic, minced
4 tsp (20 mL) chili powder
2 tsp (10 mL) ground cumin

2 tsp (10 mL) sweet paprika,
   smoked or plain
1 tsp (5 mL) crumbled dried oregano
¼ tsp (1 mL) cayenne
2 cups (500 mL) tomato sauce
2 tbsp (30 mL) each brown sugar
   and cider vinegar
1 tbsp (15 mL) Dijon mustard
12 kaiser rolls
Creamy Coleslaw (page 170)

TIE THE PORK 4 times across and twice lengthwise to hold the meat together. Season with salt and pepper.

In a heavy-bottomed saucepan, heat the oil over medium-high heat. Brown the pork all over, using wooden spatulas or lifters to turn the roast without piercing the meat. Transfer the pork to a plate.

Drain and discard all but 1 tbsp (15 mL) of the fat in the pan. Return the pan to medium heat; add the onions, garlic, chili powder, cumin, paprika, oregano and cayenne. Fry, stirring almost constantly, until the onion softens and the spices darken, about 4 minutes. Stir in the tomato sauce, brown sugar, vinegar and mustard. Reduce the heat to low and simmer to blend the flavours, about 3 minutes.

FOR STOVETOP-BRAISING → Place the pork in the sauce and spoon the sauce over the top and sides. Cover and simmer over very low heat, turning the pork every hour or so, until the meat is so tender it can be pulled into strands with a fork, about 4 hours. If needed, add a little water to the pan.

FOR A SLOW COOKER → Place the pork in a medium-size slow cooker, 5 to 6 quarts (5 to 6 L). Pour the sauce over the pork. Cover and cook on low heat until the meat is so tender it can be pulled into strands with a fork, about 8 hours.

Lift the pork into a large wide bowl. Cover and let stand for 10 minutes.

Meanwhile, skim as much of the liquid fat as possible off the top of the braising liquid. Measure the braising liquid; there should be about 3½ cups (875 mL), thick enough to coat a spoon. (If you have used a slow cooker, transfer the liquid to a saucepan.) Adjust the amount by boiling for a few minutes or by adding water.

Pull off any obvious fat from the pork and, with 2 forks, pull the meat into strands. Return the pulled pork and braising liquid to the pan and heat until steaming hot.

Meanwhile, heat the rolls. Split and serve in a basket, with the pulled pork and a bowl of Creamy Coleslaw on the side. To assemble, pile the pork and then coleslaw on the bottom of a bun, then set the top of the bun on and enjoy.

> **NOTE**
> The pork can be braised ahead of time. After braising or slow-cooking, let the pork and braising liquid cool separately. Wrap the pork and cover the liquid. Refrigerate for up to 1 day. Remove all visible fat from the pork and lift the congealed fat off the surface of the liquid.

Hoisin-Glazed Ribs

Makes 8 servings

....

ROSE: Everyone will love these barbecued, Asian-flavoured, finger-licking-good ribs I developed for a summer celebration featured in *Family* magazine. Look for hoisin sauce, sesame oil and chili paste in the Asian section of your supermarket, adding more chili paste if you like spicier ribs. *Pictured with Asian Cabbage Salad (page 171).*

....

6 to 8 lb (2.7 to 3.5 kg) meaty pork back ribs
 or side ribs
1 cup (250 mL) hoisin sauce
¾ cup (175 mL) ketchup
⅓ cup (75 mL) liquid honey
¼ cup (60 mL) fresh lemon or lime juice

¼ cup (60 mL) rice vinegar
3 cloves garlic, minced
1 tbsp (15 mL) chopped fresh ginger
1 tbsp (15 mL) sesame oil
1 tsp (5 mL) Asian hot chili sauce
 or ½ tsp (2 mL) hot pepper flakes

USING A FORK, lift the membrane from a corner of the rib bones on the non-meaty side and gently peel it away from the ribs. Place the ribs in a single layer in a shallow roasting pan, meaty-side up. Add 1½ cups (375 mL) water to the pan, cover with foil and bake in a 325°F (160°C) oven until the meat is tender when pierced with a knife, about 1 hour (1¾ hours if using side ribs). Remove to a glass baking dish.

In a medium bowl, whisk together the hoisin sauce, ketchup, honey, lemon juice, vinegar, garlic, ginger, sesame oil and chili sauce. Brush the ribs on both sides with some of the hoisin mixture. Pour any remaining hoisin mixture over them. Let cool; cover and refrigerate for at least 4 hours or up to 24 hours.

About 30 minutes before cooking, remove the ribs from the refrigerator. Preheat the barbecue to medium-low. Remove the ribs from the dish, shaking off and reserving the marinade. Put the ribs meaty-side down (in batches if necessary) on a greased grill. Cook, covered, moving the ribs occasionally so that they don't get too brown in one spot, and turning and basting with some of the reserved marinade halfway through cooking, until heated through and glazed, about 20 minutes. Slice the ribs into serving pieces.

Pour the reserved marinade into a small saucepan and heat it over medium heat until piping hot. Serve as a sauce with the ribs. (Since the ribs are cooked before being marinated, there will be no uncooked meat juices in the marinade.)

Porchetta, Two Ways

Makes 8 servings

. . . .

"LUSTY" IS HOW to describe this pork loin cooked in two ways, either roasted in cool weather or barbecued for summer get-togethers. Porchetta has its origins in Italian alfresco feasts and is newly trendy in Canada. It does take some time seasoning, stuffing and rolling the loin, but its dramatic spiral appearance makes it worthwhile. An excellent accompaniment for this roast would be Do-Ahead Scalloped Potatoes (page 158).

. . . .

ROAST PORCHETTA

1 boneless centre loin pork roast (single
   loin, 3 lb/1.5 kg)
3 tbsp (45 mL) extra virgin olive oil, divided
4 large cloves garlic, minced
2 tbsp (30 mL) minced fresh rosemary

1 tbsp (15 mL) dry vermouth
4 tsp (20 mL) minced fresh sage
¾ tsp (4 mL) fennel seeds, crushed
½ tsp (2 mL) salt
¼ tsp (1 mL) freshly ground black pepper

PLACE THE PORK, fat-side up, on a cutting board. Starting at the right side with a knife parallel to the board, cut the loin in half almost but not all the way through. Open up the loin like a book. Starting in the centre of the opened loin and with the knife parallel to the board, cut the loin in half on the left side almost but not all the way through. Repeat on the right side and open flat. Cover the loin with waxed paper and pound with a mallet to an even thickness.

In a small skillet, heat half the oil over medium-low heat. Fry the garlic, stirring often, until softened, about 5 minutes. Scrape into a large bowl. Stir in the remaining oil, rosemary, vermouth, sage, fennel seeds, salt and pepper. Spread about ¾ of the garlic mixture over the inside of the loin, leaving a 1-inch (2.5 cm) border along one short end. Starting at the other end of the loin, roll up firmly towards the border. Tie with kitchen string at 1-inch (2.5 cm) intervals.

Lay the stuffed and rolled loin in the remaining garlic mixture in the bowl, turning to coat. Cover and marinate in the refrigerator, turning occasionally, for 2 hours. (MAKE-AHEAD: Refrigerate for up to 24 hours.)

Place the loin on a rack in a shallow roasting pan. Roast in a 375°F (190°C) oven until a meat thermometer registers 160°F (70°C), about 1 hour and 20 minutes. Transfer the roast to a cutting board and tent with foil. Let it rest for 15 minutes. Remove the string and slice the roast thinly across the grain.

CONTINUED . . .

Skillet Sausages

Makes 4 servings

IN THE WATERLOO region, home of Canada's largest Oktoberfest, plump, zesty farmer's sausages are specialties as well as good, locally brewed beer and ale. Beer or ale give this simple, everyday dish a distinctive flavour. Accompanied by Buttermilk Mashed Potatoes (page 109) and steamed green beans, this is comfort in a skillet.

1 tbsp (15 mL) canola oil

1 lb (500 g) fresh farmer's sausages

2 cups (500 mL) thinly sliced onions

1 cup (250 mL) sliced peeled apples

2 tbsp (30 mL) all-purpose flour

½ tsp (2 mL) paprika

1 bottle (340 mL) dark ale

1 tbsp (15 mL) Worcestershire sauce

6 black peppercorns

1 bay leaf

salt to taste

IN A LARGE skillet, heat the oil over medium-high heat. Prick the sausages in several places with the point of a sharp knife and brown them on all sides. Remove them to a plate.

Drain off all but 2 tbsp (30 mL) of the drippings from the skillet. Cook the onions over medium heat for 3 minutes. Add the apples and cook for 2 minutes. With a slotted spoon, transfer the onions and apples to the plate.

Stir the flour and paprika into the skillet and cook, stirring, for 2 minutes. Remove from the heat and gradually stir in the ale. Cook, whisking constantly, until smooth and thickened. Stir in the Worcestershire sauce, peppercorns and bay leaf. Return the sausages, onions and apples to the skillet. Cover tightly and cook over low heat until the sausages are cooked through, about 20 minutes. Taste and add salt if necessary. Discard the bay leaf.

VARIATION: Skillet Sausages and Sauerkraut

Brown the sausages as in the Skillet Sausages recipe and remove from the skillet.

Drain off all but 2 tbsp (30 mL) of the drippings from the skillet. Add 2 cups (500 mL) rinsed sauerkraut, 1 chopped apple, ½ tsp (2 mL) caraway seeds, 1 bay leaf and ¼ tsp (1 mL) freshly ground black pepper. Stir to combine well and place the sausages on top. Cover tightly and cook over low heat until the sausages are cooked through, about 20 minutes. Discard the bay leaf.

Peameal Bacon Roast

Makes 6 to 8 servings

ELIZABETH: It's hard to believe that such a delicious nosh as peameal bacon could now be such a mystery in Canada. It certainly wasn't when I grew up in Stratford, Ontario. It's true that there was side bacon—the crispness of which made it the *ne plus ultra* for bacon and tomato sandwiches. But as sure as my father's trip to the Stratford market on Saturday morning was the Sunday-morning peameal-bacon fry-up. Peameal bacon was part of a Southwestern Ontario diet. But we all took it for granted.

Fast-forward to the 1960s and Toronto's St. Lawrence Market. Joe Homer and Elso Biancolin ran two stalls in the South Market—an old-fashioned butcher shop and a bake shop that sold breads, buns and all manner of baked goods from bakeries around the city—and had a little challenge they solved together. Perfectly good rib-end cuts of peameal bacon were being left over in the butcher shop as shoppers opted for the prestigious centre cut of the cured loin. Solution: Slice and fry up the bacon and pop it into buns and sell said "sandwich" to eager and increasingly regular shoppers. But the sandwich didn't become world famous until the South Market was renovated in 1977. Stalls shuffled ownership and were jazzed up and, in the new bright and airy market, the Biancolin family (sons Robert and Maurice) made the sandwich a feature of their expanded Carousel Bakery.

And people noticed. The thick mittful of fried peameal bacon stuffed in a soft kaiser roll got rave reviews from television chefs and international publications.

In addition to sandwiches, take advantage of whole peameal bacon roasts, available at many butcher stores, markets and supermarkets. The roasted loin makes a perfect brunch dish and a nice weekend roast dinner.

2 lb (1 kg) whole peameal bacon roast

2 tbsp (30 ml) brown sugar

3 tbsp (45 ml) rum or orange juice

1 tsp (15 ml) Dijon mustard

PLACE THE BACON on a cutting board. Anticipate carving by making neat shallow parallel cuts over the top and upper sides of the bacon about ¼ to ½ inch (5 mm to 1.25 cm) apart. Set the bacon on a rack in a small roasting pan.

In a small bowl, mix the brown sugar, rum and mustard. Spoon over the top and sides of the roast, letting some drip down into the shallow cuts.

Roast in a 350°F (180°C) oven until the top is crusty and the interior temperature is 140 F° (60°C), about 1 hour. Let rest 10 minutes before slicing.

VARIATION: Barbecued Peameal Bacon

Cut 2 lb (1 kg) uncooked peameal bacon roast into ½-inch (1.25 cm) thick slices, brush lightly with oil, and cook on both sides on a greased grill over medium heat until nicely marked and crisp around the edges, about 5 minutes per side. Brush with dark maple syrup if you fancy a touch of sweet.

VARIATION: Peameal Bacon Sandwich

On a griddle or in a frying pan set over medium-high heat, melt 2 tsp (10 mL) butter. Add 12 slices of uncooked peameal bacon and fry until opaque and crisp around the edges, about 5 minutes per side. Stuff into soft kaiser rolls; add a squirt of honey mustard or ketchup, if you must.

SO WHAT IS PEAMEAL BACON?

For those baffled by the fuss about peameal bacon, here's what you need to know. Peameal bacon is a well-trimmed and lean pork loin, cured in a salt and sugar brine, but neither smoked nor cooked. It is rolled in cornmeal: years ago the coating was crushed peas, hence the "pea" meal. It is different from back bacon (Canadian bacon, as Americans call it), which is the same pork loin cut, but brined, smoked and cooked (like cooked ham) and not rolled in cornmeal.

Hachis Parmentier
(Shepherd's Pie)

Makes 6 to 8 servings

THIS RECIPE WAS handed down to Michelle Gélinas (a Quebec food writer, caterer and culinary researcher, and the author of the cookbook *Michelle Gélinas tout simplement*) from her paternal grandmother, Elizabeth McCaffrey. According to Michelle, her grandmother always made her *hachis Parmentier* with leftover roast pork, including its drippings, tasty with garlic and herbs. What makes this shepherd's pie a Quebec shepherd's pie (also known as *pâté chinois*) is the corn in the layer between the meat and mashed potato topping.

Hachis means a chopped concoction, and *Parmentier* signals that the dish includes potatoes—the dish is named to honour Antoine-Augustin Parmentier, who introduced potatoes to France in the 18th century.

Serve this dish with green or yellow beans, steamed then sautéed in butter. Accompany with Fruit Chili Sauce (page 306), Pickled Baby Beets (page 316) or Crunchy Bread-and-Butter Pickles (page 315).

FILLING

1 large onion, diced
2 cloves garlic, minced
2 tbsp (30 mL) canola oil
1 tsp (5 mL) dried savory* or sage
½ tsp (2 mL) each salt and freshly ground
  black pepper
¼ cup (60 mL) leftover gravy or apple juice
4 cups (1 L) coarsely ground cold leftover
  roast pork**
½ cup (125 mL) minced flat-leaf parsley
1 can (14 oz/398 mL) creamed corn
2 cups (500 mL) corn kernels, fresh
  or frozen

MASHED POTATO TOPPING

6 medium Yukon Gold potatoes, peeled
  and quartered (2 lb/1 kg)
½ cup (125 mL) 18% cream, heated
½ cup (125 mL) whole milk, heated (approx)
½ tsp (2 mL) each salt and freshly ground
  black pepper

*Summer savory, often just called savory,
  is a narrow-leafed herb that tastes like
  a combination of thyme, rosemary and
  oregano. It is popular in Quebec and Atlantic Canada, especially Newfoundland.

**The best way to grind cooked meat is to
  cut it into cubes and use a food processor
  to chop it finely.

FILLING → In a skillet over medium heat, fry the onion and garlic in the oil. Add the savory, salt and pepper; fry until the onion is softened, about 5 minutes. Add the gravy, pork and parsley; mix well. (The meat layer should be moist but not soupy.) Spread evenly over the bottom of a greased 13- × 9-inch (3.5 L) baking dish or shallow dish of similar capacity.

Mix the creamed corn and corn kernels; spread over the layer; set aside.

MASHED POTATO TOPPING → Meanwhile, in a saucepan of boiling salted water, cover and cook the potatoes until fork tender, about 15 minutes. Drain; return to the heat to dry, shaking the pot. Rice or mash the potatoes until smooth. Beat in the cream and enough of the milk to make a light purée. Mix in the salt and pepper. Spread over the corn. (MAKE-AHEAD: Let cool for 30 minutes; cover and refrigerate for up to 1 day.)

Bake in the centre of a 350°F (180°C) oven until the filling is bubbling around the mashed potatoes, about 30 to 40 minutes (longer if the potatoes have been refrigerated).

VARIATION: Shepherd's Pie with Peas

This is a leftover in the best sense of the word—thrifty, yes, but the last word in delicious comfort. And while this Southwestern-Ontario version shares the general method of *hachis Parmentier*, the meat layer is beef, enhanced (some might say souped up) with more gravy, and peas alone replace the more liquid corn layer. (It all balances out.) The potato topping bridges the two culinary cultures, as do the vegetable accompaniment and tangy condiments.

1 large onion, diced	1 cup (250 mL) leftover beef gravy
2 large cloves garlic, minced	4 cups (1 L) coarsely ground cold
2 tbsp (30 mL) canola oil	leftover roast beef
1 tsp (5 mL) dried thyme	½ cup (125 mL) minced fresh parsley
½ tsp (2 mL) each salt and freshly	2 cups (500 mL) frozen peas
ground black pepper	1 recipe Mashed Potato Topping

In a skillet over medium heat, fry the onion and garlic in the oil. Add the thyme, salt and pepper; fry until the onion is softened, about 5 minutes. Add the gravy, beef and parsley; mix well. Spread evenly over the bottom of a greased 13- × 9-inch (3.5 L) baking dish or shallow dish of similar capacity. Sprinkle with the peas. Spread the mashed potato topping overtop.

    Bake in the centre of a 350°F (180°C) oven until the filling is bubbling around the mashed potatoes, about 30 to 40 minutes.

Baked Beans

Makes 8 servings

ELIZABETH: A bubbling pot of baked beans is a dish about which many Canadians rhapsodize. Many of us have fond memories of "Granny"—or "Mimi"—spooning out steaming bowlfuls of beans. Alas, in the kitchen of my childhood, beans came out of a can, although my father was always eager to doctor them up with a little extra mustard, brown sugar and onion. That doesn't mean we didn't love beans on crunchy brown toast, but it wasn't until I was grown up and my parents moved to Montreal that we started to bake beans from scratch. While salt pork is the bean's meat of tradition, I prefer smoked bacon. Take your pick.

2 cups (500 mL) navy (white pea) beans
1 large onion, diced
½ cup (125 mL) chili sauce or ketchup
¼ cup (60 mL) fancy molasses
1 tbsp (15 mL) dry mustard
1 tbsp (15 mL) Worcestershire sauce

2 tsp (10 mL) cider vinegar
1 tsp (5 mL) salt
½ tsp (2 mL) freshly ground black pepper
4 oz (125 g) slab or thick-cut bacon,
   or salt pork
3 cups (750 mL) boiling water

PLACE THE BEANS and 8 cups (2 L) cold water in a large saucepan; cover. Bring to a boil over high heat; reduce the heat and boil gently for 2 minutes. Remove from the heat and let stand for 1 hour.

Drain and return to the pan. Cover with 12 cups (3 L) cold water; bring to a boil, covered. Reduce the heat and simmer, covered, until the beans are fork tender and their skins split when you blow on them, about 30 to 45 minutes. Drain the beans.

In a large bean pot or Dutch oven, stir together the beans, onion, chili sauce, molasses, mustard, Worcestershire sauce, vinegar, salt and pepper. Dice the bacon and add it to the bean mixture, with the boiling water. Stir well and cover.

Bake in a 300°F (150°C) oven until the liquid forms a luscious sauce around the beans, about 4 hours. Stir well. For a little crust on top, remove the cover and bake 30 minutes longer.

VARIATION: Slow-Cooker Baked Beans
Combine all the ingredients in a medium-size slow cooker, about 5 quarts
(5 L). Cover and cook on low until the beans are tender and the liquid forms
a thin sauce, about 6 to 7 hours. Uncover and cook on high until the sauce
thickens, about 30 minutes.

CASSOULET

The French version of baked beans, *cassoulet*, is a slow-cooked dish, usually
containing a variety of meats, starting with the southwest French specialty
confit of duck (or goose), along with lamb, sausage and perhaps another bit
of plain pork. Traditional cassoulet takes several days to make, but is such a
delicious dish that cooks over the years have tried to make quicker versions.

Julia Aitken, a food writer, editor and cookbook author, fondly remembers
her British mother making a quick cassoulet she called Bean Mess, which
contained dried navy beans, pork belly and kielbasa: "My mother, Margaret
Browne, had two food 'bibles', *Mrs. Beeton's All About Cookery* and *French
Country Cooking* by Elizabeth David. I treasure her food-spattered copy of
the David book, which still falls open naturally to the recipe for Le Cassoulet
de Castelnaudary. This dish was a cheap way to feed a family of six in
postwar Britain and quickly became one of Mum's standbys. But, with duck
confit being thin on the ground in northwest England, she simplified the
recipe, omitting the duck and using cheap-as-chips pork belly to create her
own tasty version. She renamed it, of course—its original title being thought
a mouthful and a bit pretentious, and Bean Mess remained a favourite family
supper for years."

MAINS
Lamb

Lamb Racks Provençal

Makes 8 servings

....

LAMB RACKS ARE so easy to cook and carve, yet provide a most elegant main course, especially teamed with our Do-Ahead Scalloped Potatoes (page 158). Seek out oven-ready "Frenched" lamb racks or French them yourself. (To French the racks, scrape the rib bones clean of meat, fat and gristle to about 1 inch/2.5 cm down from the tips.)

....

4 lamb racks (7 to 8 ribs each)

5 cloves garlic

½ cup (125 mL) loosely packed
   parsley sprigs

2 tbsp (30 mL) olive oil

2 tbsp (30 mL) anchovy paste

1 tbsp (15 mL) red wine vinegar

2 tsp (10 mL) dried rosemary, crushed

1 tsp (5 mL) coarsely ground black pepper

½ tsp (2 mL) crumbled dried thyme

DRY THE LAMB racks well and score the outside layer of fat diagonally to make small diamonds. In a blender or food processor, process the garlic, parsley, oil, anchovy paste, vinegar, rosemary, pepper and thyme until smooth. Rub all over the racks. Marinate the racks, covered, in the refrigerator for at least 1 hour or up to 4 hours. Remove from the refrigerator 30 minutes before roasting.

Place the racks bone side down in a shallow roasting pan. Roast in a 450°F (230°C) oven for 10 minutes. Lower the temperature to 350°F (180°C); roast until a thermometer registers 140°F (60°C), another 20 to 30 minutes longer for rare. Let stand, loosely covered with foil, for 10 minutes before carving between the ribs to serve.

VARIATION: Lamb Loin Chops Provençal
Prepare the marinade for Lamb Racks Provençal. Marinate 16 lamb loin chops for up to 4 hours. Place the chops on a greased barbecue grill 4 inches (10 cm) from medium-high heat or on a greased broiler rack in the oven; barbecue or broil until just pink inside, about 5 minutes a side, turning once.

Braised Lamb Stew
with Rosemary Dumplings

Makes 6 servings

JOHN BISHOP IS a Vancouver cookbook author and restaurateur whose restaurant, Bishop's, was one of the first fine dining establishments in Canada to offer local and seasonal menus. John has a culinary diary for his children: "I've jotted down the recipes that have been most popular with them. It's tentatively called *A Month of Meals Cooking for You: Recipes for Families,* and I've made notes on how the book might look. It's a little legacy for me to pass on to my kids." This recipe is part of that legacy.

STEW
1¼ lb (625 g) boneless lamb shoulder or leg
salt and freshly ground black pepper
½ cup (125 mL) all-purpose flour
2 tbsp (30 mL) canola oil
½ cup (125 mL) each finely chopped onion,
    carrot and celery
2 cloves garlic, chopped
2 tbsp (30 mL) tomato paste
1 cup (250 mL) dry red wine

1 tsp (5 mL) fennel seeds
2 cups (500 mL) lamb or beef broth or water

DUMPLINGS
1 cup (250 mL) all-purpose flour
1 tsp (5 mL) baking powder
½ tsp (2 mL) salt
1 tsp (5 mL) chopped fresh rosemary leaves
2 tbsp (30 mL) olive oil
½ cup (125 mL) milk

STEW → Trim off the sinew and excess fat from the lamb and cut the meat into 2-inch (5 cm) cubes. Season with salt and pepper. Dip each cube into the flour, coating all sides. In a large skillet over medium-high heat, heat the oil and brown the lamb in batches, removing the cubes with a slotted spoon to a casserole or baking dish as they brown.

In the same skillet over medium heat, cook the onion, carrot, celery and garlic, stirring, for about 5 minutes. Stir in the tomato paste, red wine and fennel seeds until well combined, scraping up any brown bits from the bottom of the skillet. Pour over the lamb and top with the broth. Cover tightly and bake for 2 hours in a 350°F (180°C) oven.

Just before the stew is cooked, prepare the dumpling mixture and turn the oven to 375°F (190°C).

DUMPLINGS → In a large bowl, stir together the flour, baking powder, salt and rosemary. Stir in the oil and milk to make a soft dough. Divide into six portions and place on a flour-coated plate. Taste the stew and adjust the seasoning if necessary. Place the dumplings overtop; cover and bake until the dumplings are light and fluffy, about 20 minutes. Serve immediately.

Piri Piri Chicken

Makes 6 generous servings

....

ELIZABETH: A roasted chicken is a thing of beauty. A chicken roasted with Portuguese flavours—paprika, lemon, garlic, oregano and piri piri sauce—is an item of perfection. The secret that makes it so terrific is not such a secret: it's the piri piri sauce, a hot sauce made from bird's eye chilis and available bottled, especially in Portuguese neighbourhood grocery stores. The piri piri does add piquancy to the chicken, but it is not one of those scary hot sauces that can ruin perfectly good food. Consider roasted potatoes or rice to go along with the chicken. This recipe comes from Rosa Carvalho.

....

6 large cloves garlic, minced
6 bay leaves, halved
2 tbsp (30 mL) fresh lemon juice
2 tbsp (30 mL) olive oil
1 tbsp (15 mL) white wine
2 tsp (10 mL) sweet paprika
1 tsp (5 mL) dried oregano
½ tsp (2 mL) each salt and freshly
   ground black pepper

½ tsp (2 mL) piri piri sauce
1 air-chilled whole roasting chicken,*
   about 3¾ lb (1.7 kg)
1 small lemon

*Chicken chilled in blasts of cold air,
   rather than cold water, has a dried,
   creamier-coloured skin that roasts crispy
   and golden brown.

IN A LARGE bowl, combine the garlic, bay leaves, lemon juice, oil, wine, paprika, oregano, salt, pepper and piri piri sauce. Prick the chicken in several places over the breasts and thighs. Add the chicken to the bowl and, wearing rubber gloves, rub the chicken all over, inside and out, with this piri piri mixture.

Cut the ends off the lemon; prick all over with a pointy knife. Push the lemon into the chicken's body cavity. Tie the chicken legs together; twist the wings back. Cover and refrigerate the chicken for at least 1 hour and up to 8 hours.

Place the chicken in a small roasting pan. Cover the roasting pan with a lid, or with foil arched generously over the chicken. Roast in the centre of a 350°F (180°C) oven for 1 hour. Remove the covering and baste the chicken with the pan juices. Continue roasting, basting 3 or 4 more times, until the juices in the thigh run clear when pierced, the skin has puffed, the legs can be wiggled easily and a thermometer inserted into the thickest part of the thigh registers 185°F (85°C), about 1 hour.

Transfer to a cutting board and tent loosely with foil. Let rest up to 20 minutes before cutting into 10 pieces (drumsticks, thighs, wings, upper halves of breasts and remaining lower breasts) with kitchen shears. Skim the fat from the pan juices; discard the fat and bay leaves. Drizzle the tasty pan juices over the chicken pieces.

Tarragon-Butter
Roasted Chicken with Gravy

Makes 6 generous servings

A GOOD ROAST chicken is like a go-everywhere black dress: indispensable. Dress it up, dress it down—the variations are endless. This particular roast chicken with a fresh tarragon butter epitomizes everything likeable about a perfect bird: crisp golden skin, moist breast and dark meat nicely but not overwhelmingly scented with herbs, plus a delicious gravy enriched with roasted garlic. There's nothing better with or over Buttermilk Mashed Potatoes (recipe follows).

CHICKEN

1 air-chilled whole roasting chicken,*
   about 3¾ lb (1.7 kg)
1 lemon
¼ cup (60 mL) chopped fresh tarragon
½ cup (125 mL) butter, softened
½ tsp (2 ml) each salt and freshly
   ground black pepper
2 heads garlic

GRAVY

2 tbsp (30 mL) all-purpose flour
2 cups (500 mL) chicken broth (approx)
1 tbsp (15 mL) red currant or wine jelly
   (optional)
salt and freshly ground pepper

*Chicken chilled in blasts of cold air, rather than cold water, has a dried, creamier-coloured skin that roasts crispy and golden brown.

CHICKEN → Starting at the neck end of the chicken, lift the skin up, separating it from the breasts. Slide one hand between the skin and meat, gently lifting and separating the skin, and extending the pocket down to and over the thighs. Cut the lemon in half; squeezing and pressing gently, rub one half of the lemon over the whole chicken. Place the spent lemon half in the chicken cavity, squeezing any remaining juices into the cavity.

From the remaining lemon half, grate 1 tsp (5 mL) lemon zest; place the zest in a bowl with the tarragon, butter, salt and pepper. Mash together to make a smooth paste. Spread about half of the tarragon butter into the pocket over the breast and thighs. Close the pocket: press on the skin to even out the tarragon butter. Spread all but 1 tsp (5 mL) of the remaining tarragon butter over the chicken. Tuck the wings under the back and set the chicken on a rack in a roasting pan just large enough to contain it comfortably.

Rub off any loose papery skin from the whole garlic heads; cut off the top of each head just enough to expose the tips of the garlic inside. Spread the exposed tips with the remaining tarragon butter. Cut the remaining lemon half into 6 wedges. Nestle the lemon wedges and garlic heads around the chicken. Roast in a 375°F (190°C) oven, basting every 20 minutes or so, until the skin puffs golden brown over the breasts, the legs can be wiggled easily in their sockets and the juices run clear when pierced in the thickest part of the thigh, about 1 hour. A thermometer inserted into the thickest part of the thigh should register 185°F (85°C). Transfer to a cutting board and tent with foil. Let rest for up to 20 minutes.

GRAVY → While the chicken is resting, remove the garlic heads and lemon wedges from the roasting pan; set aside. Tip up the pan; skim off any fat. Squeeze out the garlic into the pan; add the flour. With a flat whisk or wooden spoon, work the garlic and flour into the drippings. Whisk in 1 cup (250 mL) of the broth to make a smooth paste. Set over medium heat, whisking constantly and adding the remaining broth in ½ cup (125 mL) increments; bring to a boil. Whisk in a little more broth for a thinner gravy, if desired. Whisk in the jelly (if using) until it melts. Taste, adding salt and pepper to taste. Serve in a warmed gravy boat.

Using sturdy kitchen or poultry shears, cut into 10 pieces (drumsticks, thighs, wings, upper halves of breasts and remaining lower breasts). Serve on a warmed platter, garnished with the roasted lemon wedges to squeeze over the chicken.

BUTTERMILK MASHED POTATOES

ALLOW FOR 1 medium potato per person, plus 1 for the pot. Choose russet or Yukon Gold potatoes. Scrub and trim the potatoes, and pare if desired (we usually desire to). Quarter and cook, covered, in boiling salted water until fork tender, about 15 minutes. Drain; return to low heat to dry out for about half a minute. Remove from the heat and either put through a ricer or mash well by hand, removing all the lumps. Moisten with a spoonful of butter, season to taste with salt and freshly ground black pepper, and stir in enough buttermilk, about 1¼ cups (300 mL) per 6 to 7 potatoes, to create a smooth, creamy mash. Depending on the season, stir in some fresh herbs: finely minced parsley, or chopped chives or dill or a mixture.

Jamaican Jerk Chicken

Makes 6 servings

....

ELIZABETH: Jerk seasoning came like a hot flash from Jamaica back in the 1980s. It was Michael Bryne, then food and beverage manager of what's now that country's Boscabel Beach Resort, who shared with me the recipe his cooks used when making jerk pork or chicken. Before trying out this jerk marinade on a crowd of friends, Michael and I spent a morning in Kensington Market, searching out Jamaican thyme and scallions (young red onions) and tasting peppers to get ones hot enough to create an authentic experience. The heat has been toned down in this recipe, but feel free to ramp it up with another Scotch bonnet pepper if you are feeling adventurous.

....

4 Jamaican scallions or regular plump
   green onions, chopped
3 large cloves garlic, chopped
1 onion, diced
½ to 1 Scotch bonnet pepper,*
   trimmed and seeded
¼ cup (60 mL) orange juice
3 tbsp (45 mL) soy sauce
1 tbsp (15 mL) canola oil
2 tsp (10 mL) ground allspice

2 tsp (10 mL) white vinegar
1 tsp (5 ml) chopped fresh thyme
½ tsp (2 mL) each salt and freshly ground
   black pepper
½ tsp (2 mL) curry powder or paste
¼ tsp (1 mL) cinnamon
12 chicken thighs (about 3 lb/1.5 kg)

*Substitute jalapeño or other hot pepper
   for Scotch bonnet.

IN A FOOD processor, whirl together until smooth the scallions, garlic, onion, Scotch bonnet pepper, orange juice, soy sauce, oil, allspice, vinegar, thyme, salt, pepper, curry powder and cinnamon.

Scrape the marinade ingredients into a large bowl. Trim off any obvious skin flaps and fat from the chicken thighs. Add the thighs to the marinade and toss to coat. Cover and marinate in the refrigerator for at least 1 hour, or up to 1 day, turning occasionally as time permits.

Arrange the thighs, bony-side up, not touching each other, in a shallow roasting pan. Roast in a 400°F (200°C) oven for 30 minutes. Turn the pieces and roast until the juices in the thickest part of the thighs run clear when pierced, about 20 to 30 minutes. Broil to crisp the skin, watching carefully, for about 2 to 3 minutes.

VARIATION: Barbecued Jerk Chicken

Chicken cooks through to the bone more reliably and without burning the outside if the pieces are grilled over medium indirect heat.

Reserve any marinade leftover after marinating the chicken thighs. Arrange the thighs, bony-side down, on a greased grill over medium indirect heat (see Indirect Heat Grilling, page 84). Spoon on any remaining marinade.

Lower the lid and grill for 25 minutes, turning the pieces and grilling until the skin is a glorious golden brown and the juices in the thickest part of the thighs run clear when pierced, about 20 minutes.

Baba's Oven-Fried Chicken

Makes 8 servings

ADELL SHNEER, former test-kitchen manager at *Canadian Living* contributes a favourite recipe to this book from her grandmother. Adell told us: "In our family, this chicken is affectionately named after my grandmother, Sarah Taradash, who was a fabulous cook. The flour coating gets crisp and irresistible. Make extra because it is equally delicious cold the next day. If you are using kosher chicken, reduce the salt to one teaspoon [5 mL]."

½ cup (125 mL) all-purpose flour
2 tsp (10 mL) kosher salt, divided
1½ tsp (7 mL) garlic powder
1 tsp (5 mL) paprika

½ tsp (2 mL) freshly ground black pepper
¼ tsp (1 mL) dry mustard
8 chicken thighs, drumsticks or breast
halves, bone-in

IN A FLAT dish, stir together the flour, 1 tsp (5 mL) of the salt, the garlic powder, paprika, pepper and mustard.

Rinse the chicken under water; sprinkle with the remaining salt. One piece at a time, coat the chicken in the flour mixture. Place, skin-side down, on a greased rimmed baking sheet. Bake in a 375°F (190°C) oven for 20 minutes. Turn the pieces over and continue baking until golden and the juices run clear when the chicken is pierced, about 40 more minutes.

Hot and Glossy Asian Wings

Makes 3 to 4 main-course servings

....

SPICY CHICKEN WINGS are always popular, as a family dinner with rice and stir-fried vegetables or as a snack for watching "the game." Pass lots of serviettes.

....

¼ cup (60 mL) hoisin sauce

2 tbsp (30 mL) each soy sauce, dry sherry or rice wine, ketchup and liquid honey

3 cloves garlic, minced

1 tbsp (15 mL) grated fresh ginger

1 tbsp (15 mL) Asian hot chili sauce

3 lb (1.5 kg) chicken wings, split*

1 green onion, finely chopped

*If the wings are not already split, remove and discard the tips. Divide the wings at the joints.

IN A LARGE bowl, combine the hoisin sauce, soy sauce, sherry, ketchup, honey, garlic, ginger and chili sauce. Pat the wings dry; add them to the bowl and toss in the marinade mixture to coat well. Cover and marinate in the refrigerator for at least 4 hours, turning occasionally. (MAKE-AHEAD: Cover the wings and refrigerate for up to 1 day ahead. Bring to room temperature for 30 minutes before roasting.)

Arrange the wings, meaty-side down, on parchment paper–lined baking sheets so that there is some room between them. Spoon half the marinade overtop. Bake in a 425°F (220°C) oven for 15 minutes. Turn the wings over and brush with the remaining marinade; bake until golden brown, crisp and the juices run clear, another 15 to 20 minutes. For crisper wings, broil for 2 minutes. Arrange the wings on a platter. Pour any pan juices overtop and sprinkle with the green onion to serve.

VARIATION: Black Bean Chicken Wings

For the marinade, stir together ⅓ cup (75 mL) black bean garlic sauce, ¼ cup (60 mL) each liquid honey and ketchup, 2 tbsp (30 mL) each sesame oil, rice vinegar and Dijon mustard and ½ tsp (2 mL) chili oil or hot pepper sauce. Marinate and bake as in the Hot and Glossy Asian Wings recipe. Garnish with the green onion if desired.

Lemon Chicken Souvlaki

Makes 6 servings

GEORGE KAPELOS: "Squeeze me a lemon," my mother would say, when I volunteered to help her cook. I soon learned to roll the fruit to extract more juice, before cutting it in half and squeezing it on the glass lemon-juicer she would pull down from the cabinet and put on the counter. In our kitchen, lemons turned up everywhere: in soups, on rice, in meat dishes and in desserts. We ate avgolemono—a lemon and egg soup—to ward off colds and provide comfort on winter nights. Lemon was a staple (along with oregano and olive oil) in the marinade for summer barbecues (often my mother added the squeezed lemon halves as well—"just for flavouring") and in Sunday roasted chicken as well. Always present on the dinner table were lemons—just in case an extra squirt was needed.

In my mid-twenties I travelled to Greece for the first time. It was Easter and the streets around the Royal Palace (now Parliament) and gardens were full of lemon trees. The scent of the blossoms was intoxicating. And, as in my mother's kitchen, lemon was served with everything—fish, chicken, spring greens, fried potatoes—and plopped on the table just in case you needed more. I had come home, home to my *patrida*.

After the memorial service (40 days after my mother's death, as is the custom in the Greek Orthodox church), my sister, brother and I hosted a lunch. We grilled lemon chicken souvlaki for the guests who came to honour our mother's memory. Here is the recipe—it's very simple—for you to share in my family's love for lemon. *Pictured with Rice Pilaf (page 116).*

3 large lemons
½ cup (125 mL) extra virgin olive oil
2 tsp (10 mL) crumbled dried oregano
½ tsp (2 mL) each salt and freshly ground
    black pepper

4 large boneless skinless chicken
    breasts (2 lb/1 kg)
6 bamboo or wooden skewers,
    soaked in water for 1 hour

ROLL 2 OF the lemons firmly on the counter; squeeze out the juice, removing the seeds. In a large bowl, whisk together the juice, oil, oregano, salt and pepper. Pour about a third of the mixture into a container for basting. Set aside. Add the squeezed lemon halves to the bowl "just for flavouring."

On a cutting board, cut the breasts lengthwise in half. Cut these halves crosswise into generous 1-inch (2.5 cm) slices, then into cubes. Add to the lemon marinade; cover and refrigerate for at least 1 hour or up to 8 hours.

CONTINUED . . .

Thread the chicken cubes onto the skewers; discard any remaining marinade. Place on a greased grill over medium-high heat; drizzle with a little of the reserved basting mixture. Grill until golden brown underneath, about 7 minutes. Turn, drizzle with the basting mixture and grill, turning as the chicken firms and browns, until golden and glazed on all sides and the juices run clear, about 8 minutes.

Cut the remaining lemon into 6 wedges. Arrange the wedges on a warm platter with the souvlaki. Serve with Rice Pilaf (recipe follows).

RICE PILAF
Makes 6 servings

MY MOTHER ALWAYS made a rice pilaf to go with the skewers. Here's how she did it: In a medium saucepan, fry 1 diced onion in 2 tbsp (30 ml) of good Greek olive oil over medium heat until translucent. Add 1½ cups (375 mL) parboiled long-grain rice; fry, stirring, for 2 minutes. Add ¼ cup (60 mL) currants and 1 bay leaf. Pour in 3 cups (750 mL) water or chicken broth and ½ tsp each (2 mL) salt and pepper. Bring to a boil, stirring once or twice. Cover and simmer over low heat until the rice is tender and the liquid is absorbed, about 25 minutes. Fluff with a fork and discard the bay leaf; add ⅓ cup (75 mL) toasted slivered almonds or pine nuts, 2 tbsp (30 ml) minced parsley and as much mint as you like.

An Excellent Chicken Pot Pie

Makes 8 servings

WHY IS THE mild chicken pot pie so popular? We think it's because you can really taste the chicken. The creamy sauce is made with the poaching broth, so it just adds more chicken-ness. The vegetables are so inoffensive and pleasant that the eater can focus on the chicken and crusty pastry topping. Buy the best chicken your budget allows.

FILLING

4 cups (1 L) water (approx)
2 cups (500 mL) chicken broth (approx)
2 bay leaves
2 sprigs thyme or 1 tsp (5 mL) dried thyme
1 stalk celery with leaves, chopped
5 parsley sprigs
1 air-chilled whole roasting chicken, or
   chicken parts, 3½ lb (1.5 kg)
8 small carrots (1 bunch)
2 medium-large potatoes (12 oz/375 g)
24 pearl onions (8 oz/250 g), peeled

SAUCE

⅓ cup (75 mL) butter
⅔ cup (150 mL) all-purpose flour

½ tsp (2 mL) each salt, dried thyme and
   freshly ground black pepper
½ tsp (2 mL) Worcestershire sauce
¼ tsp (1 mL) hot pepper sauce
½ cup (125 mL) 18% cream
1½ cups (375 mL) frozen peas
⅓ cup (75 mL) minced fresh parsley

PASTRY

2 cups (500 mL) all-purpose flour
½ tsp (2 mL) salt
⅓ cup (75 mL) cold butter, cubed
⅓ cup (75 mL) cold lard, cubed
1 large egg yolk
1½ tsp (7 mL) white wine vinegar
ice water

FILLING → In a large stockpot or saucepan, combine the water and broth with the flavouring items: the bay leaves, thyme, celery and parsley. If using a whole chicken, use kitchen shears to cut into quarters; add the chicken to the pot, adding more water if needed to just cover the chicken. Bring to a boil over medium heat, skimming off any foam on the surface. Reduce the heat and simmer, covered, until the chicken is tender, about 25 minutes. Check the breasts first and remove them if their juices run clear, before the juices run clear in the thighs and legs. Remove the chicken to a tray to cool.

Skim the flavouring items from the poaching broth and discard. Peel and cut the carrots and potatoes into bite-size chunks. Simmer, covered, in the broth until just tender, about 8 minutes. With a slotted spoon, transfer to a tray. Add the onions to the broth; simmer, covered, until just tender, about 12 minutes. Transfer to the tray with the potatoes and carrots and set aside.

CONTINUED . . .

While the vegetables are cooking, pull the skin off the chicken. Pull the meat away from the bones and chop the meat into bite-size pieces.

Return the bones to the poaching broth and simmer gently, uncovered, for 20 minutes (see Note 1). Remove and discard the bones; strain the broth into a large measuring cup or bowl. You should have about 4½ cups (1.125 L). If less, top up with chicken broth; if more, freeze for another dish.

SAUCE → In a large saucepan, melt the butter over medium heat. Stir in the flour, salt, thyme and pepper. Cook, stirring, for 2 minutes. Whisk in the chicken poaching broth, about a quarter at a time. Bring to a simmer, whisking, until the sauce thickens and becomes smooth; simmer for 3 or 4 minutes. Stir in the Worcestershire sauce, hot pepper sauce and cream. Let cool while making the pastry.

PASTRY → Using a food processor or in a bowl, combine the flour and salt. Sprinkle the butter and lard over the flour and salt. Pulse or use a pastry blender to combine the ingredients until the mixture is coarse and crumbly. In a measuring cup, stir together the yolk and vinegar; add ice water to the ½ cup (125 mL) mark. Drizzle over the crumbly mixture and pulse about 6 times or stir until the dough is ragged and blended. Turn out onto a floured counter and press into a flat rectangular shape. Wrap, and let rest in the refrigerator for 20 minutes.

Gently mix the chicken, potatoes, carrots, onions, peas, parsley and sauce in a 13- × 9-inch (3.5 L) glass baking dish. On a floured surface, roll out the pastry to a rectangle about ¼ inch (5 mm) thick, large enough to fit over the filling without stretching and about ½ inch (1.25 cm) down the four sides. Place over the filling; trim the edges and press to the dish. (MAKE-AHEAD: Refrigerate, covered, for up to 1 day; add about 10 minutes to baking time.) Cut a few slashes down the centre to let steam escape. Brush with the egg wash (see Note 2). Press the pastry scraps together and reroll; cut out decorative shapes and press onto the pastry. Brush the shapes with egg wash. Place the pot pie on a large rimmed baking sheet.

Bake in the centre of a 400°(200°C) oven until the filling is bubbling and the pastry a lovely golden brown, about 45 minutes.

NOTE 1

A homemade pot pie is certainly not a 30-minute supper project. Rather, it is something to do on a weekend afternoon, listening to music or sharing time and work with a cooking buddy. Returning the chicken bones to simmer longer in the poaching broth may look like a bother, but the bones really do enrich the broth. If you're pressed for time, substitute purchased puff pastry for the pastry topping and replace the pesky little onions with 6 small cooking onions, peeled and quartered.

NOTE 2

To make an egg wash, stir together 1 large egg yolk with 2 tbsp (30 mL) cream, milk or water.

Chicken Stew
with Fluffy Dumplings

Makes 4 servings

....

ROSE: Each time I appear on Rogers TV's *Daytime* in Kitchener, co-host and associate producer Susan Cook-Scheerer and I compare notes on growing up on a farm—the wood stove, even the cot in the corner of the kitchen, where each of our dads would have a "shut-eye" after lunch every day. The other thing we talk about is that old-fashioned farm dish chicken and dumplings. For all the chicken and dumpling lovers, here's a recipe that I hope will bring back good memories.

....

SUSAN COOK-SCHEERER: As a kid growing up in rural Ontario, there were two things I always looked forward to on a blustery winter's day: one was seeing my dad's cronies, who would often be gathered in our big country kitchen to play Solo (a card game that was popular in our area). The other was the incredible smell coming from a pot on our old wood stove, where one of my favourite winter comfort foods would be bubbling away—chicken and dumplings.

Mom would start a large pot of water boiling and then add in a roasting chicken (a big one—there were six kids to feed, after all!). After it had cooked for most of the afternoon, she would remove the chicken, which would be served separately, then she would add cut-up potatoes and the dumpling mixture to the broth. (Yes, this recipe comes from "back in the day," when I was blissfully unaware of what "carbs" were.)

Although many people will talk about their love for "light, fluffy" dumplings, the kids in our family preferred a heartier dumpling—the kind that could be achieved only by lifting the lid of the pot during the cooking process. This would produce a dumpling with a somewhat rubbery texture—just the way we liked them. Not a stormy winter's day goes by that I don't think of this special dish.

....

STEW

4 chicken breasts, bone-in
salt and freshly ground black pepper
2 tbsp (30 mL) all-purpose flour
1 tbsp (15 mL) each butter and canola oil
16 tiny carrots
12 pearl onions or 6 cipolline onions

10 tiny red potatoes, unpeeled
8 oz (250 g) tiny mushrooms
2 stalks celery, diagonally sliced
4 cups (1 L) chicken broth
½ tsp (2 mL) each salt, dried thyme
    and crumbled dried sage
1 cup (250 mL) frozen peas

FLUFFY DUMPLINGS

2 cups (500 mL) sifted cake-and-pastry
   flour (approx)*

4 tsp (20 mL) baking powder

¾ tsp (4 mL) salt

2 tbsp (30 mL) lard

⅔ cup (150 mL) milk (approx)

*Sift flour before measuring.

STEW → Dry the chicken well and spread out on a plate. Sprinkle with salt and pepper; then dredge with the flour. Reserve the remaining flour.

In a saucepan large enough to allow 3 inches (8 cm) of space for the dumplings to rise, melt the butter in the oil over medium heat, brown the chicken on all sides in batches and remove to a plate.

Add the carrots, onions, potatoes, mushrooms and celery to the pan and cook for 5 minutes. Stir in the flour remaining from dredging the chicken and cook for 1 minute. Gradually add the broth, stirring to scrape up any brown bits from the bottom of the pan. Stir in the salt, thyme and sage. Add back the chicken and return to a boil; reduce the heat, cover and simmer until the chicken is no longer pink inside, about 30 minutes. Stir in the peas. (MAKE-AHEAD: Cool, cover and refrigerate for up to 1 day. Bring to a simmer to proceed.)

FLUFFY DUMPLINGS → Sprinkle a large plate with a light covering of flour. Into a large bowl, sift together the 2 cups (500 mL) flour, baking powder and salt. Cut in the lard until the mixture has the texture of meal. Stir in the milk, adding a few more drops if necessary to make a sticky dough.

With a tablespoon, cut out the dumplings and drop them onto the floured plate. Quickly drop the dumplings onto the gently simmering stew, spacing them evenly; cover the pan tightly and simmer, without lifting the lid, until the dumplings are cooked through, about 15 minutes.

> **NOTE**
> If you freeze the stew and dumplings, thaw them in the refrigerator and reheat them together; the dumplings stay remarkably fluffy.

Roast Turkey with Hazelnut-Cranberry Stuffing

Makes 18 servings

IF THERE'S ONE iconic Canadian holiday dish, it's roast turkey. Plump, golden and ready to serve to a crowd, turkey is on the table for big holidays throughout the year. Paramount to a roast turkey is an excellent stuffing, and this herbed, fruity, nutty bread dressing is generous and in the festive tradition. Reputation-Making Gravy (recipe follows) completes the meal.

STUFFING

1½ cups (375 mL) hazelnuts (filberts)

⅓ cup (75 mL) butter

4 large onions, diced

3 large tender celery stalks with leaves, diced

4 tsp (20 mL) each crumbled dried sage and thyme

¾ tsp (4 mL) each salt and freshly ground black pepper (approx)

1½ cups (375 mL) dried cranberries

½ cup (125 mL) minced fresh parsley

16 cups (4 L) cubed homestyle or sourdough white bread

1 cup (250 mL) chicken broth

TURKEY

18 lb (8 kg) turkey

½ cup (125 mL) butter, melted

2 tsp (10 mL) each crumbled dried sage and thyme

½ tsp (2 mL) each salt and freshly ground black pepper

STUFFING → Toast the hazelnuts on a baking sheet in a 350°F (180°C) oven or toaster oven until the skins loosen and the hazelnuts turn golden, about 10 minutes. When cool enough to handle, wrap in a towel and rub vigorously to remove most of the skins; chop coarsely and set aside.

In a large skillet, melt the butter over medium heat; add the onions, celery, sage, thyme, salt and pepper. Cook, stirring regularly, until the onions are tender and fragrant, about 15 minutes. Stir in the cranberries and parsley.

Place the bread in a large bowl; scrape the onion mixture over the bread and toss to coat. While tossing, drizzle with the chicken broth. (MAKE-AHEAD: Let cool. Cover and refrigerate for up to 1 day or place in an airtight container and freeze for up to 2 weeks. Let thaw in the refrigerator, about 1 day.) Stir in the hazelnuts; taste, adjusting the salt and pepper if necessary.

TURKEY → Remove the giblets and wipe the turkey dry. Loosely pack the stuffing into the body and neck cavities, and any remaining stuffing (see Note 1) into a casserole dish. Skewer the neck to the body, and tie the legs together. Fold the wing tips under the back. Place, breast-side up, on a rack in a large roasting pan; brush all over with the butter and sprinkle with the sage, thyme, salt and pepper. Tent loosely with foil, tucking in the sides but leaving the ends open. Roast in a 325°F (160°C) oven for 3½ hours, basting every 30 minutes. Uncover, baste and roast until the proverbial golden brown, and a meat thermometer inserted in the thickest part of the thigh registers 180°F (82°C), about 1 hour.

Reserving the pan juices to make gravy, lift the turkey onto a carving board (see Note 2) and tent loosely with foil. Let stand for 30 minutes before carving.

REPUTATION-MAKING GRAVY
Makes about 4 cups (1 L)

AFTER REMOVING THE bird from the roasting pan, skim off the fat from the pan juices. Place the pan over medium heat. With a flat whisk or wooden spoon, whisk in 2 cups (500 mL) turkey or chicken broth (see Note 3), scraping up any brown bits from the bottom of the pan. Reduce the heat to low. In a jar, shake together ⅓ cup (75 mL) all-purpose flour and ½ tsp (2 mL) each salt and freshly ground black pepper with another 2 cups (500 mL) turkey or chicken broth. Pour into the pan, whisking or stirring until blended and smooth; simmer for 3 minutes. For thicker gravy, simmer longer; for thinner, add more broth. Taste and adjust the seasoning. Strain the gravy through a sieve into a clean saucepan or large pitcher, for reheating just before serving in a warmed gravy boat.

NOTE 1
That extra stuffing? Bake, covered, in a 375°F (190°C) oven for about 40 minutes, while the turkey rests and is being carved. Uncover briefly to toast the top layer of bread.

NOTE 2
A carving board has a shallow ditch around the sides to collect the juices and may have prongs to hold the turkey steady during carving.

NOTE 3
You can use the turkey neck, heart and gizzard, a bay leaf, 2 celery stalks with leaves (chopped), parsley stems, ½ tsp (2 mL) dried thyme and 1 small onion (chopped) to make broth for gravy. Simply cover all the ingredients listed here with 6 cups (1.5 L) cold water and simmer, uncovered, over low heat for 2 hours. Strain. *Makes 4 cups (1 L) broth*

Grilled Salmon
with Tarragon Mayonnaise

Makes 8 servings

SALMON HAS ALWAYS been a favourite fish with Canadians from coast to coast. Put on the barbecue, it is an unbeatable hit with a summer crowd. This method of grilling it slowly over low heat leaves the cook free to join the guests for drinks and appetizers. *Pictured with Tarragon Mayonnaise (recipe follows) and Edna Staebler's Bean Salad (page 172).*

3 lb (1.5 kg) wild salmon fillet or fillets (with skin)
3 tbsp (45 mL) olive oil
2 tbsp (30 mL) each chopped fresh tarragon and parsley

1 tsp (5 mL) grated lemon zest
1 tbsp (15 mL) fresh lemon juice
salt and freshly ground black pepper

DIVIDE THE SKINLESS side of the fillet into 8 portions by cutting down almost to the skin, but not through it. Place the fillet skin-side down in a shallow glass dish. In a small bowl, combine the oil, tarragon, parsley, zest and lemon juice. Brush over the salmon and let sit at room temperature for at least 5 minutes or up to 30 minutes.

Place the fillet, skin-side down, on a greased grill over low heat and sprinkle with salt and pepper; close the lid and grill until the fish is opaque and flakes easily when tested with a fork, about 30 minutes. Insert a spatula between the skin and each portion of fish, removing the fish and leaving the skin on the grill. (When the grill cools, it will come off easily.)

TARRAGON MAYONNAISE
Makes about 1 cup (250 mL)

¾ cup (175 mL) mayonnaise
2 tbsp (30 mL) sour cream
1 tsp (5 mL) grated lemon zest
1 tbsp (15 mL) fresh lemon juice
2 tbsp (30 mL) chopped fresh tarragon

1 tbsp (15 mL) snipped fresh chives
1 clove garlic, minced
½ tsp (2 mL) salt
¼ tsp (1 mL) freshly ground black pepper

IN A SMALL bowl, whisk together the mayonnaise, sour cream, lemon zest and juice. Stir in the tarragon, chives, garlic, salt and pepper. (MAKE-AHEAD: Cover and refrigerate for up to 6 hours.)

Bombay Mussels

Makes 2 main-course servings or 4 appetizers

ELIZABETH: Steamed with beer, white wine, tomato sauce, herbs and cream—you name it, cultivated mussels are a favourite on Prince Edward Island restaurant menus. One of the best ways I have ever tasted mussels is with a curry, ginger and cream broth, a signature dish called Bombay Mussels served in the Charlottetown restaurant Flex Mussels, alas no longer in business.

2 lb (1kg) mussels
1 tsp (5 mL) canola oil
1 clove garlic, finely chopped
1 tsp (5 mL) finely chopped fresh ginger
2 tbsp (30 mL) finely diced or puréed mango
1 tbsp (15 mL) mild curry paste
¼ cup (60 mL) white wine

½ cup (125 mL) whipping cream
¼ tsp (1 mL) sesame oil
⅓ cup (75 mL) chopped fresh coriander (cilantro), divided
½ lime
1 crusty French baguette, sliced

CHECK THE MUSSELS, discarding any that don't close when tapped. A little gape is not unusual for cultivated mussels. Fresh, live mussels close obediently—give them a minute or two just to be sure. Discard any that continue to gape. Pull out and snip off any beards and rinse; set aside.

In a 4- to 6-quart (4 to 6 L) saucepan, heat the oil over medium heat (see Note). Add the garlic, ginger, mango and curry paste; fry for 1 to 2 minutes, stirring frequently. The goal here is to warm the ingredients just enough to awaken them. Exercise caution, as excessive heat makes the curry bitter. (The combination of fresh ginger, garlic and mango is aromatherapy of the most enchanting kind.)

Stir in the wine and, using a wooden spoon, scrape the bottom of the pot smooth. Add the cream, sesame oil and half of the coriander. Bring to a boil over high heat; add the mussels. Stir and toss to coat the shells evenly.

Cover tightly and steam until the mussels have opened wide, about 4 to 6 minutes, stirring gently midway. Be sure to check the mussels at the beginning of the suggested time. Discard any mussels that have not opened.

Using a slotted spoon, scoop the mussels into warmed bowls. Over high heat, boil the sauce hard to reduce by one-third or to desired consistency, about 2 minutes. Meanwhile, squeeze fresh lime juice over the mussels. Pour the reduced sauce over the mussels and garnish with the remaining chopped coriander. Serve with plenty of crusty baguette.

NOTE

A wide saucepan with a heavy bottom is the best for cooking mussels. There's room for the mussels to open and, covered, the liquid comes back to the boil immediately, steaming the mussels quickly, without toughening them.

MUSSELS AND THEIR BEARDS

Although today's cultured mussels arrive at the market cleaned, you may find a few that still have their beards, the super-strong threads that mussels use to attach themselves to rocks in the wild, or to the long mesh socks in which they grow when cultivated. Pull the beard out and towards the pointed end of the shell. Cut off on the sharp edge of the shell, or snip off with scissors. Then rinse the mussels in cold water. Gone are the days when you had to scrub mussels—Canadian farmed mussels, whether from Prince Edward Island, nearby Îles-de-la-Madeleine, Nova Scotia, New Brunswick or Newfoundland, are prescrubbed. Take just a few minutes to check.

Quick Curried Shrimp

Makes 4 to 5 servings

FOR A QUICK curry supper, turn to curry paste. It's faster than measuring out a half-dozen different spices, has a more mellow fresh flavour than powder and makes a very nice little curry to spoon over basmati rice and serve with a thick yogurt enhanced with diced cucumber and radish. Curry paste comes in several traditional blends and is now available in most supermarkets. We use shrimp here, but Quick Curried Chicken works just as well (recipe follows).

2 tbsp (30 mL) canola oil

1 large onion, diced

3 large cloves garlic, minced

2 tsp (10 mL) grated fresh ginger

½ tsp (2 mL) salt

¼ tsp (1 mL) freshly ground black pepper

2 tbsp (30 mL) mild curry paste

1 cup (250 mL) tomato sauce or puréed tomatoes (passata)

1 cup (250 mL) coconut milk (approx) (see Note)

1 lb (500 g) small to medium raw shrimp (31 to 40 or 26 to 30)

¼ cup (60 mL) chopped fresh coriander (cilantro)

1 tsp (5 mL) granulated sugar (optional)

1 tbsp (15 mL) lemon juice

1 tsp (5 mL) garam masala (optional)

IN A LARGE skillet, heat the oil over medium heat; fry the onion, garlic, ginger, salt and pepper until the onion is soft, about 5 minutes, stirring often. Stir in the curry paste; cook, stirring, until slightly darkened, about 2 minutes.

Stir in the tomato sauce and coconut milk; bring to a simmer. Reduce the heat and simmer, covered, for 10 minutes.

Meanwhile, peel the shrimp; rinse. Add to the sauce with 2 tbsp (30 mL) of the coriander. Cook, stirring occasionally, until the shrimp are firm and opaque, about 5 minutes. Taste the sauce, adding the sugar if desired. Stir in a little more coconut milk if you like a thinner sauce. Sprinkle with the lemon juice, garam masala (if using) and the remaining coriander.

NOTE

Before opening a can of coconut milk, shake it well to blend the thin and thicker milk. Store any unused coconut milk in an airtight container in the freezer to use again in a curry.

VARIATION: Quick Curried Chicken

Replace the shrimp with 2 large boneless skinless chicken breasts (1 lb/500 g). Cut the breasts into 1-inch (2.5 cm) cubes. Instead of adding the chicken to the already-made sauce, brown the chicken first in 1 tbsp (15 mL) of the canola oil and remove from the pan. Continue with the sauce in the same pan, adding a little more oil if needed and scraping up any brown bits. When the sauce is ready, return the chicken to the pan and simmer until the juices in the chicken run clear when the pieces are pierced, about 10 minutes.

Pad Thai

Makes 4 servings

....

LINDA STEPHEN, author of *The Complete Book of Thai Cooking* and owner of Linda's Country Kitchen Cooking School: My first taste of pad Thai was when I was working in Australia. Thai restaurants were just starting in Sydney and I found one that I really liked. I ate the whole menu over a period of three nights, ordering pad Thai each time. My challenge then became to make my own version. There are many versions of this favoured dish, but this is the one I often return to when I need a "fix."

....

8 oz (250 g) dried medium rice noodles

3 tbsp (45 mL) chicken broth, ketchup or tomato sauce

3 tbsp (45 mL) lime juice or tamarind paste*

2 tbsp (30 mL) fish sauce

2 tbsp (30 mL) palm or brown sugar

½ tsp (2 mL) Asian hot chili sauce

3 tbsp (45 mL) canola oil, divided

2 large eggs, beaten

3 cloves garlic, minced

4 oz (125 g) shrimp, peeled and deveined, cut in small pieces

4 oz (125 g) boneless chicken or pork, cut in small pieces

2 cups (500 mL) bean sprouts, divided

2 green onions, chopped

¼ cup (60 mL) chopped peanuts

¼ cup (60 mL) chopped fresh coriander (cilantro)

1 fresh red chili, cut into strips (optional)

1 lime, cut in wedges

*Tamarind paste comes in a block that is fairly solid. You may have to soften it in 3 tbsp (45 mL) of boiling water for a few minutes.

TO SOFTEN THE noodles, place them in a large bowl and cover with very hot water; let stand until softened but still firm, 10 to 12 minutes. Drain, rinse well with cold water and drain again; set aside.

In a small bowl, stir together the broth, lime juice, fish sauce, sugar and chili sauce; set aside.

Heat a wok or large skillet over medium-high heat and add 1 tbsp (15 mL) of the oil. Add the eggs and swirl to coat the bottom of the pan. Cook until starting to set, then stir to break into pieces. Remove from the wok and reserve.

Add the remaining oil to the wok. When hot, add the garlic, shrimp and chicken; stir-fry until the shrimp and chicken are just cooked, about 2 minutes. Stir in the softened noodles and reserved sauce mixture; cook until the noodles are soft but not mushy, 1 to 2 minutes.

Add half the bean sprouts and the cooked eggs; toss to combine.

Turn the noodle mixture out onto a serving platter. Sprinkle with the remaining bean sprouts and the green onions, peanuts, coriander and chili (if using). Garnish with the lime wedges.

Lobster Rolls

Makes 8 small lobster rolls

LOBSTER IS A luxury food whether you live in Atlantic Canada or inland, so it's interesting that one of the popular ways to serve it in Atlantic Canada is chopped, dressed as a salad and nestled in soft, hot dog–style rolls—its casual presentation the opposite of its elevated culinary status. These lobster rolls are delicious, and are included in honour of the many lobsters enjoyed—some in rolls, some in risotto, some butter packed and some whole with bib and crackers—on trips to the lobster shores of Atlantic Canada.

¼ cup (60 mL) light mayonnaise

1 tsp (5 mL) fresh lemon juice

¼ tsp (1 mL) Dijon mustard

pinch each salt and freshly ground
   black pepper

dash hot pepper sauce

2 cups (500 mL) bite-size lobster chunks
   (see Note)

2 tbsp (30 mL) finely diced celery heart

2 tbsp (30 mL) finely diced sweet red pepper

2 tsp (10 mL) thinly sliced chives
   or green onion

2 tsp (10 mL) finely chopped fresh parsley,
   dill or basil

8 small rolls or sliders or mini pitas

4 tender leaves butterhead lettuce, such as
   Boston or Bibb

IN A MEDIUM bowl, mix together the mayonnaise, lemon juice, mustard, salt, pepper and hot pepper sauce. Add the lobster, celery, sweet pepper, chives and parsley. Toss gently but thoroughly to coat the lobster and crisp ingredients. (MAKE-AHEAD: Cover and refrigerate for up to 4 hours.)

Split the rolls in half horizontally; line each one with a piece of lettuce and fill with the lobster salad.

> **NOTE**
> Not having to cook the lobster is convenient when you are making lobster rolls. Lobster is available cooked, canned or frozen, depending on your supermarket or fishmonger. Frozen shelled lobster is the most convenient option; let thaw in the refrigerator and drain well in a sieve. Press to remove liquid.

MAINS:

Eggs and Cheese

"All the Best" Macaroni and Cheese

Makes 4 servings.

FOR THIS ULTIMATE comfort food, a long-standing favourite at All the Best, Jane Rodmell's mid-town Toronto gourmet shop, Jane uses two-year-old Ontario Cheddar cheese. As Jane says in *All the Best Recipes*, the cookbook that showcases the shop's most popular dishes, this Cheddar cheese "gives just the right bite without overwhelming."

2 cups (500 mL) elbow macaroni
¼ cup (60 mL) butter
half onion, finely chopped
1 clove garlic, minced
¼ cup (60 mL) all-purpose flour
½ tsp (2 mL) salt
pinch freshly ground black pepper
pinch cayenne

4 cups (1 L) milk
2 cups (500 mL) packed shredded
  Cheddar cheese (about ½ lb/250 g)
2 tbsp (30 mL) freshly grated
  Parmesan cheese
Parsley Bread-Crumb Topping
  (optional, recipe follows)

IN A LARGE pot of boiling lightly salted water, cook the macaroni until *al dente*, 10 to 13 minutes. Drain, rinse in cold water, drain again and return to the pot.

In a large saucepan, melt the butter over medium heat. Add the onion and cook, stirring, until soft but not coloured, 4 to 5 minutes. Stir in the garlic, flour, salt, pepper and cayenne; cook, stirring, for 2 to 3 minutes.

In a small saucepan over medium heat or in a measuring cup in the microwave oven, heat the milk until steaming. Slowly add the hot milk to the flour mixture, whisking briskly until all the milk is incorporated and the sauce is smooth. Reduce the heat and cook the sauce gently, stirring, for 5 minutes. Remove from the heat and stir in the Cheddar and Parmesan cheeses. Pour the cheese sauce over the cooked macaroni and gently stir to combine. Taste and adjust the seasoning.

Pour into a lightly greased 11- × 7-inch (2 L) baking dish. Sprinkle with Parsley Bread-Crumb Topping (if using). Bake in a 350°F (180°C) oven until the sauce is bubbling, 20 to 25 minutes. If desired, broil briefly to lightly brown the top. Let stand for 5 to 10 minutes before serving.

PARSLEY BREAD-CRUMB TOPPING

1½ cups (375 mL) coarse fresh white
  bread crumbs
2 tbsp (30 mL) minced parsley
  (preferably flat-leaf)

pinch each salt and freshly ground black
  pepper
pinch cayenne (optional)
3 tbsp (45 mL) butter, melted

IN A BOWL, combine the bread crumbs, parsley, salt and pepper, and the cayenne if using. Pour the butter over the bread crumb mixture and toss with a fork to ensure the bread crumbs are evenly coated.

BACKYARD HOCKEY AND MACARONI AND CHEESE

ANDREW COPPOLINO, food writer, author and radio show host: My mother's dish was a simple layering of cooked elbow macaroni and cheese with a milk-egg mixture poured overtop, always made in her orange cast-iron ovenproof pot.

Each winter my father would build a rink in our backyard so that my brother Michael and I could play backyard hockey. I recall him trudging about in the snow with sundry and assorted pieces of equipment—sheets of plywood, shovels and even cross-country skis—to pack down the snow to flood and freeze. We had goals and end boards with passages cut through the snowbanks to get on and off the ice. I recall Dad even setting up a couple of floodlights so that we could play into the night.

And dedicated players we were. I was Tony Esposito to Mike's Phil. (It was helpful that we had some Italian background like these NHL brothers of whom we were fans.) We played for hours, and that often meant playing the "Stanley Cup" right through the dinner hour. Mom would set up a card table and chairs and put down some towels on the floor in the back hall so that we could come in and have a quick dinner without struggling with frozen fingers to unlace our skates. We sat fully dressed in hockey gear, wolfed down dinner (often Mom's mac and cheese) and were out on the ice again for the second period in mere minutes.

The Quiche That Started It All

Makes 6 servings

THE EGG AND bacon pie called *quiche lorraine* originally called for only bacon, eggs and cream, but gradually cheese and various other ingredients, such as cooked onions, sweet peppers and spinach, were added to the dish or replaced the bacon for a vegetarian main course. Quiche makes an easy and lovely lunch dish served with a crisp green salad.

pastry for a deep 9-inch (23 cm) single-crust pie (see Reputation-Making Pastry, page 272)
1 tbsp (15 mL) Dijon mustard
¼ lb (125 g) chopped prosciutto, cooked ham or bacon*
1 cup (250 mL) shredded Gruyère, divided
3 large eggs

1½ cups (375 mL) whipping cream or light cream
¼ tsp (1 mL) freshly ground black pepper
pinch nutmeg

*If you use bacon, fry it until it is cooked but not crisp before adding it to the quiche.

ON A LIGHTLY floured surface, roll out the pastry to a scant ¼-inch (5 mm) thickness. Fit into a deep 9-inch (23 cm) pie plate. Trim the pastry about ¾ inch (2 cm) from the edge of the plate's rim; fold the pastry under and flute. With a fork, prick the shell at 1-inch (2.5 cm) intervals and refrigerate for 30 minutes.

Line the shell with foil; fill it with pie weights or dried beans. Bake in the bottom third of a 400°F (200°C) oven until the edge is light golden, about 20 minutes. Remove the foil and weights and let the shell cool on a rack.

Brush the bottom of the shell with the mustard. Sprinkle with the prosciutto and half the cheese. In a medium bowl, whisk the eggs; whisk in the whipping cream, pepper and nutmeg. Pour the egg mixture into the shell and sprinkle with the remaining cheese. Bake in a 375°F (190°C) oven until a knife inserted in the middle comes out clean and the top is golden brown, 35 to 40 minutes.

VARIATION: Spinach Quiche
Substitute the prosciutto with 1 pkg (10 oz/284 g) spinach, cooked, drained, pressed and chopped.

VARIATION: Seafood Quiche
Substitute the prosciutto and the cheese with ½ lb (250 g) cooked small shrimp and 1 tbsp (15 mL) chopped fresh dill, or 1 cup (250 mL) cooked crabmeat and 2 tbsp (30 mL) chopped parsley.

Gnocchi con Sugo di Pomodoro (Potato Dumplings with Tomato Sauce)

Makes 8 servings

DAIENE VERNILE, anchor and producer of CTV's *ProvinceWide:* Food was beyond an obsession in my Italian family. Growing up in a north Toronto suburb, I wondered why my Canadian friends weren't killing and plucking chickens, why their backyards weren't overrun with tomato plants, and why they didn't spend endless hours making homemade pasta, like us. It was television (where, ironically, I came to forge a 30-year career with CTV News) which gave me my first glimpses into Canadian cuisine. Fast-food restaurants, TV dinners, and something called Hamburger Helper. It all looked so delectable! So why was my mother torturing us with homemade Italian food, I would ask myself. Would I ever get to taste Canadian fare?

Fast-forward a few decades, and you'll now hear me lecturing my kids on the evils of packaged and processed foods. Although I'm not as old school as Nona (my chicken comes already deceased from the market), I do like to prepare many dishes from scratch. My all-time favourite is *gnocchi con sugo di pomodoro*—perfect little Italian potato dumplings with tomato sauce, sprinkled with Parmigiano Reggiano cheese. My mother's recipe is so simple, made with just a few ingredients. I now prepare it with my daughter Claire, who actually produces better gnocchi than I! She carries on the family's cooking traditions in her own food blog, *Cooking with Claire.*

POTATO DUMPLINGS
4 oval baking potatoes (about 2 lb/1 kg)
1 tbsp (15 mL) salt
2 cups (500 mL) all-purpose flour

TOMATO SAUCE
¼ cup (60 mL) extra virgin olive oil
1 onion, finely diced
2 cloves garlic, minced
1 carrot, diced
1 can (28 oz/796 mL) tomatoes, undrained
1 large sprig fresh parsley or basil
1 tsp (5 mL) salt
1 cup (250 mL) freshly grated Parmesan cheese (approx)

POTATO DUMPLINGS → Wash the potatoes but do not peel them; bake in a 400°F (200°C) oven until tender when pierced, 45 minutes to 1 hour. When cool enough to handle, peel them and put them through a ricer or mash them.

While the potatoes are still warm, place on a floured work surface and sprinkle with the salt; slowly knead the flour into the potatoes, ½ cup (125 mL) at a time, until they are like "play dough"—slightly sticky. Divide the dough into 4 pieces. Cover and let rest for about 10 minutes.

Roll each piece of dough into a rope about ¾ inch (2 cm) thick. Cut each rope into 1-inch (2.5 cm) pieces.

Line 2 baking sheets with clean tea towels; sprinkle the towels with flour. Dip a fork into the flour. Hold the fork with the tines facing down; with the fingers of your other hand, lightly roll each piece down the tines of the fork to create ridges and an indentation to hold the sauce. Place the gnocchi on the prepared baking sheet. (MAKE-AHEAD: Cover and refrigerate for up to 1 day, or freeze for up to 3 months.)

TOMATO SAUCE → In a large deep saucepan, heat the oil over medium heat; add the onion and cook until softened, about 2 minutes. Stir in the garlic and carrot; cook for 3 more minutes.

Stir in the tomatoes and, using a potato masher, chop them into small bits. Turn the heat to high and keep stirring. Add the sprig of parsley or basil and the salt. After the mixture comes to a boil, reduce the heat to medium. Cook, stirring regularly, until the oil separates from the tomatoes and the sauce is thick (a spoon drawn over the bottom leaves a space that fills in very slowly), 20 to 30 minutes. (MAKE-AHEAD: Cool, cover and refrigerate for up to 1 week or freeze for up to 3 months.)

To prepare, drop the gnocchi in 2 batches into rapidly boiling salted water and cook until they surface, 4 to 5 minutes. With a slotted spoon, remove the gnocchi to a bowl and toss with the tomato sauce, adding a little gnocchi cooking water to loosen the sauce if desired. Sprinkle with Parmesan cheese to serve.

Pizza Dough and Pizza Sauce

Makes one 12-inch (30 cm) crust and 3½ cups (875 mL) sauce

ROSE: Check out your phone book and the street corners downtown—pizza has to be one of the most popular fast foods going. With all this choice, it is still often hard to find a good pizzeria that serves up a pizza that doesn't taste like the cardboard box in which it could be delivered. Perhaps that is too harsh. Wonderful, wood-fired, thin-crust pizzas are available in most towns, and there are other good pizzas about, but a homemade one is still tops. And not only is making pizza an easy job, it's one that kids particularly like to share.

In the neighbourhood where we lived as a young family, I was lucky enough to have fine cooks as neighbours on both sides—one who shared with me the spices her father sent from Bombay and another who taught me how to make fresh pasta and all things Italian (she just wanted me to show her how to cook a turkey). It was this neighbour, Vince Marcoccio, who shared her recipes and knowledge of pizza-making. We would often descend to her second kitchen in the basement (the upstairs kitchen was "for show," but the downstairs kitchen was just as well equipped) to make pasta or a batch of pizzas, usually ten at a time. The toppings were the traditional pepperoni, sweet peppers and cheese, but her homemade pizza sauce and crust made the ordinary spectacular.

You can easily double the recipe for the dough. You'll have enough sauce for about 6 pizzas. (Any leftover sauce freezes well.)

PIZZA DOUGH
pinch granulated sugar
⅔ cup (150 mL) warm water
2 tsp (10 mL) active dry yeast

2 tbsp (30 mL) canola oil
1½ cups (375 mL) all-purpose flour (approx)
½ tsp (2 mL) salt

IN A SMALL bowl, combine the sugar and water; sprinkle the yeast overtop and let stand until foamy and increases in volume, about 10 minutes. Stir in the oil.

In a large bowl, mix the flour with the salt; make a well in the centre and pour in the yeast mixture. With a fork, gradually blend together to form dough. With floured hands, gather into a ball.

Turn out onto a lightly floured surface; knead for about 5 minutes, adding just enough extra flour to make a soft, slightly sticky dough. Place in a greased bowl, turning once to grease all over. Cover with greased waxed paper and a tea towel. Let stand in a warm draft-free place until tripled in volume, 1½ to 3 hours.

Punch down the dough and form into a ball. Turn out onto a lightly floured surface and cover with a bowl; let stand for 10 minutes. Roll out the dough into a 12-inch (30 cm) circle, stretching with your fingers at the end.

PIZZA SAUCE

3 tbsp (45 mL) olive oil
2 cloves garlic, crushed
1 can (28 oz/796 mL) tomatoes, undrained
1 can (5½ oz/156 mL) tomato paste

1 tbsp (15 mL) finely chopped basil
  (or 1 tsp/5 mL crumbled dried)
2 tsp (10 mL) granulated sugar
1 tsp (5 mL) dried oregano
½ tsp (2 mL) salt, or to taste
freshly ground black pepper

IN A MEDIUM saucepan, heat the olive oil over medium-low heat and simmer the garlic for 2 minutes.

If the tomatoes are not diced, use scissors to cut them into chunks while still in the can; add them and their juice to the pan along with the tomato paste, basil, sugar, oregano, salt and a few grindings of pepper. Bring to a boil, breaking up the tomatoes with a wooden spoon; turn the heat to very low and slowly simmer, uncovered and stirring often, until thick and fairly smooth, about 1 hour. Remove from the heat; taste and add more salt and pepper if necessary. If you wish, purée through a food mill or rub through a sieve.

Friday Night Pizza

Makes 3 to 4 servings

THE TOPPINGS HERE are merely suggestions; feel free to use others, such as fresh tomatoes, onion, olives, anchovies, bacon (sautéed)—the list goes on. However, don't overload the crust or it will be soggy. Try other good melting cheeses too; a combination of cheeses like mozzarella, fontina and provolone works well.

3 tbsp (45 mL) olive oil, divided (approx)
¼ lb (125 g) mushrooms, sliced
½ sweet green pepper, cut into chunks
oil or cornmeal for preparing pizza pan
Pizza Dough (page 150)
2¼ cups (550 mL) shredded mozzarella
   cheese (about ½ lb/250 g), divided

½ tsp (2 mL) dried Italian herb seasoning
pinch hot pepper flakes
½ cup (125 mL) Pizza Sauce (page 151)
   or ½ cup store-bought pizza sauce
½ lb (250 g) pepperoni, sliced

IN A LARGE skillet, heat about 1 tbsp (15 mL) oil over medium heat; cook the mushrooms, stirring often, for 4 minutes. Add the green pepper; cook for 1 minute. Set aside.

Meanwhile, grease a 12-inch (30 cm) pizza pan with oil or sprinkle it with cornmeal. Top with pizza dough, stretching it to the sides. Brush lightly with some of the olive oil and sprinkle with half the cheese. Stir the Italian herb seasoning and hot pepper flakes into the pizza sauce; spread over the dough, leaving a small border. Arrange the mushroom mixture and pepperoni on top. Sprinkle with the remaining cheese; drizzle with the remaining olive oil. Bake near the bottom of a 500°F (260°C) oven until the crust is golden brown, about 15 minutes.

Company Pizza

Makes 3 to 4 servings

THERE ARE MANY combinations of toppings—prosciutto and artichokes, roasted peppers and chorizo, even bacon and eggs—all it takes is imagination! This pizza has a pear, Brie and caramelized red onion topping. Its dough gets a new flavour by kneading in a few toasted walnuts just after you punch it down (let it stand for 10 minutes).

1 pear, unpeeled
2 tsp (10 mL) butter
½ tsp (2 mL) dried thyme
freshly ground black pepper
1 tbsp (15 mL) olive oil (approx)
1 small red onion, thinly sliced in rings
1½ tsp (7 mL) red wine vinegar

½ tsp (2 mL) salt
pinch granulated sugar
Pizza Dough (page 150)
¼ cup (60 mL) finely chopped
   toasted walnuts
6 oz (175 g) Brie, unpeeled

CORE AND SLICE the pear. In a skillet, melt the butter over medium heat; cook the pear for 5 minutes. Sprinkle with the thyme and generously with pepper; with a slotted spoon, remove to a bowl.

In the same skillet, heat the oil over low heat; cook the onion, covered, for 5 minutes. Stir in the vinegar, salt and sugar; cover and cook for 5 minutes.

Meanwhile, punch down the dough; knead in the walnuts and form into a ball. Turn out onto a lightly floured surface and cover with a bowl; let stand for 10 minutes. Press into a greased 12-inch (30 cm) pizza pan; brush lightly with more of the oil. Scatter evenly with the onion and pear mixtures.

Cut the cheese (including the rind) into ½-inch (1.25 cm) cubes. Scatter over the pizza. Drizzle with any juice from the skillet. Bake near the bottom of a 500°F (260°C) oven until the crust is golden brown, 12 to 15 minutes.

Spring Risotto

Makes 3 to 4 main-course servings or 6 to 8 appetizers

JOHN SEWELL AND LIZ RYKERT: This is a great recipe in late May or very early June, when wild leeks (or ramps) are just out. We love to gather them in the bush around our Collingwood, Ontario, farm. The nice thing about leeks is you use the whole of the plant, including both the bulb (which needs very careful cleaning) and the leaves (which need to be finely chopped). When finished, the dish itself has gorgeous spring-green accents.

⅓ cup (75 mL) butter, divided

2 tbsp (30 mL) olive oil

¼ cup (60 mL) chopped onion

1 cup (250 mL) carnaroli or arborio rice

4 cups (1 L) chicken broth (approx)

1 cup (250 mL) chopped wild leeks*

6 oz (175 g) spinach, trimmed, washed and coarsely chopped (or baby spinach) (about 4 cups/1 L)

1 cup (250 mL) fresh or frozen green peas

1 cup (250 mL) freshly grated Parmesan cheese

freshly ground black pepper

*If wild leeks are not available, substitute chopped green onion and 1 clove garlic, minced.

IN A LARGE saucepan or a deep skillet over medium heat, melt 3 tbsp (45 mL) of the butter in the oil. Add the onion and cook, stirring often, until translucent, 3 to 4 minutes. Add the rice and stir to coat it well.

Meanwhile, in a small saucepan, heat the broth and keep it warm on a nearby burner.

Add one ladle (about ½ cup/125 mL) of hot broth to the rice mixture; as the rice absorbs the broth, keep stirring and adding broth, waiting until the broth is absorbed each time before adding more. After 5 minutes, stir in the leeks. Continue to stir and add broth, a ladle at a time, for another 5 minutes. Stir in the spinach; continue to stir and add broth for 10 minutes; stir in the peas and continue stirring and adding broth until the rice is creamy and just tender, about 5 minutes longer. Remove from the heat; stir in the remaining butter, Parmesan cheese and pepper. Serve immediately.

Sides and Salads

Do-Ahead Scalloped Potatoes

Makes 8 servings

ROSE: I love *gratin dauphinois*, the French version of scalloped potatoes . . . creamy, very rich and a perfect make-ahead dish for company. The potatoes are first simmered in milk to remove their acidity, then in whipping cream. A few years ago, in *A Taste of Canada*, I decided to dispense with the cream and still came up with a close facsimile of the French dish. It is probably the recipe from that book that most people mention making; probably because scalloped potatoes are so classically Canadian. Who can serve ham without them? *Pictured on page 82.*

¼ cup (60 mL) butter
4 large shallots, minced
8 large oval baking potatoes, peeled and
  thinly sliced
3 cups (750 mL) milk

¼ tsp (1 mL) nutmeg
salt and freshly ground black pepper
1 clove garlic, halved
1½ cups (375 mL) shredded Gruyère
  (4 oz/125 g)

IN A LARGE saucepan, melt the butter over medium heat; cook the shallots until softened, about 4 minutes. Add the potatoes and milk. Bring to a simmer over medium heat and cook, uncovered, for 20 minutes, lowering the heat as necessary and stirring often to prevent scorching. Season with the nutmeg and salt and pepper to taste.

Meanwhile, rub the cut sides of the garlic over the inside of a greased shallow 8-cup (2 L) baking dish. Mince the garlic and sprinkle over the bottom. Top with the potato mixture and sprinkle with the cheese. (MAKE-AHEAD: Cool, cover and refrigerate for up to 2 days. Bring to room temperature before baking.)

Bake, uncovered, in a 375°F (190°C) oven until golden brown on top and bubbly, about 30 minutes.

Latkes (Potato Pancakes)

Makes 6 servings

....

ELIZABETH: Back in the 1970s and 1980s I taught night-school cooking classes at Central Technical School in Toronto. One of the memorable parts of being an instructor then was getting to know and admire the woman who taught next door to my kitchen, Lucille Lorie. At that time Lucille must have been in her eighties, and she shared her love for entertaining with dishes she had helped create for her friend Lillian Kaplun's cooking school and Lillian's cookbooks, *For the Love of Cooking* and *For the Love of Entertaining*. Lucille, whose life included many years as a leader and consummate volunteer in the Jewish community, was a no-nonsense woman and generous with everyone. She was happy to share—not her own recipe for latkes (a crisp potato pancake served on the Jewish festival of Hannukah), but her daughter Lenore Barrett's.

Sour cream and Cider-Baked Applesauce (page 77) are the best accompaniments for latkes. You need about 1 cup (250 mL) of sour cream and 2 cups (500 mL) of applesauce for the number of latkes in this recipe. *Pictured on page 70.*

....

6 medium potatoes, peeled (2 lb/1 kg)
2 large eggs
1 small onion, very finely diced
2 tbsp (30 mL) matzo meal*
   or all-purpose flour

½ tsp (2 mL) salt (kosher recommended)
¼ tsp (1 mL) baking powder
½ cup (125 mL) canola oil (approx)

*Matso meal is unleavened crackers, crushed into crumbs.

SHRED THE POTATOES on the medium side of a box grater or with the shredding blade of a food processor. Place in a bowl, cover with cold water and refrigerate overnight.

Drain the potatoes in a sieve, pressing and squeezing them as dry as possible with your hands. In a large bowl, beat the eggs; add the potatoes, onion, matzo meal, salt and baking powder, mixing well. (There is only a little batter holding the potato shreds together.)

In a large skillet, heat 2 tbsp (30 mL) of the oil over medium-high heat until hot—shimmering but not smoking. (Test the heat by adding a strand of potato from the latke mixture. If it sizzles, proceed; if not, wait until the oil is hot enough for a new sample to sizzle.) Place the potato mixture by ¼ cup (60 mL) for large latkes (a heaping tbsp/15 mL for small) into the pan, patting each latke thin with the back of a lifter or spoon. Fry until golden around the edge, about 3 minutes. Turn and brown the other side, about 3 minutes. Regulate the heat so the latkes don't burn.

Drain the latkes on paper towel–lined racks. Between each batch, use a slotted spoon to pick out any potato strands remaining in the oil. Top up the oil and heat, as needed. Serve immediately. (MAKE-AHEAD: Arrange latkes in a single layer on rimmed baking sheets. Cover and refrigerate for up to 8 hours. Reheat in a 450°F/230°C oven until crisp and hot, about 5 minutes.)

Roasted Vegetables

Makes 4 servings

TAKE ADVANTAGE WHEN the oven is on to roast a pan of vegetables for dinner. For entertaining, multiply the amounts given here to suit the guest count.

4 medium potatoes

2 medium carrots

1 onion

2 cups (500 mL) bite-size chunks peeled
  butternut squash

1 cup (250 mL) cauliflower florets

2 tbsp (30 mL) olive or canola oil

1 tsp (5 mL) dried oregano, thyme,
  basil or rosemary

½ tsp (2 mL) salt, coarse sea salt
  (if available)

¼ tsp (1 mL) freshly ground black pepper

PEEL THE POTATOES, carrots and onion, leaving the root end on the onion (to keep the wedge intact). Cut the potatoes into quarters, the carrots into finger-size lengths and the onion lengthwise into 6 wedges. Place in a bowl with the squash and cauliflower. Drizzle the olive oil overtop, and sprinkle with the oregano, salt and pepper. Toss gently to coat.

Spread in a single layer in a shallow roasting pan or metal cake pan; a 13- × 9-inch (3.5 L) pan is ideal. Bake in the centre of a 400°F (200°C) oven for 15 minutes. Turn; bake until the potatoes and carrots are tender, about another 15 to 20 minutes. Brown, if necessary, under the broiler, just a few minutes.

Hodge Podge

Makes 2 servings as a meal in itself, 4 servings as a side dish

....

MARIE NIGHTINGALE, food writer and author of *Out of Old Nova Scotia Kitchens:* It was my first vegetable garden. I planted it at our summer cottage with significant help from the local farmer. I was particularly proud of the way the green beans were coming along. They must have been eight or ten inches high, not far from sprouting legumes. Hodge podge was on my mind.

One night I looked out the window and there was a big black and white cow looking back at me. We didn't have cows. "My beans!" I cried as I ran out the door chasing not one but two cows out of my garden. I was a city girl, not used to animals of that size, but my beans were in danger. My husband had rushed off to get the farmer, who found me on my hands and knees trying to replant the beans. Clifton, the farmer, was distraught, offering me anything from his garden to compensate. "But these were mine," I sobbed. It was my best Sarah Bernhardt performance.

There were several meals of hodge podge that summer—made with fresh green beans and other new vegetables from Clifton's garden. If there is any dish that is profoundly loved in Nova Scotia it is hodge podge, the first pickings of new summer vegetables cooked together and served up in a cream sauce. In early July, you'll hear market-going people greeting each other with "Have you had a hodge podge yet?"

....

WE HAVE ADAPTED Marie's recipe using her suggestion for the types of vegetable, but use what you have at hand, being sure to start with the vegetables that take the longest, working down to those that cook very quickly, so that none of them overcook.

....

1 cup (250 mL) tiny new potatoes, unpeeled and scrubbed

1 cup (250 mL) new-pulled baby carrots

1 cup (250 mL) each green and yellow beans, trimmed and halved

1 cup (250 mL) snow peas, trimmed and halved diagonally

1 cup (250 mL) shelled peas

2 green onions, chopped

½ cup (125 mL) whipping cream

1 tbsp (15 L) butter

salt and freshly ground black pepper

2 tbsp (30 mL) chopped fresh parsley

PLACE THE POTATOES in a large pot with about 1 inch (2.5 cm) of boiling water. Cover and boil gently for 2 to 3 minutes before adding the carrots. Cook the carrots, covered, 1 to 2 minutes; then add the beans. Cook, uncovered, for 2 minutes. Add the snow peas, shelled peas and green onions; cook gently, uncovered, until all the vegetables are just tender, 3 minutes. Drain only if a lot of water remains; add the cream and cook until thickened, 2 to 4 minutes. Stir in the butter, and salt and pepper to taste. Sprinkle with parsley to serve.

Wild Rice, Lentil and Orzo Salad

Makes 6 to 8 servings

....

ELIZABETH: There is something very satisfying about this combination of grains, pasta and legumes. Whenever I serve this salad, which I created for *Canadian Living* magazine and showcased at the Good Food Festival in Toronto, guests always ask for the recipe. Without fail. It has just enough spice to tantalize, and collaborates deliciously with roast or grilled chicken, pork, salmon or pickerel. With cold salmon . . . hmmm. Perfect picnic food.

....

SALAD
½ cup (125 mL) wild rice
⅔ cup (150 mL) green or brown lentils
½ cup (125 mL) orzo pasta
½ cup (125 mL) currants
¼ cup (60 mL) diced red onion

DRESSING
¼ cup (60 mL) white wine vinegar
1 tsp (5 mL) each cumin and Dijon mustard
½ tsp (2 mL) each granulated sugar, salt
    and ground coriander
¼ tsp (1 mL) each nutmeg, paprika,
    turmeric and ground cardamom
pinch each cinnamon, cloves and cayenne
⅓ cup (75 mL) canola oil
⅓ cup (75 mL) slivered almonds, toasted

SALAD → In a large saucepan of boiling salted water, cover and cook the wild rice until tender to the bite, but neither splayed nor mushy, about 35 minutes. In a separate saucepan of boiling salted water, cover and cook the lentils until tender, about 25 minutes. In a third saucepan of boiling salted water (The dishwasher is going to be ticked off, but the salad is worth the three pots!) cook the orzo just until tender, about 5 minutes.

Drain the rice, lentils and orzo and combine in a large bowl with the currants and red onion.

DRESSING → In a medium bowl, whisk together all the dressing ingredients except the oil and almonds (Yes, all the measuring of the spices is also worth it!) Whisk in the oil.

Pour over the rice mixture and toss gently. Let cool, cover and refrigerate for 4 hours. (MAKE-AHEAD: Refrigerate for up to 1 day.) To serve, sprinkle with almonds.

NOTE
Choose wild rice with shiny long dark brown and black grains.

Corn on the Cob
with Parsley-Garlic Butter

Makes enough for 8 cobs

THERE IS SOMETHING truly Canadian about biting into a juicy cob of corn. Since freshest corn is the best, those without kitchen gardens flock to roadside stands and farmers' markets to participate in this rite of summer.

Choose cobs whose moist, green husks completely cover the ear (don't be tempted to pull the husks back, since that allows moisture to escape). The silk should be moist and dark, the stems damp and pale green. Sweet local corn needs only butter, salt and freshly ground black pepper, but you can add a bit of pizzazz with flavoured butters.

8 fresh cobs of corn, husked
⅓ cup (75 mL) butter, at room temperature
1 tbsp (15 mL) fresh lemon juice

2 tbsp (30 mL) chopped fresh parsley
2 cloves garlic, minced
salt and freshly ground black pepper

COOK THE CORN in a large covered pot of unsalted boiling water for 3 to 5 minutes depending on the size. (Or, to grill, pull back the husks, remove the silk and replace the husks, tying them at the tip with string. Soak in cold water for 15 minutes; grill over high heat until tender, 20 to 30 minutes, turning occasionally.)

Cream the butter well; then very gradually beat in the lemon juice. Stir in the parsley, garlic, and salt and pepper to taste. Pack into a small bowl, or spoon onto plastic wrap and shape into a log. Cover or wrap tightly and refrigerate overnight. Accompany with a small spreader or slice into rounds to serve with the corn.

VARIATION: Tarragon Butter
Substitute chopped fresh tarragon for the parsley and omit the garlic.

VARIATION: Spicy Lemon-Grilled Corn
In a shallow casserole dish, combine ⅓ cup (75 mL) fresh lemon juice with 2 tbsp (30 mL) canola oil, 1 tsp (5 mL) ground cumin, ½ tsp (2 mL) sweet paprika, ¼ tsp (1 mL) each salt, pepper and cayenne (optional). Roll 6 husked cobs of corn in the mixture and marinate, covered, for up to 2 hours in the refrigerator.

Place the cobs on a greased barbecue grill, close the lid and grill until golden brown, 10 to 12 minutes, turning often and brushing with any remaining marinade.

Plum Tomato Crumble

Makes 4 to 6 servings

THE LOWER MOISTURE in plum tomatoes makes them ideal candidates for a crunchy-topped baked side dish that is just right for early fall entertaining.

TOMATOES
8 plum tomatoes (2½ lb/1.2 kg)
1 tbsp (15 mL) olive oil
1 tbsp (15 mL) dried oregano
½ tsp (2 mL) salt
¼ tsp (1 mL) freshly ground black pepper

CRUMBLE TOPPING
2 tbsp (30 mL) olive oil
2 tbsp (30 mL) butter
1 onion, diced
2 large cloves garlic, minced
1 cup (250 mL) fresh bread crumbs
    (1 to 2 slices)
¾ cup (175 mL) finely grated firm
    cheese, such as Parmesan cheese
    or Romano cheese

TOMATOES → Trim and halve the tomatoes lengthwise; arrange, cut-side up, on a parchment paper–lined rimmed baking sheet. Lightly brush the tops with olive oil and sprinkle evenly with the oregano, salt and pepper. Roast in the centre of a 375°F (190°C) oven until crinkly and browned, about 1½ hours.

CRUMBLE TOPPING → Meanwhile, in a skillet, heat the oil and butter over medium heat. Fry the onion and garlic, stirring often, until light golden, about 12 minutes. Let cool; stir in the bread crumbs and cheese.

Arrange the tomatoes, slightly overlapping if necessary, in a shallow baking dish. An 8-inch (2 L) square heatproof dish is ideal. Spoon the bread crumb mixture evenly overtop. (MAKE-AHEAD: Cover and refrigerate for up to 1 day. Add 5 minutes to the baking time.)

Bake in the centre of a 400°F (200°C) oven until the topping is crisp and the tomatoes and juices are bubbling, about 25 minutes.

Fiddleheads Vinaigrette

Makes 3 to 4 servings

....

ROSE: As distinctly Canadian as maple syrup, fiddleheads grow all across the country, but the Maliseet First Nations of New Brunswick claim to have discovered these edible ferns and their nutritional value.

The ostrich fern is the only variety that's safe to eat and, since my husband, Kent, has always been lucky enough to find a good spot to pick them wherever we've lived, I've done much research on this native food. My first encounter with what is now one of my favourite greens was over 40 years ago, when I was out with my husband and his grandfather, who showed us the wild vegetable growing by a stream. Kent's grandfather told us the story of how a First Nations person had introduced fiddleheads to Kent's great-grandmother in early spring when her winter food supply was running low.

If you also find a patch, always leave several fiddleheads in each clump and pick tightly curled heads (resembling a fiddle's neck) no higher than 6 inches (15 cm). Uncurl each head and shake off the thin brown scaly husk; then wash them several times in cool water and trim off any dark stem ends. Do not overcook them since this robs them of nutrients, flavour and colour.

My favourite way of enjoying fiddleheads is with this vinaigrette. If fiddleheads are not in season, substitute a 10-ounce (300 g) package of frozen fiddleheads (see the package for cooking times).

....

8 oz (250 g) fresh fiddleheads
2 tbsp (30 mL) fresh lemon juice
¼ tsp (1 mL) Dijon mustard
6 tbsp (90 mL) olive or canola oil

2 tbsp (30 mL) minced shallots
salt and freshly ground black pepper
thin lemon slices for garnish

STEAM OR BOIL the fiddleheads just until tender, 5 to 8 minutes. Drain and rinse under cold running water until the fiddleheads feel cold to the touch. Wrap in a tea towel and let stand at room temperature or in the refrigerator if not using immediately.

In a small bowl, stir together the lemon juice and mustard. Gradually whisk in the oil; stir in the shallots, and salt and pepper to taste.

Just before serving, gently combine the vinaigrette and fiddleheads; garnish with lemon slices. Serve immediately since the ferns may turn brown if left standing.

Classic Potato Salad

Makes 6 servings

TED BOYD: A friend of mine brings her delicious potato salad to all our neighbourhood barbecues, to rave reviews. I'm a relatively inexperienced cook, but with this recipe I make a potato salad that rivals hers.

5 potatoes (see Note)
2 tbsp (30 mL) white wine vinegar
1 tsp (5 mL) granulated sugar
4 hard-cooked eggs, finely chopped
¼ cup (60 mL) each diced red onion, celery
    and sweet green pepper

2 cornichons (or 1 small dill pickle), minced
1 cup (250 mL) light mayonnaise
1 tbsp (15 mL) Dijon mustard
pinch cayenne
salt and freshly ground black pepper

PEEL AND QUARTER the potatoes. Cook them covered in boiling, salted water until tender, about 20 minutes; drain well and coarsely chop. Place in a bowl and combine with the vinegar and sugar while still hot.

Add the eggs, onion, celery, green pepper and pickles; toss gently.

In a small bowl, stir together the mayonnaise, mustard, cayenne, and salt and pepper to taste; stir into the potato mixture. Serve warm or cold. (MAKE-AHEAD: Cover and refrigerate for up to 8 hours; bring to room temperature to serve.)

NOTE

Waxy potatoes are best for this salad. Choose any shape, red or white, when they are new, but with older potatoes, pick the red round varieties.

Cabbage Salad, Two Ways

Makes 6 to 8 servings

WITH ALL THE trendy new greens and exotic vegetables, it is comforting to know that cabbage, forever crisp and never expensive, is still a popular choice for hearty salads. We give you two versions here. One, a coleslaw, has a creamy dressing that produces just the right amount of tang and crunch to complement cold meat and hot saucy dishes like Chili Pulled Pork (page 78). The other calls on Asian flavours to give a twist to an old picnic, potluck and packed-lunch favourite.

CREAMY COLESLAW

DRESSING

½ cup (125 mL) light or regular mayonnaise

⅓ cup (75 mL) light or regular sour cream

2 tbsp (30 mL) canola oil

2 tbsp (30 mL) buttermilk or plain yogurt

2 tsp (10 mL) Dijon mustard

¼ tsp (1 mL) celery or caraway seeds

¼ tsp (1 mL) each salt and freshly ground black pepper

SLAW

4 cups (1 L) very finely shredded green cabbage

2 large red apples (Cortland recommended), unpeeled, cored and diced

1 cup (250 mL) diced or shredded carrots

½ cup (125 mL) very thinly sliced radishes

1 green onion, thinly sliced

¼ cup (60 mL) minced flat-leaf parsley (see Note)

⅓ cup (75 mL) toasted slivered almonds

DRESSING → In a large bowl, whisk together the mayonnaise, sour cream, oil, buttermilk, mustard, celery seeds, salt and pepper. (MAKE-AHEAD: Store in an airtight container in the refrigerator for up to 4 days.)

SLAW → To the dressing, add the cabbage, apples, carrots, radishes, green onion and parsley. Toss well. (MAKE-AHEAD: Cover and refrigerate for up to 4 hours.) Sprinkle the almonds overtop.

> **NOTE**
> One tbsp (15 mL) snipped fresh dill is a terrific in-season addition to the salad.

VARIATION: Asian Cabbage Salad

For the slaw use the same amounts of cabbage, apples, carrots, radishes, green onion and almonds; replace the parsley with ¼ cup (60 mL) minced fresh coriander (cilantro).

DRESSING

⅔ cup (150 mL) light or regular mayonnaise

2 tbsp (30 mL) lemon juice

1 tbsp (15 mL) seasoned rice vinegar

1 tbsp (15 mL) sesame oil

1 tbsp (15 mL) soy sauce

dash hot pepper sauce

IN A LARGE bowl, whisk together the mayonnaise, lemon juice, vinegar, sesame oil, soy sauce and hot pepper sauce.

To the dressing, add the cabbage, apples, carrots, radishes, green onion and coriander. (MAKE-AHEAD: Cover and refrigerate for up to 4 hours.) Sprinkle the almonds overtop.

Edna Staebler's "Schnippled" Bean Salad

Makes 4 to 6 servings

EDNA STAEBLER (1906–2006) was one of the first Canadian writers to extol the virtues of local (regional) food in her magazine articles and bestselling *Schmecks* cookbooks. Her sympathetic portrayal of Old Order Mennonites and Waterloo County fare lifted the region into a culinary destination in Canada. Her sour cream bean salad became one of the area's long-lasting specialties, as good today as when she made it for company.

Here's Edna's recipe (from *Food That Really Schmecks*), the introduction and instructions in her own quaint style.

EDNA STAEBLER: How many beans to use is a problem: people always eat more than they think they can; one summer Sunday I had ten guests for dinner. I used six quarts of fresh yellow beans for the salad and there was just a nappieful left.

1 quart (1 L) yellow or green string beans
  (1 lb/500 g)
1 smallish onion, sliced
salt and freshly ground black pepper

1 tbsp (15 mL) granulated sugar
1 tbsp (15 mL) white vinegar
¾ cup (175 mL) sour cream

CUT THE STEMS off the beans, wash them, then schnippel them—that means cutting the beans on a slant in very thin slices, one bean being cut into 3 or 4 long slices. (Or you could use frozen French-cut beans.) Put the beans into boiling salted water and cook them just long enough to be barely soft, 3 to 4 minutes for garden- or market-fresh beans. Drain and cool them.

Meanwhile, in a small bowl, sprinkle the onion liberally with salt and stir it around; let it stand at least 15 minutes, giving it a stir now and then. In a bowl large enough to contain the beans, put the sugar, vinegar, half a teaspoon [2 mL] of salt, a good sprinkling of pepper and the sour cream. Stir all together. Now take the salted onion into your hand and with the other hand squeeze as much of the juice out of the onion as you can. Put the squeezed onion into the dressing, pour the drained beans into the bowl and mix with the dressing till all the beans are generously coated—you might need more cream.

Some people like the beans to be slightly warm or hot—but then the dressing becomes thin and runny and doesn't properly coat the beans. Some like the squeezed juice of the onion in the dressing as well as the onion. Some like more onion. If by some strange miscalculation the bean salad isn't all eaten, you can put it in your refrigerator and keep it for a day or two.

Salad Dressing, Old and New

Makes about 1¼ cups (300 mL)

ELIZABETH: This old-fashioned cooked dressing is neither a vinaigrette nor a mayonnaise, rather a tangy and sweet custardy dressing that was, until the 1960s, the go-to dressing in my family for Devilled Eggs (page 18), ham, tuna, salmon and egg sandwich fillings. We also used it for potato salads and especially Cabbage Salad, Two Ways (page 170), where it was always mixed with cream, sometimes sour cream too. It provided just the right zippy lubrication. I'm nostalgic for this salad dressing's sweet and sour qualities, and I still leave space for it in my refrigerator—right beside the mayonnaise.

OLD-FASHIONED COOKED DRESSING

½ cup (125 mL) granulated sugar
2 tsp (10 mL) dry mustard
½ tsp (2 mL) salt

½ cup (125 mL) cider or white vinegar
2 large eggs
1 tbsp (15 mL) butter

IN THE TOP of a double boiler or a heatproof bowl, whisk together the sugar, mustard and salt; whisk in the vinegar, then the eggs. Set over simmering water; cook, whisking often, until the dressing is thick, smooth and creamy like custard, about 8 minutes. Stir in the butter.

Strain through a sieve into a clean jar or airtight container; let cool for 30 minutes. Refrigerate until cold; then cover. Refrigerate for up to 2 weeks.

YOUR HOUSE DRESSING

Makes about 1¼ cups (300 mL)

THIS IS A modern vinaigrette to coat all the wide variety of greens available now. Just remember the classic formula for vinaigrette: 1 part acid (vinegar or lemon juice) to 3 or 4 parts oil (olive or canola). We prefer the 1 to 4 ratio most of the time since the 1 to 3 ratio can be a little tangy. There's enough dressing here for three large salads.

1 cup (250 mL) extra virgin olive oil
   (see Note)
¼ cup (60 mL) red or white wine vinegar
1 clove garlic

½ tsp (2 mL) salt
¼ tsp (1 mL) freshly ground black pepper
1 tsp (5 mL) Dijon mustard

MEASURE THE OIL and vinegar into a jar with a screw top.

On a cutting board, press the garlic with the broad blade of a knife. Sprinkle the garlic with the salt; mash together with the knife or a fork to make a paste. Add to the jar with the pepper and mustard. Shake until well blended. (MAKE-AHEAD: Refrigerate for up to 4 to 5 days. Bring out to room temperature for a few minutes and shake well before using.)

NOTE
To reduce fat, replace ¼ cup (60 mL) of the oil with apple juice or water. Or go back to the 1 to 3 ratio by reducing the oil to ¾ cup (175 mL) and adding ½ tsp (2 mL) granulated sugar or honey.

VARIATIONS: Twists on Your House Dressing
› SUNDRIED TOMATO AND OREGANO DRESSING: Reduce the salt to ¼ tsp (1 mL) and add 1 tbsp (15 mL) minced oil-packed sundried tomato and 1 tbsp (15 mL) minced fresh oregano or 1 tsp (5 mL) dried oregano.
› PARMESAN CHEESE DRESSING: Reduce the salt to a pinch. Add ¼ cup (60 mL) freshly grated Parmesan cheese or other hard grating cheese, such as Grana Padano or Romano cheese.
› ANY-HERB DRESSING: Yes, use whatever you have growing: basil, dill, thyme, oregano and rosemary are top of the list. Add about 1 generous tablespoon (15 mL) chopped, per batch.

Breads

Down East Oatmeal Bread

Makes 2 loaves and a happy gang around the toaster

. . . .

FIRST YOU SETTLE down at the table, ocean view recommended, and then the waiter brings the bread basket, the opening act for a grand meal to come. And front and centre in the selection: thick slices of bread, moist with oats, yielding just a little tang of molasses, culinary vestiges of Nova Scotia's Scottish heritage and Caribbean connection. This is the kind of bread recipe with which even beginners have success.

. . . .

⅓ cup (75 mL) packed brown sugar, divided

½ cup (125 mL) lukewarm water

4 tsp (20 mL) active dry yeast

1 cup (250 mL) quick cooking rolled oats (not instant)

1¼ cups (300 mL) boiling water

⅓ cup (75 mL) butter, cubed

2 tbsp (30 mL) fancy molasses

1½ tsp (7 mL) salt

2 large eggs

1 cup (250 mL) whole wheat flour

4 cups (1 L) all-purpose flour (approx)

1 large egg

¼ cup (60 mL) quick cooking rolled oats

IN A LARGE liquid measuring cup, stir 1 tsp (5 mL) of the sugar into the water. Sprinkle the yeast overtop; stir and let stand until foamy and increases in volume, about 10 minutes. Stir again.

Meanwhile, in a large bowl, combine the 1 cup (250 mL) rolled oats and boiling water. Add the remaining sugar and the butter, molasses and salt; stir occasionally until smooth and the butter has melted. Let cool to warm room temperature; whisk in the 2 eggs, then the yeast mixture.

With a mixer or a wooden spoon, beat in the whole wheat flour and half of the all-purpose flour. Stir in enough of the remaining flour to form a soft, slightly sticky dough. Scrape onto a work surface well sprinkled with some of the flour. Knead, incorporating flour as needed until the dough is smooth and springy but still slightly soft, about 8 minutes.

Place the dough in a clean greased bowl, turning to grease all over. Cover and let rise in a warm spot until doubled in bulk, about 1 hour. Grease two 8- × 4-inch (1.5 L) loaf pans. Gently flatten the dough; divide in half. On a lightly floured surface, gently pull the dough into 11- × 8-inch (28 × 20 cm) rectangles. Starting at one narrow end, roll the dough up into a cylinder; pinch the ends and along the bottom to seal. Fit into the prepared pans. Cover the loaves and let rise in a warm spot until doubled in bulk, about 45 minutes.

Beat the 1 egg until frothy. Without pressing, brush over the loaves; sprinkle the loaves with the ¼ cup (60 mL) rolled oats. Bake in the centre of a preheated 375°F (190°C) oven until the loaves sound hollow when lightly tapped on the bottom, about 25 to 30 minutes. Remove from the pans and let cool on racks. (MAKE-AHEAD: Wrap in plastic wrap, place in an airtight container and freeze for up to 1 month.)

Egg Bread

Makes 1 loaf, about 12 slices

THIS BEAUTIFUL BRAIDED egg bread appeals to bread-lovers everywhere. It makes for superb French toast and, especially, fine bread pudding.

2 tsp (10 mL) granulated sugar
¾ cup (175 mL) lukewarm water
2 tsp (10 mL) active dry yeast
2 large eggs, at room temperature
2 tbsp (30 mL) canola oil
1 tsp (5 mL) salt

3 to 3½ cups (750 to 875 mL) all-purpose
   flour (approx)
1 egg yolk
½ tsp (2 mL) water
1 tbsp (15 mL) poppy or sesame seeds

IN A LARGE bowl, or a stand mixer if available, dissolve the sugar in the water. Sprinkle the yeast over the surface; let stand until foamy and increases in volume, about 10 minutes.

Beat in the eggs, oil and salt. Beat in 2 cups (500 mL) of the flour, beating until the batter is stretchy and smooth. By hand, beat in the remaining flour, as much as is needed to make a soft, rather sticky dough. Sprinkle some of the remaining flour onto the counter; scrape the dough out onto the floured surface and knead until the dough is no longer sticky but still soft and smooth, about 6 to 8 minutes.

Place the dough in a lightly oiled clean bowl; turn to coat the dough with a film of oil. Cover with a damp towel; place in a warm spot to rise until doubled, about 1 hour. Press the dough down; gather into a ball. Cover the bowl and let the dough relax for 5 minutes.

Meanwhile, lightly oil a 9- × 5-inch (2 L) loaf pan; set aside. Cut the dough into 3 equal portions. Roll and shape each third into a rope about 14 inches (35 cm) long. Pinch the ropes together at one end and, overlapping the ropes firmly but not tightly, braid the dough, pinching the other ends of the ropes together firmly. Fit neatly into the loaf pan, tucking the ends under (see Note). Cover the dough with lightly oiled plastic wrap and place in a warm spot to rise until doubled in bulk, about 45 minutes.

Meanwhile in a small bowl, mix the egg yolk and water; brush over the top of the loaf, being careful not to let the egg wash touch the rim of the pan. Sprinkle with the poppy seeds.

Bake in the centre of a 375°F (190°C) oven until golden brown and the bottom of the loaf sounds hollow when tapped, about 40 minutes. Remove from the pan and let cool on a rack. (MAKE-AHEAD: Wrap in plastic wrap, place in an airtight container and freeze for up to 1 month.)

NOTE
You can set the braided dough onto a parchment paper–lined baking sheet and let it rise free-form, without the loaf pan. Bake as for the loaf, reducing the baking time slightly.

Light Rye Bread

Makes 3 loaves

ROSE: I have served this easy-to-make bread for many years. Its flavour is especially complemented when paired with smoked salmon or in sandwiches of cold cuts or ham.

2 cups (500 mL) light rye flour
2 cups (500 mL) boiling water
¾ cup (175 m) fancy molasses
⅓ cup (75 mL) lard or butter
1 tbsp (15 mL) salt

1 envelope (8 g) active dry yeast
 (2¼ tsp/11 mL)
½ cup (125 mL) warm water
6 cups (1.5 L) all-purpose flour (approx)
cornmeal (optional)

IN A LARGE bowl, stir together the rye flour, boiling water, molasses, lard and salt. Let cool.

Meanwhile, sprinkle the yeast over the warm water and let stand until foamy and increases in volume, about 10 minutes. Stir and add to the rye flour mixture. Gradually add enough all-purpose flour to make a stiff dough. Turn out onto a floured surface and knead until the dough is smooth and bounces back when a finger is poked into it, 3 to 4 minutes.

Divide the dough into 3 equal portions and shape each into a round loaf. Place on baking sheets sprinkled with cornmeal (if using) or on greased baking sheets. Cover and let rise in a warm place until doubled in bulk, about 2 hours.

Bake in the centre of a 350°F (180°C) oven until dark brown and hollow sounding when rapped on the bottom with a knuckle, 40 to 50 minutes. Cool on racks. (MAKE-AHEAD: Place in an airtight container and freeze for up to 1 month.)

Refrigerator Rolls

Makes 2 dozen dinner rolls or 1 dozen hamburger or sandwich-size rolls

ROSE: Before we had access to good bakery rolls, many cooks would make these soft round dinner rolls for entertaining because they could be prepared a few days ahead and were delicious warm from the oven. My mother often made them and sometimes would form them into flat mounds twice the size of dinner rolls so that we could use them as hamburger buns. These buns beat any commercial hamburger bun I've ever met!

¼ cup (60 mL) warm water
¼ cup (60 mL) granulated sugar
1 tbsp (15 mL) active dry yeast
1 cup (250 mL) milk
¼ cup (60 mL) butter

1 tsp (5 mL) salt
1 large egg, well beaten
4 cups (1 L) all-purpose flour (approx)
melted butter or oil for greasing the rolls

MEASURE THE WARM water into a large mixing bowl. Stir in 1 tsp (5 mL) of the sugar until dissolved; sprinkle the yeast overtop and let stand until foamy and increases in volume, about 10 minutes. Stir well.

Meanwhile, heat the milk in a small saucepan until small bubbles appear around the edge of the pan. Stir in the butter, the remaining sugar and the salt. Stir until the butter is melted and then cool to lukewarm. Add to the yeast mixture along with the egg and 2 cups (500 mL) of the flour. Beat well with a wooden spoon or, if you are using the dough hook of your mixer, beat on medium speed for 5 minutes.

Gradually add enough of the remaining flour to make a soft dough you can handle, keeping it as soft as possible. Turn out onto a floured surface, rubbing out any remaining dough from the bowl, and knead until smooth and elastic, about 5 minutes. Shape into a smooth, round ball and transfer to a large clean greased bowl; turn the dough to grease the top, cover with plastic wrap and refrigerate until needed, up to 5 days. (If using the same day, let rise at room temperature until doubled in volume, about 1 hour, before punching down and forming into balls.) Punch down once during the first day and once every other day after that.

When needed, let rest, covered, at room temperature for about 2 hours. (If you use only a portion of the dough, put the remainder back into the refrigerator.)

Punch the dough down and knead 2 or 3 times. Shape into 12 or 24 rolls, depending on the size of roll you want. Place on greased baking sheets, a 2-inch (5 cm) space between them; grease the tops well and let sit, covered with a piece of greased waxed paper and tea towel, in a warm place until doubled in volume, 1 to 1¼ hours.

Bake in the centre of a 400°F (200°C) oven until light brown and the rolls sound hollow when lightly tapped, about 15 to 20 minutes (depending on size). Cool on racks or serve hot.

Cinnamon Buns and Chelsea Buns

Makes 18 buns

....

FROM ONE SWEET yeast dough come two delicious progeny: cinnamon buns and Chelsea buns. Both are studded with fruit and spices but come out of their pans in different shapes: round for cinnamon buns, square for Chelsea buns. While cinnamon buns have pulled ahead in popularity in Canada (could this be because of their generous, even lavish, amounts of brown sugar and butter, as well as the ubiquitous cinnamon?), Chelsea buns, with a more modest level of sweetening, have enjoyed a long history, which began in the 18th century at the Bun House of Chelsea, England, and still rank highly. Both buns turn weekend breakfasts and brunches into occasions, especially if you finish baking them, filling the kitchen with welcoming aromas, as the family descends or guests arrive. *Cinnamon Buns pictured here.*

....

SWEET DOUGH
¼ cup (60 mL) granulated sugar
½ cup (125 mL) lukewarm water
1 envelope (8 g) active dry yeast
   (2¼ tsp/11 mL)

¼ cup (60 mL) butter, cubed
½ cup (125 mL) milk
1 tsp (5 mL) salt
2 large eggs
3½ cups (875 mL) all-purpose flour (approx)

IN A LIQUID measuring cup, mix 1 tsp (5 mL) of the sugar into the water. With a fork, stir in the yeast. Let stand until foamy and increases in volume, about 10 minutes.

Meanwhile, in a small saucepan, heat the remaining sugar with the butter, milk and salt, stirring occasionally, until the sugar dissolves and the butter melts. Let cool to lukewarm. Scrape into a large bowl; beat in the eggs, then the yeast mixture.

With a mixer or by hand, beat in 2 cups (500 mL) of the flour, 1 cup (250 mL) at a time. Beat until the batter is smooth and stretchy. By hand, beat in enough of the remaining flour, about ½ cup (125 mL) at a time, to make a soft, sticky dough. Turn out onto a counter dusted with some of the remaining flour and knead, incorporating the remaining flour or additional flour as needed to make a smooth, soft and satiny dough, about 5 minutes. Place the dough in a clean greased bowl, turning to grease all over. Cover and let rise in a warm spot until doubled in bulk, about 1 hour. Press gently to deflate; let rest for 5 minutes. Divide the dough in half. Proceed with either the Cinnamon Buns or Chelsea Buns (recipes follow).

CONTINUED . . .

CINNAMON BUNS

¾ cup (175 mL) chopped pecan halves
½ cup (125 mL) butter, softened
1 cup (250 mL) packed brown sugar

1 tbsp (15 mL) cinnamon
1 recipe Sweet Dough
½ cup (125 mL) small sultana raisins

GREASE THE BOTTOM and sides of two 8- or 9-inch (20 or 23 cm) round cake pans. Divide the pecans between the pans. In a bowl, blend together half of the butter, half of the sugar and half of the cinnamon. Drop the butter mixture by bits evenly over the pecans. Set aside.

On a floured work surface, roll each half of the Sweet Dough into a 15- × 8-inch (38 × 20 cm) rectangle. Spread each with half of the remaining butter; sprinkle evenly with the remaining sugar, the remaining cinnamon and the raisins. Starting at the long side, tightly roll up the Sweet Dough into a cylinder. Pinch the ends and sides to seal. Cut each roll into 9 slices. Arrange 9 slices, cut-side down, in each prepared pan. Cover and let rise in a warm spot until doubled in bulk, about 45 minutes.

Bake the buns in the centre of a 375°F (190°C) oven until golden brown and fragrant, about 15 minutes. Let the pans cool for 2 minutes on a rack. Place a plate over the top of the buns and, gripping the plate and pan with oven mitts, turn the buns out onto the plate. Scrape any sugary mixture back onto the buns. Slide off the plate onto racks to cool. Best served warm or rewarmed. (MAKE-AHEAD: Wrap in plastic wrap and freeze in an airtight container for up to 1 month.)

CHELSEA BUNS

1 recipe Sweet Dough*
1 tsp (5 mL) grated lemon zest
3 tbsp (45 mL) butter, melted
½ cup (125 mL) packed brown sugar
½ cup (125 mL) currants
¼ cup (60 mL) candied orange
   or mixed citrus peel
1 large egg
1 tbsp (15 mL) coarse granulated
   sugar (optional)

*Follow the Sweet Dough recipe; before heating the butter and milk mixture, add the grated lemon zest. Continue with the Sweet Dough recipe until the dough has risen. Press gently to deflate, let rest for 5 minutes.

GREASE THE BOTTOM and sides of two 8- or 9-inch (20 or 23 cm) square cake pans.

On a floured work surface, roll each half of the Sweet Dough into an 18- × 12-inch (45 × 30 cm) rectangle. Brush with the butter; sprinkle evenly with the sugar, currants and orange peel. Starting at the long side, tightly roll up the dough into a cylinder. Pinch the ends and sides to seal. Cut each roll into 9 slices. Arrange 9 slices, cut-side down, in each prepared pan. Cover and let rise in a warm spot until doubled in bulk, about 45 minutes. Beat the egg lightly; brush over the surface of the buns. Sprinkle with the coarse sugar (if using).

Bake the buns in the centre of a 375°F (190°C) oven until golden brown and fragrant, about 15 minutes. Let the pans cool for 2 minutes on a rack. Turn out onto a rack to cool. Best served warm or rewarmed. (MAKE-AHEAD: Wrap in plastic wrap and freeze in an airtight container for up to 1 month.)

Hot Cross Buns

Makes 16 buns

....

ELIZABETH: I've always lamented that hot cross buns, for centuries a Good Friday tradition, tend to show up in supermarkets almost as soon as revellers down their last sip of Christmas cheer. Where is the anticipation? Then my sybaritic side comments that these currant-rich, sweetly spiced buns are too good to be restricted to a spring weekend and I encourage everyone to enjoy them year round.

This recipe features a gently kneaded dough, stickier than most bread doughs and softer, which makes for particularly moist and tender buns. The finishing touches include crosses cut into the dough and a honey glaze for shine.

....

⅓ cup (75 mL) granulated sugar
½ cup (125 mL) lukewarm water
4 tsp (20 mL) active dry yeast
¾ cup (175 mL) milk
¼ cup (60 mL) butter, cubed
1 tsp (5 mL) salt
2 large eggs plus 1 egg yolk
1½ tsp (7 mL) cinnamon

½ tsp (2 mL) nutmeg
generous pinch each cloves and allspice
    (or ¼ tsp/1 mL cloves)
4 cups (1 L) all-purpose flour
1 cup (250 mL) currants
½ cup (125 mL) candied orange or mixed
    citrus peel
3 tbsp (45 mL) liquid honey

IN A LIQUID measuring cup, stir 1 tsp (5 ml) of the sugar into the water. Sprinkle the yeast overtop and stir with a fork; let stand until foamy and increases in volume, about 10 minutes. Stir well.

Meanwhile, in a small saucepan, heat the remaining sugar with the milk, butter and salt just until the butter is melted and the sugar has dissolved. Let cool to lukewarm.

In a large bowl, beat the eggs and yolk with the cinnamon, nutmeg, cloves and allspice. Beat in the milk and yeast mixtures. Beat in 2 cups (500 mL) of the flour, 1 cup (250 mL) at a time. Beat at medium speed for 3 minutes to make a smooth, stretchy batter. (This is when a stand mixer is handy, but you can use your good beating arm and a wooden spoon. Consider this part of your fitness program.)

By hand, stir in the remaining flour, 1 cup (250 mL) at a time, to make a soft, rather sticky dough. Mix in the currants and candied orange peel.

Turn out onto a lightly floured surface and, with floured hands, shape into a soft, smooth round. Dust your hands with flour, as needed, and use a dough scraper or metal spatula to release dough from the surface. Place the dough in a clean greased bowl, turning to grease all over. Cover and let the dough rise in a warm spot until doubled in bulk, about 1½ hours. Press gently to deflate; let rest for 10 minutes.

Meanwhile, line a large baking sheet with parchment paper, or grease it; set aside.

Turn the dough out onto a lightly floured surface. Cut in half; roll each half into two 16-inch (40 cm) ropes. Cut each rope into 8 sections to make 16 pieces of dough.

One at a time, shape the pieces of dough into smooth round balls, keeping a smooth rounded surface on top and pulling and pinching the dough underneath. Lightly dust your hands with flour if necessary to prevent sticking. Leaving 2 inches (5 cm) of space between them, place the balls evenly on the prepared baking sheet. Let rest until the dough relaxes, about 5 minutes. Press each ball into a puck, about ¾ inch (2 cm) thick.

Cover the buns with lightly greased plastic wrap and let them rise in a warm spot until doubled in bulk, about 45 minutes. Using a very sharp knife and a light stroke, cut a shallow cross in the top of each bun. Let stand for 5 minutes.

Bake in the centre of a 375°F (190°C) oven until golden brown on top and the buns sound hollow when tapped on the bottom, about 15 minutes. Place the pan on a rack. Warm the honey; brush over the buns. Lift the buns onto the rack to cool.

NOTE

Hot Cross Buns are best warm from the oven but stay fresh for about 3 days if enclosed in an airtight container or bag. Reheat in a toaster oven or oven for fresh-baked taste. You can also freeze Hot Cross Buns, but do so before glazing or they become far too sticky.

Yule Raisin Bread

Makes 4 loaves

THIS RECIPE COMES from Catherine Betts, a caterer and photographer based in New Brunswick. Catherine hails from England, where every Christmas her sisters make this old-fashioned raisin bread, which came from their great-grandmother. They like it served with Wensleydale cheese.

1 cup (250 mL) milk

½ cup (125mL) water

½ cup (125 mL) granulated sugar, divided

2 envelopes (8 g each) active dry yeast
    (4½ tsp/22 mL total)

½ cup (125 mL) butter, softened

2 tbsp (30 mL) lard or butter

2 large eggs

6 cups (1.5 L) all-purpose flour (approx)

1½ tsp (7 mL) salt

1 tsp (5 mL) nutmeg

1½ cups (375 mL) sultana raisins

1½ cups (375 mL) currants

1 cup (250 mL) candied mixed citrus peel

1 large egg yolk, beaten

IN A SAUCEPAN, heat the milk and water with 1 tsp (5 mL) of the sugar to lukewarm. Remove from the heat and sprinkle in the yeast; let stand until foamy and increases in volume, about 10 minutes. Whisk in the butter and lard. Whisk in the eggs.

Meanwhile, in a large bowl, whisk together 3 cups (750 mL) of the flour, the remaining sugar, the salt and nutmeg; add the yeast mixture and, with a wooden spoon, stir until smooth. Gradually, 1 cup (250 mL) at a time, stir in enough of the remaining flour to make a soft dough, working in the last of the flour with a rotating motion of your hand and adding up to ¼ cup (60 mL) extra flour if necessary. Turn out onto a floured surface and knead until smooth and elastic, 10 to 12 minutes. Cover with the bowl and let rest for 5 minutes. Meanwhile, in a small bowl, stir together the raisins, currants and peel.

Flatten the dough into a large rectangle. Scatter with half the fruit mixture and fold the dough over it; knead until the fruit is evenly distributed. Cover as before and let rest 5 minutes. Repeat with the remaining fruit. Place the dough in a clean greased bowl, turning to grease all over. Cover with plastic wrap and let rise in a warm place until doubled in bulk, about 1½ hours (a heating pad underneath turned to low works well).

Punch down the dough and divide into 4 equal portions. Form each into a loaf and place each in a greased 8- × 4-inch (1.5 L) loaf pan, turning to grease all over; cover with a clean tea towel and let rise in a warm place until doubled in bulk, about 45 minutes.

Gently brush the loaves with the egg yolk and bake in the centre of a 375°F (190°C) oven until browned and the loaves sound hollow when tapped on the bottom, about 30 minutes. Transfer to racks to cool. (MAKE-AHEAD: Wrap in plastic wrap and place in an airtight container and freeze for up to 1 month.)

Buttermilk Cornbread

Makes 8 servings

CORNBREAD, SOMETIMES CALLED johnny cake, is an old tradition in Canada. The addition of creamed corn makes this spicy version very moist.

1¼ cups (300 mL) cornmeal
1 cup (250 mL) shredded old
  Cheddar cheese
¾ cup (175 mL) all-purpose flour
½ tsp (2 mL) each salt and baking soda
½ sweet red pepper, finely diced
1 jalapeño pepper, seeded and minced

3 large eggs, beaten
1¼ cups (300 mL) creamed corn
  (one 10-oz/284 mL can)
¾ cup (175 mL) well-shaken buttermilk
⅓ cup (75 mL) canola oil

IN A LARGE bowl, whisk together the cornmeal, cheese, flour, salt and baking soda. Stir in the peppers.

In another bowl, whisk together the eggs, creamed corn, buttermilk and oil; stir into the cornmeal mixture just until combined. Pour into a greased 8-inch (2 L) square cake pan, smoothing the top; bake in the centre of a 400°F (200°C) oven until golden and a tester inserted into the centre comes out clean, 35 to 40 minutes.

Cream Tea Scones

Makes about 12 scones

CAROL FERGUSON, founding food editor of *Canadian Living* magazine, award-winning food writer, educator and consultant: Many of my favourite recipes—traditional scones, shortbread, saskatoon berry pie—evoke fond memories of my prairie childhood, especially of family gatherings at my grandmother's big farmhouse in southern Saskatchewan. Everyone looked forward to the fresh-baked scones that appeared at the daily ritual of afternoon tea, which my very Scottish granny carried on just like in the old country. I remember standing, in a long apron, on a stool at her baking counter, watching her gentle deftness with shortbread and scones. I also remember helping to arrange the tea table with pretty cups and saucers and big vases of fragrant lilacs or sweet peas, whether for a gathering of our clan or just one or two of her lady friends from neighbouring farms.

In my hometown farther north, my mother carried on the same traditions—frequent afternoon teas with friends and visitors, and lots of home baking. In the kitchen, I watched and learned as she modestly produced mouth-watering pies and tarts, poppy seed cake, cream puffs, cinnamon buns and several varieties of shortbread and scones. After a lot of practice, I mastered my first recipes—for tea biscuits and scones. Over the years, I've developed many variations on the scone theme. This one for cream tea scones is a sweet, flaky version ideal for traditional English cream tea. Serve the scones with butter, jam and thick, rich Devonshire cream or clotted cream (available in some Canadian grocery stores; stiffly whipped cream may be substituted). These scones are also excellent as a base for Old-fashioned Strawberry Shortcake (page 252). *Pictured with Seville Orange Marmalade (page 300).*

2 cups (500 mL) all-purpose flour
2 tbsp (30 mL) granulated sugar
1 tbsp (15 mL) baking powder
½ tsp (2 mL) salt

½ cup (125 mL) cold butter
1 large egg
⅔ cup (150 mL) milk

IN A LARGE bowl, mix together the flour, sugar, baking powder and salt. Cut in the butter until the mixture looks like coarse crumbs. In a small bowl, beat the egg lightly; remove 1 tbsp (15 mL) of the beaten egg and reserve for the topping. To the remaining egg, add the milk; add the mixture all at once to the dry ingredients, stirring quickly with a fork to make a soft dough. With floured hands, gather into a ball and turn out onto a lightly floured surface. Knead lightly a few times until smooth. Roll or pat out to a ¾-inch (2 cm) thickness. Cut into 2½-inch (7 cm) rounds. Place on an ungreased baking sheet. Brush the tops with the reserved egg. Bake in the centre of a 425°F (220°C) oven until golden brown, 12 to 14 minutes.

Banana Bread

Makes 10 slices

DANA MCCAULEY, food writer, cookbook author and trend consultant: I make this banana bread at least a couple of times a month, whenever the bananas on the counter get too "skanky" to eat—that's when they are perfect.

⅔ cup (150 mL) butter, softened
½ cup (125 mL) lightly packed brown sugar
2 large eggs, beaten
1 cup (250 mL) mashed, very ripe banana
   (about 3 medium bananas)
1 tsp (5 mL) vanilla

2 cups (500 mL) all-purpose flour
1 tbsp (15 mL) baking powder
½ tsp (2 mL) each baking soda and salt
1 cup (250 mL) chopped pecans, walnuts
   or chocolate chunks (optional)

IN A LARGE bowl, beat the butter until light and fluffy (feel free to use a mixer if you prefer). Blend in the brown sugar and beat until light. Beat in the eggs, adding one at a time. Blend in the banana and vanilla until well incorporated.

Place the flour in a separate bowl; sprinkle the baking powder, baking soda and salt over the flour and stir together. Using deep strokes, blend the dry ingredients into the butter mixture until almost fully combined. Fold in the nuts or chocolate, if using. Scrape the batter into a lightly greased 9- × 5-inch (2 L) loaf pan and smooth evenly to fill to the edges of the pan. Bake in the centre of a 350°F (180°C) oven until the loaf springs back when lightly touched on top, 50 to 60 minutes. Cool in the pan on a rack for 10 minutes. Turn out onto a rack and cool completely before slicing. (MAKE-AHEAD: Store in an airtight container at room temperature for up to 5 days. Or wrap the loaf or individual slices in plastic wrap in an airtight container and freeze for up to 1 month.)

Nut and Date Loaf

Makes 10 slices

THIS KIND OF moist fruity loaf—a "quick bread" in baking talk—bridges the gap between muffins and a full-fledged fancy (read fussy) layer cake. It's as easy to whip up as a snacking cake. The dates make this loaf a great keeper—to almost 1 week at room temperature if you can keep it hidden that long. Or frozen in slices for up to 1 month, handy to take out for lunches or to go with an afternoon latte or tea. Some people have been known to spread butter or soft cream cheese over a slice . . . or two.

1 cup (250 mL) packed chopped pitted dates
1¼ cups (300 mL) boiling water
½ cup (125 mL) butter, softened
1⅓ cups (325 mL) packed brown sugar
1 large egg
2 tsp (10 mL) finely grated orange zest

1 tsp (5 mL) vanilla
2⅓ cups (575 mL) all-purpose flour
1 tsp (5 mL) baking soda
½ tsp (2 mL) each salt and nutmeg
¾ cup (175 mL) chopped walnut
    or pecan halves (see Note)

LINE A 9- × 5-inch (2 L) loaf pan with parchment paper or grease the bottom and sides; set aside.

In a heatproof bowl, stir together the dates and boiling water. Let cool to room temperature.

Meanwhile, in a large bowl, beat the butter until creamy. Beat in the sugar; beat until fluffy. Beat in the egg, orange zest and vanilla.

In a separate bowl, whisk together the flour, baking soda, salt and nutmeg. Stir a third of these dry ingredients into the butter mixture, followed by half of the date mixture, then half of the remaining dry ingredients, then the remaining date mixture and then the remaining dry ingredients. Sprinkle the nuts over the batter and fold in.

Scrape into the prepared pan; smooth the top. Tap smartly on the counter to remove any air bubbles. Bake in the centre of a 350°F (180°C) oven until a tester inserted into the centre comes out clean, about 60 to 70 minutes. Let cool in the pan on a rack for 20 minutes. Transfer the loaf to the rack and let cool, upright. (MAKE-AHEAD: Remove the parchment paper and store in an airtight container at room temperature for up to 5 days. Or wrap the loaf or individual slices in plastic wrap and freeze in an airtight container for up to 1 month.)

NOTE
If you are making this loaf for school lunches or other occasions where nut allergies may be an issue, simply omit the nuts or replace them with chocolate chips or raisins.

Muffins Many, Many Ways

Dry Muffin Mix makes 6 portions, each enough for 12 muffins

JENNIFER MACKENZIE, professional home economist, food writer and cookbook author: Muffins are one of the earliest creations I remember making with my mom, Patricia, who is a fabulous cook. I would stand on a chair beside her, both of us wearing matching hand-sewn aprons, as she taught me how to measure, whisk and stir, "just enough" to make sure the muffins stayed tender. Mom taught me the wonders of baking from scratch and using healthy ingredients, which steered me towards becoming a professional home economist and cookbook author. Many years after those initial lessons, I created this recipe for a homemade muffin mix for the café (Nuttshell Next Door, in Lakefield, Ontario) I co-own with my husband, chef Jay Nutt. Our staff loves the recipe because it's easy to whip up muffins in just a few minutes early in the morning; our customers love it because it creates wonderful muffins.

DRY MUFFIN MIX

9 cups (2.25 L) all-purpose flour
8 cups (2 L) whole wheat flour
3¼ cups (800 mL) granulated sugar

¼ cup (60 mL) baking powder
1 tbsp (15 mL) baking soda
1 tbsp (15 mL) salt

IN A LARGE bowl, whisk together the all-purpose flour, whole wheat flour, sugar, baking powder, baking soda and salt. Divide into 6 equal portions, each about 3⅓ cups (825 mL), and transfer the portions to airtight containers or sealable storage bags (dividing any remaining mix equally between the portions). Store in a cool, dry place for up to 2 months or freeze for up to 6 months. If frozen, let warm to room temperature before using.

MUFFINS

Makes 12 muffins

1 portion Dry Muffin Mix
1 large egg
1¼ cups (300 mL) unsweetened applesauce
  or mashed ripe bananas (3 large)

¾ cup (175 mL) milk
⅓ cup (75 mL) canola oil or melted butter

LINE 12 MUFFIN cups with paper liners, or grease them.

In a large bowl, whisk the Dry Muffin Mix to distribute any settled ingredients. Stir in the muffin ingredients of your choice (see Variations: Add-Ins and Toppings).

In a medium bowl, whisk together the egg, applesauce, milk and oil until blended. Pour over the dry ingredients and stir just until moistened. Spoon the batter evenly into the prepared muffin cups. Add a topping, if using (see Variations: Add-Ins and Toppings).

Bake in the centre of a 375°F (190°C) oven until the muffin tops spring back when lightly touched, 25 to 30 minutes. Let cool in the pan on a rack for 10 minutes. Transfer muffins to the rack to cool completely.

VARIATIONS: Add-Ins and Toppings

These amounts are for 1 batch of 12 muffins.

› APPLE SPICE: Use applesauce (not mashed bananas) and add 1 cup (250 mL) each diced apples and raisins, 1½ tsp (7 mL) cinnamon and ¼ tsp (1 mL) nutmeg. Optional topping: Thin apple slice.

› PEAR GINGER: Use applesauce (not mashed bananas) and add 1¼ cups (300 mL) diced pears and 2 tbsp (30 mL) minced crystallized ginger. Optional topping: Thin pear slice.

› BERRY-BERRY: Use applesauce or mashed bananas and add 1½ cups (375 mL) mixed fresh or frozen raspberries and blueberries.

› LEMON CRANBERRY: Use applesauce (not mashed bananas) and add ¾ cup (175 mL) dried cranberries and 1 tbsp (15 mL) grated lemon zest.

› BANANA CHOCOLATE-CHOCOLATE: Use mashed bananas (not applesauce) and add ½ cup (125 mL) miniature semisweet chocolate chips and ¼ cup (60 mL) white chocolate chips (or chopped chocolate for both).

› RAISIN CINNAMON PECAN: Use applesauce or mashed bananas and add ¾ cup (175 mL) raisins, ½ cup (125 mL) chopped toasted pecans and 1½ tsp (7 mL) cinnamon.

Soaker Lemon Loaf

Makes 10 slices

QUICK BREADS OR tea breads are great to have on hand because they stay lovely and moist, especially when drenched in a lemony syrup like this one. Slices, buttered or not, disappear quickly with a cup of afternoon tea . . . or coffee in the morning, for that matter.

1½ cups (375 mL) all-purpose flour
1 tsp (5 mL) baking powder
½ tsp (2 mL) salt
½ cup (125 mL) chopped walnuts
1 tbsp (15 mL) grated lemon zest, divided

½ cup (125 mL) butter, softened
1¼ cups (300 mL) granulated sugar, divided
2 large eggs
½ cup (125 mL) milk
¼ cup (60 mL) fresh lemon juice

LINE A 9- × 5-inch (2 L) loaf pan with parchment paper and set aside.

In a medium bowl, whisk together the flour, baking powder and salt. Stir in the walnuts and 2 tsp (10 mL) of the lemon zest.

In a large bowl, cream the butter; beat in 1 cup (250 mL) of the sugar until light and fluffy. Beat in the eggs, one at a time, incorporating each well.

Add the dry ingredients alternately with the milk, making 3 dry and 2 liquid additions, combining lightly after each. Turn into the prepared pan and bake in the centre of a 350°F (180°C) oven until a tester inserted into the centre comes out clean, about 70 minutes. Place on a rack to cool for 5 minutes.

Meanwhile, in a measuring cup in the microwave oven or in a small saucepan on the stovetop, heat the remaining ¼ cup (60 mL) sugar with the lemon juice and remaining 1 tsp (5 mL) grated lemon zest until the sugar is dissolved. With a long skewer, poke about 12 holes in the loaf, right to the bottom of the pan. Drizzle the syrup slowly overtop until completely used. Let cool another 5 minutes, then carefully remove the loaf using the parchment paper as handles. Let cool completely on the rack before removing the paper. Wrap in plastic wrap and let stand 1 day before using. (MAKE-AHEAD: Wrap and store at room temperature for up to 3 days or place in an airtight container and freeze for up to 1 month.)

Oatmeal Pancakes

Makes 10 to 12 pancakes

....

ELIZABETH: When cooking teacher Pam Collacott and I travelled to Whitehorse to headline a cooking show that raises funds for children's breakfast programs in Yukon Territory, we had the good fortune to stay at Sandra Henderson's bed and breakfast. What a treat was in store for us. These healthy pancakes are just one of the dishes Sandra cooked, she in her kitchen and we right beside her, dashing any good dieting intentions by generously dousing the pancakes with maple syrup. In season, you can add diced apple, pear or berries to the batter.

....

2 cups (500 mL) large-flake rolled oats
2 cups (500 mL) well-shaken buttermilk
   (approx, see Note)
½ cup (125 mL) all-purpose flour
2 tbsp (30 mL) granulated sugar

1 tsp (5 mL) baking powder
1 tsp (5 mL) baking soda
½ tsp (2 mL) salt
2 large eggs
¼ cup (60 mL) canola oil

IN A LARGE bowl, combine the oats and buttermilk. Cover and refrigerate overnight.

In a medium bowl, combine the flour, sugar, baking powder, baking soda and salt. Stir into the rolled oat mixture. In a small bowl, beat the eggs and oil. Stir into the oat mixture. The mixture should be pourable; if not, add a bit more buttermilk.

Heat a griddle or skillet over medium heat until drops of water dance and sputter; grease lightly. Drop the batter in ¼-cup (60 mL) amounts onto the hot surface. Cook until the pancake tops are covered with fine bubbles. Turn the pancakes over and cook until the bubbly side is well browned. Serve immediately.

NOTE

If you don't have buttermilk handy, simply stir 2 tsp (10 mL) fresh lemon juice or vinegar into 2 cups (500 mL) milk and let the mixture stand for 5 minutes before incorporating it into the recipe.

VARIATION: Buttermilk Pancakes

Increase the baking powder to 1½ tsp (7 mL) and decrease the oil to 2 tbsp (30 mL). Replace the oats and the all-purpose flour with 2 cups (500 mL) all-purpose flour. Combine the flour with the other dry ingredients in a large bowl, and the buttermilk with the eggs and oil in a small bowl. Pour the buttermilk mixture into the dry ingredients and stir just enough to combine, ignoring lumps. Let rest for 5 minutes (not overnight). Add blueberries or other fruit as desired. Cook as in the main recipe.

Puddings and Desserts

Rice Pudding, Two Ways

Makes 8 servings

....

ELIZABETH: Just how do you describe rice pudding? According to skeptics who have moved on from childhood favourites to the more sophisticated *panna cotta* or *crème brûlée*, it's "bland." From the mouths of fans of rice pudding comes the word "comforting," as they imagine digging a spoon into rich creamy rice, still warm, studded with plump raisins. For me, rice pudding is a lovely homey dessert, fondly remembered from my mother's kitchen. There, she added plenty of raisins to please my father, and picked them out of her portion to please herself. I like dressing rice pudding up and exploring its variations from around the world. This rice pudding is a stovetop version and uses arborio (or another short-grain) rice, high in the kind of starch that provides the pudding's velvety texture.

....

CREAMY RICE PUDDING

½ cup (125 mL) Thompson raisins (see Raisins, page 206)

2 tbsp (30 mL) rum or orange juice

⅔ cup (150 mL) arborio or short-grain rice

5 cups (1.25 L) whole milk

⅓ cup (75 mL) granulated sugar

pinch salt

1 strip (6 inches/15 cm) orange zest

1 cinnamon stick

½ cup (125 mL) 10% or 18% cream

IN A SMALL covered bowl, soak the raisins in the rum while the pudding cooks.

In a medium-large saucepan, stir together the rice, milk, sugar, salt and orange zest. Break the cinnamon stick into rough shards and add.

Bring to a simmer over medium heat, stirring regularly. Simmer gently, stirring often, until the rice swells, is tender and the milk thickens into a velvety sauce around the rice, about 1 hour. Be especially vigilant with the stirring as the pudding thickens or it will scorch. Cover and let stand for 10 minutes. Remove the orange zest and cinnamon.

Stir in the cream, raisins and rum. Serve warm. (MAKE-AHEAD: Cover the surface of the pudding with plastic wrap; let cool for 30 minutes. Refrigerate for up to 4 days. Rewarm in the microwave oven or on the stovetop on very low heat. Before serving, add a little more milk or cream to lighten the pudding.)

TWISTS

› Instead of Thompson raisins, use golden raisins, currants, dried cranberries or cherries, or slivered dried apricots or prunes, adding a little more for a fruitier pudding. Try a strip of lemon zest instead of orange zest.

› Instead of the cinnamon stick and orange zest, slit 1 vanilla bean lengthwise. Scrape the seeds into the rice mixture; add the pod too. Remove the pod for serving.

VARIATION: Brûlée Rice Pudding

Spoon the still-warm, firm rice pudding into heatproof ramekins (see Note) and smooth the surface. Sprinkle with brown sugar to coat the surface, about 1 tbsp (15 mL) per bowl. Heat using a *crème brûlée* torch, or briefly under the broiler until the sugar melts and caramelizes. Let stand for a few minutes in the refrigerator for surface to harden and crackle.

NOTE

Ramekins are small, usually round dishes for baking and serving an individual portion.

CARDAMOM RICE PUDDING

Makes 6 to 8 servings

ONE OF OUR go-to restaurants when we lived near the Danforth in Toronto was the Sheri-Punjab. At the end of every meal, proprietor Mr. Singh presented the table with little dishes of homemade rice pudding (*kheer*), fragrant with cardamom. Just the ticket after our spicy choices.

⅓ cup (75 mL) white basmati rice
4 cups (1 L) whole milk (approx)
½ cup (125 mL) granulated sugar
pinch salt

6 green or white cardamom pods
⅔ cup (150 mL) slivered dried apricots
⅓ cup (75 mL) sliced almonds

SOAK THE RICE in a large bowl of cold water for 30 minutes; drain well.

In a medium-large saucepan, stir together the rice, milk, sugar and salt. With the bottom of a cup, lightly crush the cardamom pods and add to the rice mixture.

Bring to a simmer over medium heat, stirring regularly. Simmer gently, stirring often, until the rice starts to swell, about 1 hour. Pick out the cardamom pods; stir in the apricots. Simmer until the rice is tender and the pudding has thickened, about 20 to 30 minutes. Be especially vigilant with the stirring as the pudding thickens or it will scorch. Cover and let stand for 10 minutes. Add a little more milk if desired to thin the pudding. (MAKE-AHEAD: Cover the surface of the pudding with plastic wrap; let cool for 30 minutes. Refrigerate for up to 4 days. Rewarm in the microwave oven or on the stovetop on very low heat. Before serving, add a little more milk or cream to lighten the pudding.)

Meanwhile, toast the almonds in a dry skillet over medium heat. Stir half into the pudding and use the remainder to garnish each serving.

RAISINS

There are 3 kinds of raisins; all are dried grapes:

› SULTANAS: The most common and available raisins, made from varieties of seedless grapes. Among the varieties are the less expensive, generic sultanas. Supermarkets also stock golden raisins and dark Thompson raisins (considered by many bakers to be the best of the seedless raisins).

› LEXIA AND MUSCAT: Dried grapes with seeds (the traditional raisins). Years ago, bakers needed to remove the seeds, a tedious and time-consuming task. Now these raisins are available without seeds and, while more expensive and harder to find (check bulk food stores), they are loved for their rich wine flavour.

› CURRANTS: Dried grapes of a small black variety, originally from Corinth, Greece (the "Corinth" evolved into "currrant"). Do not confuse dried currants with currants (red, black or white), which are a totally different species.

Blueberry Bread Pudding
with Whisky Sauce

Makes 8 to 10 servings

THIS RECIPE IS inspired by a delicious bread pudding we once had at Pictou Lodge Resort, when we were in search of Nova Scotia's finest fare for a *Canadian Living* magazine story.

The Whisky Sauce brings back memories of Cape Breton's Glenora Inn and Distillery in the Mabou Highlands. It was Canada's first single-malt whisky distillery, where Donnie Campbell, the inn's whisky ambassador, coached us on the fine technique of nosing whisky.

6 large eggs
2 cups (500 mL) 18% cream
1 cup (250 mL) granulated sugar, divided
1 cup (250 mL) whipping cream
1 cup (250 mL) milk
1 tbsp (15 mL) maple extract

1 tsp (5 mL) vanilla
12 cups (3 L) cubed white sandwich bread, about 1¼ loaves, crusts trimmed off
2 cups (500 mL) fresh blueberries
½ cup (125 mL) finely chopped pecans
Whisky Sauce (recipe follows)

IN A LARGE bowl, whisk the eggs. Whisk in the 18% cream, all but 2 tbsp (30 mL) of the sugar, and the whipping cream, milk, maple extract and vanilla. Stir in the bread and blueberries; stir gently but thoroughly to moisten evenly. Scrape into a lightly greased 13- × 9-inch (3.5 L) glass baking dish. (MAKE-AHEAD: Cover and refrigerate for up to 8 hours; add 10 minutes to the baking time.)

Toss the pecans with the remaining sugar; sprinkle over the surface. Bake in the centre of a 375°F (190°C) oven until puffed and golden brown and the tip of a knife inserted into the centre comes out clean, about 45 minutes. Let cool on a rack for 15 minutes to serve hot or for up to 1 hour to serve warm. Serve with Whisky Sauce.

WHISKY SAUCE
Makes about 1¼ cups (300 mL)

1 large egg
½ cup (125 mL) granulated sugar
1 tsp (5 mL) cornstarch

⅓ cup (75 mL) unsalted butter, melted
¼ cup (60 mL) whisky

IN A HEATPROOF bowl, whisk together the egg, sugar and cornstarch until smooth; whisk in the butter. Set over a saucepan of simmering water; cook, whisking, until thickened enough to coat the back of a spoon, about 4 minutes. Remove from the heat; whisk in the whisky. (MAKE-AHEAD: Cool, cover and refrigerate for up to 24 hours. Reheat in a heatproof bowl over hot but not boiling water.)

Saucy-Bottom Lemon Pudding

Make 6 to 8 servings

....

ELIZABETH: My grandmother, Elizabeth Maud Davis, was still young in body and spirit when my grandfather left her a widow. In those days before pensions, she needed to work, and so she became a housekeeper. Always a storyteller, her letters were full of news about the people she worked for—a retired general, a Great Lakes sea captain and Dr. and Mrs. Lindsay, back in Canada from lifetime careers in the service of the United Church in China. In each of the households, she added to her repertoire of recipes and passed them to my sister Janey and me. The biggest hit, a lemon pudding with a light spongy cake on top and a saucy bottom, remains a favourite to this day, and my grandmother's handwritten recipe, used so often it's batter-stained, is framed and has a place of honour in my kitchen.

....

1 cup (250 mL) granulated sugar, divided
3 tbsp (45 mL) all-purpose flour
¼ tsp (1 mL) salt
1 cup (250 mL) milk
3 tbsp (45 mL) butter, melted
3 large eggs, separated

1 tbsp (15 mL) finely grated lemon zest
⅓ cup (75 mL) lemon juice
1½ cups (375 mL) fresh blueberries
    or raspberries
1 tbsp (15 mL) icing sugar

IN A LARGE bowl, whisk together ¾ cup (175 mL) of the sugar, the flour and the salt. Add the milk, butter and egg yolks; whisk to combine. Whisk in the lemon zest and juice; set aside.

In a separate bowl, beat the egg whites until soft peaks form; beat in the remaining sugar, 1 tbsp (15 mL) at a time, beating until stiff shiny peaks form. Stir about one-quarter of the egg-white mixture into the lemon batter. Fold in the remaining egg white mixture.

Scrape into an 8-inch (2 L) glass baking dish or metal cake pan. Place the dish in a larger shallow pan. Pour enough boiling water into the outer pan to come halfway up the sides of the dish holding the batter. Bake in the centre of a 350°F (180°C) oven until the top is lightly browned and the pudding has pulled away from the sides of the dish, about 30 to 40 minutes.

Remove the dish with the baked pudding from the outer pan and let cool on a rack to the desired temperature (still a little warm or at room temperature). (MAKE-AHEAD: Cover the pudding and refrigerate for up to 1 day.) Spoon into dessert bowls; top with a scattering of blueberries and a dusting of icing sugar.

Peach Upside-Down Pudding

Makes 6 servings

THIS IS ONE of those puddings where the fruit starts on top, but ends up—well, almost all of it—in a saucy layer under a soft cake topping. Time your dessert so it comes out of the oven about 45 minutes before you serve it up—with all the usual suspects: ice cream, frozen yogurt, whipped cream, *crème fraîche* or simply pouring cream.

BATTER

⅓ cup (75 mL) butter
1¼ cups (300 mL) all-purpose flour
¾ cup (175 mL) granulated sugar
2 tsp (10 mL) baking powder
½ tsp (2 mL) nutmeg or cinnamon
¼ tsp (1 mL) salt
1 large egg
¾ cup (175 mL) milk

SAUCE

4 cups (1 L) sliced peeled peaches (6 or 7)
¾ cup (175 mL) packed brown sugar
1 tsp (5 mL) grated lemon or orange zest
2 tbsp (30 mL) lemon or orange juice

BATTER → Melt the butter and let it cool. In a large bowl, whisk together the flour, sugar, baking powder, nutmeg and salt.

In a separate bowl, whisk together the egg, milk and butter. Pour over the dry ingredients; whisk just until smooth and scrape into a greased 8-inch (2 L) square baking dish or cake pan.

SAUCE → In a medium saucepan, bring the peaches, sugar, lemon zest and juice to a boil over medium-high heat. Reduce the heat to simmer and cook for 2 minutes. (There will be a lot of liquid that will be absorbed in the baking.) Spoon evenly over the batter. Bake in the centre of a 350°F (180°C) oven until the cake has risen to cover (or almost cover) the peaches and the top is golden brown, about 40 minutes.

Pouding Chômeur à l'Ancienne (Poor Man's Pudding)

Makes 6 servings

THIS RECIPE, WHICH can be also translated as "old-fashioned economy pudding," comes from Rollande DesBois, a Montreal cookbook author, cooking teacher and food writer. This self-saucing butterscotch pudding cake is so popular in Quebec that myths have grown up about its origins. Some say it was invented in the Depression by female factory workers or by the wife of the mayor of Montreal, but culinary historians believe that the origin of the recipe is earlier.

BATTER
¼ cup (60 mL) butter, softened
¾ cup (175 mL) granulated sugar
1 large egg (see Note)
1½ cups (375 mL) all-purpose flour
2 tsp (10 mL) baking powder
¼ tsp (1 mL) salt
¾ cup (175 mL) milk

SAUCE
1½ cups (375 mL) packed light
    brown sugar
1½ cups (375 mL) water
½ cup (125 mL) medium or amber
    maple syrup

BATTER → In a large bowl, beat the butter with the sugar until light and fluffy. Beat in the egg. In a separate bowl, whisk together the flour, baking powder and salt to combine. Stir into the butter mixture in 3 parts, alternating with the milk in 2 parts. Scrape into a greased 8-inch (2 L) metal cake pan; smooth the top. Set aside.

SAUCE → In a medium saucepan, bring the sugar, water and maple syrup to a boil, stirring until the sugar dissolves. Boil for 2 minutes. With one hand, hold a rubber spatula over the centre of the batter. With the other hand, slowly pour the syrup over the spatula, dispersing the hot liquid evenly over the batter rather than making holes in the batter. Do not stir. The sauce seeps down underneath the cake batter, making the yummy layer of butterscotch.

Bake in the centre of a 350°F (180°C) oven until a tester inserted into the top of the golden-brown pudding comes out clean, about 40 to 45 minutes. Let cool for a few minutes on a rack.

Scoop into warmed bowls. Lovely with ice cream or pouring cream.

NOTE
If you like, add ½ tsp (2 mL) vanilla to the cake batter along with the egg, and to the sauce just before pouring it over the batter.

Carrot Pudding
with Brown Sugar Sauce

Makes 8 to 10 servings

DOROTHY DUNCAN, Canadian food historian and prize-winning author: Among my happiest childhood memories are those of the visits to my grandparents' farm and the magic realm known as the farmhouse kitchen. This was the undisputed domain of my Scottish grandmother, Georgina Gibson, where every day, with apparent ease, she produced three hearty meals for her family, friends, neighbours and anyone else who happened to drop in at the right time. I always wanted to join her as she stood beside her enormous (to my eyes) wood-burning cookstove as I was fascinated as she stirred, tasted, rearranged her cooking pots, and occasionally opened the oven door to check on whatever she had baking, warming or roasting there. I knew that it would not be long before we would all be seated around the equally enormous kitchen table enjoying the hearty, no-nonsense meal that she had produced.

As I grew older, and taller, one of her big white aprons would be folded and tied around me so that I could help create the miracle of the next meal. For breakfast there would be oatmeal porridge, eggs, fried pork, fried potatoes, her own homemade bread, butter and preserves. For dinner at noon there would be a roast of beef or pork, vegetables from her garden, pickles and more preserves, made on that same stove, carefully sealed in crocks or glass jars, labelled and stored on shelves in the cellar.

Dessert was an important part of both dinner at noon and supper after the chores were finished in the evening. Puddings and pies were the favourites, and it was in that kitchen, beside that stove, that I met and fell in love with carrot pudding with brown sugar sauce. As I grew older I learned that my grandmother, like many of her neighbours, made many carrot puddings every fall after she harvested the root vegetables from her garden and the local storekeeper received fresh supplies of dried fruit and spices in readiness for the orders from all his lady customers. Grandmother steamed her puddings in a large tub on the back of the stove, allowed them to cool and wrapped each one in a clean cotton cloth ready to hang on a peg in the cellar. As winter set in she could turn to her puddings for special occasions, Sunday dinners, unexpected visitors—in fact, any emergency! She simply re-steamed them while she made a large quantity of brown sugar sauce.

My grandmother did not own a printed cookbook, but she did keep some handwritten "receipts"—as she called them—so my mother, Margaret Gibson, carried on the tradition of the carrot puddings. My mother's habit was to make two generous puddings in November, to be stored in a cool, dry place and brought out for Christmas Day and New Year's Day dinners. And yes, she carried on the miracle of the sauce as well, and I was again pressed into service to stir the flour, brown sugar, butter and water as it slowly turned into that succulent liquid that we ladled so generously over the pudding time after time.

I have been amazed as the years passed, and I collected and studied Canadian cookbooks, to see how often variations of these two simple recipes have appeared.

1 cup (250 mL) finely chopped beef suet*

1 cup (250 mL) granulated sugar

1 cup (250 mL) each grated carrot
 and potato

1 tsp (5 mL) baking soda

¼ cup (60 mL) milk

1½ cups (375 mL) all-purpose flour

1 tsp (5 mL) each salt, cinnamon
 and nutmeg

¼ tsp (1 mL) cloves

1 cup (250 mL) Lexia or Muscat raisins
 (see Raisins, page 206)

1 cup (250 mL) currants

*Suet is white kidney fat. Ask for it from a
 butcher or look for it already chopped and
 frozen in most supermarkets.

GREASE ONE 6-CUP (1.5 L) or two 3-cup (750 mL) heatproof bowls or pudding moulds and sprinkle the inside with granulated sugar.

Beat together the suet and sugar. Stir in the carrot and potato. In a liquid measuring cup, stir the baking soda into the milk and set aside.

In a large bowl, whisk together the flour, salt, cinnamon, nutmeg and cloves. Stir in the raisins and currants. Stir in the suet mixture, then the milk mixture. Turn into the prepared bowl or bowls (the bowl should be no more than three-quarters full). Cover with a double thickness of waxed paper, then a large piece of foil, leaving a 2-inch (5 cm) overhang. Tie string securely around the top of the bowl to hold the covers. Place on a rack in a large pot and pour boiling water around the bowl to two-thirds of the way up the bowl. Cover and simmer over medium-low heat, adding more water if needed, until the top is no longer sticky, 2½ to 3 hours. Let stand for 5 minutes before unmoulding. (MAKE-AHEAD: Cool, wrap well and freeze, or store in a cool, dry place for up to 2 months. To reheat, return to the original bowl and steam until heated through, 20 minutes for smaller puddings and up to 1 hour for a larger pudding.) Serve with the hot Brown Sugar Sauce.

BROWN SUGAR SAUCE
Makes about 2 cups (500 mL)

¼ cup (60 mL) butter

1 cup (250 mL) packed brown sugar

¼ cup (60 mL) all-purpose flour

2 cups (500 mL) hot water

IN A HEAVY saucepan, melt the butter over medium heat. Meanwhile, stir together the sugar and flour; add to the butter, stirring constantly. Gradually stir in the hot water; bring to a boil, stirring. Serve hot. (MAKE-AHEAD: Cool, cover and let the sauce sit at room temperature up to 2 hours ahead. Or refrigerate for up to 1 day if left over. Reheat gently to serve.)

Fruit Cobbler

Makes 6 servings

FOR MANY SPRINGS, we drove to Stratford to attend classes with Neil Baxter at Rundles Restaurant. Making good use of his expertise and the restaurant's professional facilities, these weekend events were an excellent way to bridge the closing of the chefs' school in March until the opening of the Shakespeare festival season in May. Along with usually ten other eager students, we would gather in time to prepare Friday night's supper and leave, happily sated, after an exquisite Sunday lunch. Neil taught us the fine points of making everything we longed to master—the most tender pasta, the creamiest Armagnac ice cream, the thinnest strudel pastry, the puffiest of puff pastry—but one recipe we both remembered with great fondness was his simple fruit cobbler. No great mysterious techniques here, just a straightforward vehicle to celebrate Canada's array of summer fruit. Neil suggests that this cobbler even works quite well with frozen fruit. (Don't thaw it first.) Our favourite mix will always include blackberries, which are great with sliced peaches as their companion, but try blueberries, raspberries, strawberries, rhubarb—anything you have on hand. Serve warm with pouring or softly whipped cream.

FILLING
5 cups (1.25 L) mixed fruit
⅓ cup (75 mL) granulated sugar
1½ to 2 tbsp (20 to 30 mL) all-purpose flour

TOPPING
1½ cups (375 mL) sifted
   cake-and-pastry flour
2 tbsp (30 mL) granulated sugar
1 tbsp (15 mL) baking powder
¼ tsp (1 mL) salt
⅓ cup (75 mL) cold unsalted butter
¾ cup (175 mL) whipping cream

FILLING → In a 6-cup (1.5 L) gratin or shallow baking dish, combine the fruit with the sugar and flour, using the larger amount of flour if the fruit is very juicy. Set aside while preparing the topping.

TOPPING → In a large bowl, whisk together the flour, sugar, baking powder and salt. With a pastry blender, cut in the butter until the mixture looks like coarse meal. (MAKE-AHEAD: Cover and refrigerate up to several days ahead.) Add the cream and stir lightly until the dry ingredients are just moistened. Spoon the mixture over the fruit in a single layer or in 6 individual patties, no more than ½ inch (1.25 cm) thick. Bake in the centre of a 375°F (190°C) oven until the topping is brown, the berry juices bubble thickly around it and the topping is no longer doughy underneath, 40 to 45 minutes.

Georgian Bay Apple Crisp

Makes 4 to 6 servings

ROSE: My mother, Josephine Varty, made the most delicious apple crisp—buttery with a true apple flavour, the apples from one of the trees on our farm that overlooked Georgian Bay. Mom made a dessert for both lunch (called dinner on the farm) and dinner (called supper on the farm), and I particularly remember relishing a cold dish of apple crisp when I finished the long walk home from public school at the end of the day. But this family favourite is best served warm with cheese or with ice cream. *Pictured with Very Vanilla Ice Cream (page 222).*

8 tart apples (about 2 lb/1 kg)
½ cup (125 mL) water
¼ cup (60 mL) granulated sugar
1 tsp (5 mL) cinnamon, divided
½ tsp (2 mL) vanilla

pinch salt
¾ cup (175 mL) packed brown sugar
¾ cup (175 mL) all-purpose flour
¼ tsp (1 mL) nutmeg
⅓ cup (75 mL) cold butter

PEEL, CORE AND thinly slice the apples. Place in a greased 8-inch (2 L) square baking dish. Stir in the water, granulated sugar, ½ tsp (2 mL) of the cinnamon, the vanilla and the salt.

In a small bowl, stir together the brown sugar, flour, the remaining cinnamon and the nutmeg. With a pastry blender, cut in the butter until the mixture is crumbly. Sprinkle over the apple mixture. Bake, uncovered, in the centre of a 375°F (180°C) oven until the apples are very tender and the top is golden brown, about 45 minutes.

Maple Crème Brûlée

Makes 6 servings

....

IT'S MAPLE SYRUP'S unique and earthy sweet flavour that makes the sugaring-off season such a special rite of spring in Canada. Easy elegance personified, this creamy dessert gains a whole new dimension of flavour when finely grated maple sugar is caramelized on top. If you can't find maple sugar, grate or finely chop the maple leaf candy moulds found in farmers' markets or even special gift shops; in a pinch, use granulated sugar. The broiler works well for caramelizing the sugar, but you could also use a small kitchen blowtorch.

....

1½ cups (375 mL) whipping cream

¼ cup (60 mL) maple syrup, preferably amber or dark

4 large egg yolks

⅓ cup (75 mL) finely grated maple sugar

IN A SMALL heavy saucepan, heat the cream and maple syrup together just until bubbles start to form around the outside. Remove from the heat. In a bowl, whisk the egg yolks slightly without allowing them to foam. Very gradually pour the hot cream into the yolks, stirring constantly.

Strain this custard through a fine sieve into a pitcher or liquid measuring cup. Pour into six ½-cup (125 mL) heatproof ramekins (see Note). Place them in a baking pan just big enough to hold them; pour hot water into the pan to come two-thirds up the sides of the ramekins. Cover with foil; bake in a 325°F (160°C) oven until the custards are just set but still slightly jiggly in the centres, about 25 minutes. Remove the ramekins to cool on a rack; refrigerate until very cold. (MAKE-AHEAD: Make up to 1 day ahead.)

Just before serving, sprinkle the custards with the maple sugar; broil on the rack nearest the heat until the sugar caramelizes to a golden brown, about 3½ minutes, watching carefully. Serve immediately.

NOTE
Ramekins are small, usually round dishes for baking and serving individual portions.

Very Vanilla Ice Cream
with Hot Fudge Chocolate Sauce

Makes about 1 quart (1 L), enough for 6 to 8 servings

THE SECRET IS, of course, a vanilla bean. Once an exotic, hard-to-find ingredient, vanilla beans are now available in most supermarkets, and often in good cookware and fancy food shops. Look for lustrous rich brown beans, pliable ones if you're able to do more than look at the selection of beans. A multitude of tiny seeds from the vanilla bean pod give the ice cream a lovely fine speckled look and a rich vanilla flavour. And the favourite topping for ice cream? Hot Fudge Chocolate Sauce (recipe follows). See Making and Storing Ice Cream (page 224) for an alternative to using an ice-cream machine.

1 vanilla bean or vanilla extract (see Note)
2 cups (500 mL) 10% or 18% cream
1 cup (250 mL) whipping cream

6 large egg yolks
⅔ cup (150 mL) granulated sugar

PLACE THE VANILLA bean flat on a cutting board. With a knife held parallel to the board, split the bean in half lengthwise. With the sharp blade, scrape out the seeds from one end to the other. Place the seeds and pod in a medium saucepan with the 10% cream and the whipping cream. Whisk gently and press the seeds with a rubber spatula to disperse them in the cream. Heat over medium heat, watching carefully, until little bubbles form around the edge of the pan. Remove the pan from the heat; cover and let stand for 30 minutes. Remove the pod. (Discard if you like, but if you rinse it and let it dry you can press it into a canister of sugar, where it will give the sugar a lovely vanilla flavour.)

In a large bowl, beat the egg yolks and sugar. Gradually pour the warm cream into the yolk mixture, whisking constantly. Whisk the yolk mixture back into the saucepan. Cook over low heat without boiling, stirring constantly, until the custard is thick enough to coat a wooden spoon, about 5 to 8 minutes. Remove from the heat. Pour through a sieve into a bowl. Discard any egg bits. Chill the bowl of custard in a larger bowl of ice water, stirring often, until the custard is cold.

Transfer to an ice-cream machine and freeze according to the manufacturer's instructions.

NOTE

For ice cream using vanilla extract, omit the vanilla bean. Start by heating the 2 creams until bubbles form around the edge of the pan. Whisk gradually into the beaten egg yolks and sugar. Return to the pan; cook and chill as directed, and add 1 tbsp (15 mL) vanilla extract. Always add vanilla extract to already-cooked custard.

HOT FUDGE CHOCOLATE SAUCE

Makes about 2 cups (500 mL), enough for about 16 servings, as long as you
don't spoon it out of the jar in the refrigerator, feigning a midnight snack attack

⅔ cup (150 mL) unsweetened cocoa
1 cup (250 mL) water
1 cup (250 mL) corn syrup

8 oz (250 g) bittersweet chocolate, chopped
1 tbsp (15 mL) vanilla
pinch cinnamon

IN A MEDIUM saucepan, whisk together the cocoa, water and corn syrup. Bring to a boil over medium heat, whisking constantly. Boil for 3 minutes, whisking often.

Reduce the heat to low; stir in the chopped chocolate. When about three-quarters of the chocolate has melted, remove from the heat and let remaining chocolate melt, stirring often. Stir in the vanilla and cinnamon. Let cool slightly before serving over vanilla ice cream. (MAKE-AHEAD: Pour into clean, hot jars; seal. Store in the refrigerator for up to 2 weeks. To warm to pouring consistency, heat in microwaveable pitcher at low power, stirring 2 or 3 times, or in a heatproof bowl over hot, not boiling, water.)

Strawberry Ice Cream

Makes about 8 cups (2 L), a good 10 servings

SIMPLER THAN VERY Vanilla Ice Cream (page 222), which is based on making a custard, this strawberry ice cream doesn't require any cooking. The fresh flavour of the berries will surprise you. See Making and Storing Ice Cream for an alternative to using an ice-cream machine.

4 cups (1 L) hulled sliced strawberries
1 cup (250 mL) fruit or berry sugar
   (instant dissolving)

1 tbsp (15 mL) fresh lemon juice
1½ cups (375 mL) 10% or 18% cream
1 cup (250 mL) whipping cream

IN A FOOD processor, purée the strawberries, sugar and lemon juice together until smooth; transfer to a bowl and let stand at room temperature for 30 minutes to sweeten the berries and completely dissolve the sugar. Stir well.

Whisk in the 10% cream and whipping cream. Transfer to an ice-cream machine and freeze according to the manufacturer's instructions.

MAKING AND STORING ICE CREAM

An ice-cream machine is a big help when making ice cream, whether it be a hand-cranked model with rock salt and ice to provide the chill or an electric one that delivers ice cream sinfully quickly. (Follow the manufacturer's instructions when you are using an ice-cream machine to freeze ice cream.)

You can still make ice cream quite easily if you have a food processor. Here's how: Freeze the ice-cream mixture in a 13- × 9-inch (3.5 L) metal cake pan until firm, almost solid. Break it into chunks and whirl, a few chunks at a time, in a food processor until smooth. Pack into an airtight container and freeze until solid yet easy to scoop, about 4 hours.

Most fresh ice creams are good for about 2 to 3 days so plan to enjoy them, if not right away, soon. And why not?

SWEETS
Cakes

Maple Carrot Cake with Maple-Butter Icing

Makes 16 servings

MONDA ROSENBERG, food consultant, cookbook author and former food editor of *Chatelaine* and the *Toronto Star:* My first encounter with carrot cake was less than stellar. Growing up in small-town Brockville, Ontario, I was totally food obsessed (yes, even at that stage), so the excitement of an upcoming birthday party was inevitably focused on the cake. Would it be white or chocolate or, on very rare occasions, marble? Then came the wondering whether I would be lucky enough to get a shiny quarter in my wedge or just a dull penny.

I remember the thrill of getting an invitation to the new-girl-in-town's party. (She had just moved from the States.) But when the cake was brought out, my heart sank. It did not even have a chocolate icing, just some white filling between the layers. And the layers looked like Christmas cake. How weird at a kid's party in the spring.

Finally someone got up the nerve to ask what kind of cake it was. When I heard "carrot," I was sure I had not heard correctly. Who would put carrots in a cake? That is what you had with roast beef. I stared at my wedge for a long time. I knew I had to try it. If I didn't, my new friend would think I was ungrateful and my mother would be on the warpath. Surprise: it wasn't as bad as I had feared!

Oh, how times and tastes have changed. The natural moistness that carrots impart to this spiced cake have sent it soaring to the top of the Canadian—and my personal—hit parade list. Here's my current fave. It's a truly Canadian version, laced with maple syrup and encased in a decadent maple-butter cream.

CAKE

1 cup (250 mL) butter, softened
1 cup (250 mL) packed brown sugar
4 large eggs
2 tsp (10 mL) vanilla
2½ cups (625 mL) all-purpose flour
1 tbsp (15 mL) baking powder
1 tsp (5 mL) baking soda
1 tsp (5 mL) salt
½ tsp (2 mL) cinnamon
½ tsp (2 mL) nutmeg
¾ cup (175 mL) amber or dark maple syrup
½ cup (125 mL) milk
4 cups (1 L) grated carrots

ICING

1½ cups (375 mL) butter, softened
¾ cup (175 mL) amber or dark maple syrup
1 tsp (5 mL) vanilla
3 to 3½ cups (750 to 825 mL) icing sugar

CONTINUED . . .

CAKE → Grease two 9-inch (2 L) round cake pans; line the bottoms with parchment paper.

In a large bowl, using a mixer, beat the butter until creamy. Gradually beat in the sugar; beat on medium until fluffy, 3 minutes. On low speed, beat in the eggs, one at a time, then the vanilla. (The mixture may look curdled.)

In a separate bowl, whisk together the flour, baking powder, baking soda, salt, cinnamon and nutmeg.

On low speed, gradually add about a third of the flour mixture to the butter mixture. Beat just until combined; add the maple syrup. Beat in half of the remaining flour mixture, followed by the milk, then end with the flour mixture. Sprinkle the carrots over the batter and fold in with a spatula.

Divide the batter between the pans. Spread evenly to the sides of the pans. Tap the pans smartly on the counter 5 to 6 times to remove any air bubbles. Bake in the centre of a 350°F (180°C) oven until a tester inserted into the centre comes out clean, the centre of the cake springs back when lightly touched and the cake comes away from the sides of the pans, about 40 minutes.

Let cool in the pans on racks for 15 minutes; turn out onto racks to cool completely. (MAKE-AHEAD: Wrap the layers and leave at room temperature overnight. Or double-wrap and freeze for up to 2 months. Thaw before icing.)

ICING → In a large bowl, using a mixer, beat the butter until creamy. On low speed, gradually beat in ¼ cup (60 mL) of the maple syrup. Add the vanilla. Beating on low speed, add ½ cup (125 mL) of the icing sugar. Repeat, adding the maple syrup and icing sugar twice. Beat in enough of the remaining icing sugar, about ¼ cup (60 mL) at a time, until the icing reaches spreading consistency. Stop and scrape down the beaters occasionally. If not firm enough to spread, refrigerate for a few minutes.

To assemble, with a long serrated knife, slice the layers in half horizontally. Place the top of one layer, dome-side down, on a flat cake plate. Tuck 4 strips of waxed paper, like a frame, under and around the cake to keep the plate clean.

Spread a generous ½ cup (125 mL) of the icing on the cut surface, leaving a narrow border of cake around the edge. Lay the bottom of the layer, cut-side down, on top. Ice in the same way, leaving a border. Add the bottom half of the second layer, cut-side down. Repeat spreading. Top with the final layer, cut-side down. Brush the side and top of the cake to remove any crumbs.

Smoothly spread a thin layer of icing over the side of the cake, then the top. Chill for 30 minutes to set this masking layer. Spread the remaining icing over the cake. Refrigerate several hours or overnight before serving. (MAKE-AHEAD: Refrigerate in an airtight container for up to 2 days.)

Three-Ginger Cake

Makes 12 servings

....

ELIZABETH: In the early 2000s, Sharol Josephson was the host of *Canadian Living Cooks* on Food Network Canada. This lively, entertaining and warm-hearted program covered everything from parenting and decor to potting plants and, of course, cooking. Sharol often joined me, the food editor of *Canadian Living* magazine, in the kitchen during cooking segments that showcased the magazine's top recipes. This gingerbread cake is from Sharon's own repertoire, however, and I think it's one of the best and most moist and gingery I've ever tasted. It's lovely as is, but a slice topped with ginger-scented whipped cream and served alongside fresh peaches is a big hit of deliciousness—and handsome too.

....

3 cups (750 mL) all-purpose flour

1 tbsp (15 mL) cinnamon

2 tsp (10 mL) baking soda

1½ tsp (7 mL) ground cloves

1 tsp (5 mL) ground ginger

¾ tsp (4 mL) salt

1½ cups (375 mL) granulated sugar

1 cup (250 mL) each canola oil
  and fancy molasses

2 large eggs

½ cup (125 mL) water

2 tbsp (30 mL) grated or minced
  fresh ginger

½ cup (125 mL) finely diced crystallized
  ginger (see Note)

1 tbsp (15 mL) icing sugar

USING A PASTRY brush, grease a 10-inch (3 L) Bundt pan; add enough flour to coat the inside of the pan. Tap out the excess flour and set aside.

In a medium bowl, whisk together the flour, cinnamon, baking soda, cloves, ground ginger and salt. In a large bowl, whisk together the sugar, oil, molasses, eggs, water and fresh ginger. Stir the flour mixture, one-third at a time, into the molasses mixture. Sprinkle the crystallized ginger overtop; fold in gently. Scrape into the prepared pan, pushing the batter into the crevices; tap the pan smartly on the counter to eliminate air bubbles.

Bake in the centre of a 350°F (180°C) oven until a tester inserted into the centre of the cake comes out clean, about 1 hour. Let the cake cool in the pan set on a rack for 30 minutes. Loosen the edge of the cake with a narrow knife. Place a small rack on top of cake; turn the cake over and let cool, decorative-side up. (MAKE-AHEAD: Wrap and store at room temperature for up to 2 days. Or overwrap with heavy-duty foil or place in a rigid airtight container and freeze for up to 1 month.) Dust with icing sugar.

> **NOTE**
> You can use preserved ginger in syrup for the crystallized ginger; just be sure it's well drained. Then you can use the syrup to flavour the whipped cream.

Chocolate Cake with Brown Sugar Fudge Icing

Makes 12 to 16 servings

MARGARET FRASER, home economist, cookbook author and retired associate food editor of *Canadian Living* magazine: Remembering my mother's cake stirs up memories from her kitchen: a wood stove, a pull-out flour bin containing a cotton sack of flour, a big brown mixing bowl, wooden spoons, a hand-cranked flour sifter and a big black cake pan. Her cake, made from scratch without an electric mixer, was moist, coarser than today's standard and very chocolaty. The fudge frosting only made it more delicious. As a kid who loved desserts best, I was prone to helping myself to an extra portion when no one was looking. It was easy to climb into a very deep pantry and carefully slice along the cut edge, nibbling as I went. Invariably the cut was crooked, necessitating one or two more thin slices to even things out. I was always surprised to hear my mother ask, "Who's been into the cake?" I wondered how she knew—until I became a mother!

CAKE

1⅔ cups (400 mL) all-purpose flour
⅔ cup (150 mL) unsweetened cocoa
1½ tsp (7 mL) baking soda
½ tsp (2 mL) salt
½ cup (125 mL) butter, softened
1½ cups (375 mL) granulated sugar
2 large eggs
1 tsp (5 mL) vanilla
1½ cups (375 mL) buttermilk or sour milk*

ICING

1 cup (250 mL) packed brown sugar
¼ cup (60 mL) light cream
2 tbsp (30 mL) butter, softened
1 tsp (5 mL) vanilla
1 cup (250 mL) sifted icing sugar

*To sour milk, pour 2 tbsp (30 mL) vinegar into a measuring cup. Add milk to make 1½ cups (375 mL) and let stand for 10 minutes.

CAKE → In a medium bowl, whisk together the flour, cocoa, baking soda and salt.

In a large bowl, cream together the butter and sugar until light and fluffy. Add the eggs, one at a time, beating well. Blend in the vanilla. Stir in the dry ingredients alternately with the buttermilk, making 4 dry and 3 liquid additions. Beat well after each addition.

Pour into a greased 13 × 9 inch (3.5 L) metal cake pan. Bake in the centre of a 350°F (180°C) oven until the centre is firm and the cake pulls away from the sides of the pan, 35 to 40 minutes. Cool on a rack.

ICING → In a small saucepan, stir together the brown sugar, cream and butter. Bring to a boil. Reduce the heat and boil gently for 3 minutes. Remove from the heat and stir in the vanilla. Cool to lukewarm, about 6 minutes.

Gradually add the icing sugar and beat until thick and spreadable. (The icing will lose its sheen.) Quickly spread onto the cooled cake.

VARIATION: Chocolate Icing

1 cup (250 mL) semisweet
   chocolate chips
3 tbsp (45 mL) butter

½ cup (125 mL) sour cream
1 tbsp (15 mL) corn syrup
½ tsp (2 mL) vanilla

IN A HEATPROOF bowl over hot water (not boiling), melt the chocolate chips with the butter. Remove from the heat and stir in the sour cream, corn syrup and vanilla until smooth. Cover and refrigerate until of spreading consistency, about 15 minutes. After icing the cake, keep it refrigerated.

Vanilla Cupcakes
with Sour Cream Vanilla Icing

Makes 16 cupcakes

ONE OF THE secrets of making a deliciously moist cake or cupcakes is to have the key ingredients at room temperature: butter, eggs and milk. In the real world, though, the urge for cake or cupcakes comes over you when all these ingredients are still cold from the refrigerator. Don't let this stop you. Warm the milk in the microwave and the eggs in a mixing bowl of just-warm water. As for the butter, shred it with a box grater into the bottom of the bowl. Set the bowl in a larger bowl of barely lukewarm water. Keep an eye on it, stirring it from time to time to smooth it out as it warms. By the time you have the other ingredients measured, and the paper liners in the pans, all these chilly ingredients will be at room temperature and ready to mix into a fine cake . . . or cupcakes.

CUPCAKES

⅔ cup (150 mL) butter, softened
1 cup (250 mL) granulated sugar
2 large eggs
2 tsp (10 mL) vanilla
1¾ cup (425 mL) all-purpose flour
2 tsp (10 mL) baking powder
½ tsp (2 mL) salt
¾ cup (175 mL) milk

ICING

¼ cup (60 mL) butter, softened
2 cups (500 mL) icing sugar, sifted, divided
1 tsp (5 mL) vanilla
¼ cup (60 mL) sour cream (approx), divided
chocolate sprinkles, small candies
  or silver dragée

CUPCAKES → Line 16 muffin cups with paper liners, or grease them.

In a large bowl, using a mixer, beat the butter until light. Gradually beat in the sugar, beating until blended and very light and creamy. Beat in the eggs, one at a time, beating well after each addition. Add the vanilla.

In a separate bowl, whisk together the flour, baking powder and salt. Mix into the butter mixture alternately with the milk, making 3 additions of the dry ingredients and 2 of the milk.

Divide equally among the prepared muffin cups, a generous ¼ cup (60 mL) in each. Tap the pans smartly on the counter. Bake in the centre of a 350°F (180°C) oven until golden, gently domed and a tester inserted into the centre comes out clean, about 20 minutes. Let firm up in the pans on a rack for 5 minutes. Remove the cupcakes to cool on a rack. (MAKE-AHEAD: Store in an airtight container at room temperature for up to 2 days. Or wrap individually and freeze in an airtight container for up to 1 month.)

ICING → In a bowl, beat the butter and half of the icing sugar just until blended. Add the vanilla, 2 tbsp (30 mL) of the sour cream and the remaining sugar; beat until smooth and easily spreadable, adding all of the remaining sour cream as needed. Pipe or spread the icing over the tops of the cupcakes; decorate with sprinkles.

VARIATION: Lemon Cupcakes with Sour Cream Lemon Icing
In the batter, replace the vanilla with 2 tsp (10 mL) finely grated lemon zest; in the icing, replace the vanilla with 1 tsp (5 mL) grated lemon zest and 1 tbsp (15 mL) of the sour cream with lemon juice.

Pastel de Tres Leches (Three-Milk Cake)

Makes 12 servings

....

MARY LUZ MEJIA, television director and producer, publicist and food and travel journalist: The first time I sampled a piece of *pastel de tres leches* (Spanish for "three milk cake"), I was in south Miami at the home of an American politician, being featured for a series that I was directing. It just so happened there was a family birthday the day of our filming. All of the crew was graciously cut a piece of this delectable cake, oozing a sweet, wonderful "milk." That was my introduction to this Latin American favourite that has become a hit in the United States and to a lesser extent here in Canada. It's a timeless favourite amongst Latinos and non-Latinos alike.

Theories abound as to how it was first introduced, which is interesting because I had no idea its origins were debatable. Some claim the cake was created in Mexico, while others argue that it was perfected in Nicaragua and later adopted by Cuba. Another theory posits that in order to get Latin American housewives to use evaporated milk, a company crafted the recipe and hence the popularity of the cake. Whatever theory you're partial to, the important thing is that you try this wonderful cake. Today there are as many adaptations as there are cake recipes—some use coconut milk, others melted chocolate or *cajeta* (Mexico's answer to *dulce de leche*—the most amazing spreadable caramel).

This recipe, with its light-as-air, sponge-like texture—that's how it soaks up all the delicious milk syrup—has become a staple in our house, and for good reason. Try it and taste for yourselves!

....

CAKE
5 large eggs, separated
½ tsp (2 mL) cream of tartar
1 cup (250 mL) granulated sugar, divided
1 cup (250 mL) all-purpose flour
1½ tsp (7 mL) baking powder
pinch salt
⅓ cup (75 mL) milk
½ tsp (2 mL) vanilla

MILK SYRUP
1 can (370 mL/12½ oz) evaporated milk
1 can (300 mL/10 oz) condensed milk
1 cup (250mL) whipping cream
½ tsp (2 mL) vanilla
1 tbsp (15 mL) dark rum (Cuban recommended)
unsweetened cocoa (optional)
whipped cream or vanilla ice cream
2 fresh mangoes or other fruit, preferably tropical, of your choice

CAKE → In a large bowl, using a mixer, beat the egg whites until foamy. Add the cream of tartar; beat until soft peaks form. Gradually add ¼ cup (60 mL) of the sugar, beating the whites to stiff shiny peaks; set aside.

In a small bowl, whisk together the flour, baking powder and salt; set aside.

In a separate large bowl, using a mixer, beat the egg yolks and remaining ¾ cup (175 mL) sugar until thick and the batter falls in ribbons from raised beaters, about 5 minutes. Fold the milk and vanilla into the yolk mixture. Sift the flour mixture over the surface; fold in.

Gently stir in about a third of the egg-white mixture. Fold in the remaining egg-white mixture. Scrape into a greased 13- × 9-inch (3.5 L) metal cake pan, smoothing the top. Bake the cake in the centre of a 350°F (180°C) oven until firm to a gentle touch and a tester inserted into the centre comes out clean, about 30 to 45 minutes. Let the cake cool completely in the cake pan. Pierce the cake all over with a skewer or fork, taking care not to tear it.

MILK SYRUP → In a large bowl, whisk together the evaporated milk, condensed milk, cream, vanilla and rum. Gently pour as much of the syrup over the cake as the cake will absorb; repeat until the cake has absorbed all the liquid—which it will do! Refrigerate until cold, about 2 hours. (MAKE-AHEAD: Cover and refrigerate for up to 24 hours.)

To serve, cut into 12 squares. Place a square on a dessert plate; dust with cocoa (if using). Garnish with whipping cream or ice cream and fruit.

Tosca Cake

Makes 8 servings

MARJA NEVALAINEN GATES: My mother, Eila Nevalainen, was a businesswoman who independently ran a family inn in Finland for over 50 years. She was also a good cook, preparing family meals, preserves and baking on a large wood-burning brick stove in the inn's kitchen.

One of my favourite memories from home is the afternoon coffee break, an important daily event in Finnish homes. The large kitchen table was set and as assortment of baking laid out. Most days it was *pulla* (a sweet yeast bread flavoured with cardamom and raisins), some cookies or dry cakes. Not only my parents, but also their clients, staff, friends and relatives—anybody who happened to be around—would sit down, exchange news, tell stories and joke around. The postman would know what day and time his favourite cinnamon buns came out of the oven and he timed his mail delivery accordingly.

In addition to the everyday coffee break in Finnish homes, life's important events— such as baptism, graduation, engagements, milestone birthdays and anniversaries— were celebrated with family and friends and a special occasion coffee table was set out. Traditionally, this festive coffee table, set with an elaborately embroidered white tablecloth, has seven different sorts of baking. Everyone knew the order of this special occasion coffee table—the unwritten rules required that you taste the sweet yeast bread with the first cup of coffee, with the second cup, the dry sponge or pound cakes and cookies and, with the third cup, you could finally enjoy a slice of frosted or cream-covered layer cake. This almond cake was my favourite, since it was not too sweet and heavy—just right.

CAKE
¼ cup (60 mL) butter
1 cup (250 mL) all-purpose flour
2 tsp (10 mL) baking powder
¼ tsp (1 mL) salt
2 large eggs
¾ cup (175 mL) granulated sugar
1 tsp (5 mL) vanilla
⅓ cup (75 mL) milk

TOPPING
2 tbsp (30 mL) butter
¼ cup (60 mL) granulated sugar
1 tbsp (15 mL) all-purpose flour
2 tbsp (30 mL) milk
½ cup (125 mL) sliced blanched almonds
½ tsp (2 mL) vanilla

CAKE → Grease an 8- or 9-inch (2 or 2.5 L) springform pan; line the bottom with parchment paper.

Melt the butter; let cool. In a bowl, whisk together the flour, baking powder and salt.

In a large bowl, using a mixer, beat the eggs and sugar until thick and the batter falls in ribbons from raised beaters. Gently stir in the vanilla, followed by half of the dry ingredients, then the milk and finally the remaining dry ingredients. Drizzle the butter over the surface; fold in.

Scrape into the prepared pan; tap on the counter to release air bubbles. Smooth the top. Bake in the centre of a 350°F (180°C) oven until just firm to the touch and a tester inserted into the centre comes out clean, about 25 to 30 minutes.

TOPPING → Meanwhile, in a small saucepan, melt the butter with the sugar over medium heat; stir in the flour. Cook 1 minute, stirring; mix in the milk and when the mixture thickens, remove from the heat. Add the almonds and vanilla, stirring until the almonds are evenly coated.

Spread the topping over the just-baked hot cake, extending it to the edge. Broil 8 inches (10 cm) from the heat, watching every second, until the topping bubbles and turns golden, about 1 to 2 minutes.

Remove from the oven; let cool on a rack for 10 minutes. Run a knife tightly against the inside of the cake pan. Undo the springform latch and remove the cake pan ring. Let cool completely. Use a lifter to remove the cake from the pan bottom; peel off the paper. Transfer to a small cake stand; cut with a serrated knife.

> **NOTE**
> This cake is very fine on its own, but if you're in the gussying-up mood,
> serve it with a big bowl of berries and some whipped cream.

Pecan-Cinnamon Coffee Cake

Makes 16 servings

DAPHNA RABINOVITCH WALTERS, chef, cookbook author and consultant: Although over the years I have tried hundreds of coffee cake recipes, this is one I keep coming back to. Simple, easy and so very moist, it epitomizes the classic coffee cake, redolent of sour cream, butter, brown sugar and nuts.

PECAN LAYER
1½ cups (375 mL) toasted pecans, finely chopped
¼ cup (60 mL) each granulated and packed brown sugar
1 tsp (5 mL) cinnamon

BATTER
1½ cups (375 mL) sour cream
1 tsp (5 mL) baking soda
1 cup (250 mL) unsalted butter, softened
1½ cups (375 mL) granulated sugar
3 large eggs
1 tsp (5 mL) vanilla
3 cups (750 mL) all-purpose flour
2 tsp (10 mL) baking powder
1 tsp (5 mL) salt

PECAN LAYER → In a small bowl, combine the pecans, the granulated and brown sugars and the cinnamon; set aside.

BATTER → In a 2-cup (500 mL) liquid measuring cup, combine the sour cream and baking soda; set aside. In a large bowl, using a mixer, beat the butter for 1 minute. Gradually add the sugar, beating until light and fluffy. Beat in the eggs, one at a time, beating well after each addition. Beat in the vanilla.

In a separate bowl, whisk together the flour, baking powder and salt. Using a wooden spoon, stir the flour mixture and sour cream mixture alternately into the butter mixture, making 3 additions of the flour mixture and 2 of the sour cream mixture. Spoon one-third of the batter into the bottom of a greased 10-inch (4 L) angel food cake pan. Sprinkle with one-third of the pecan mixture. Top with another third of the cake batter, smoothing the batter carefully over the pecan mixture. Sprinkle with another third of the pecan mixture. Top with the remaining cake batter, again spreading carefully. Top with the remaining pecan mixture.

Bake in the centre of a 350°F (180°C) oven until a tester inserted into the centre comes out clean, about 60 to 70 minutes. Let cool in the pan on a rack for 30 minutes. Remove from the pan to cool completely on the rack.

VARIATION: Dress-Up
To the pecan filling, add ¼ cup (60 mL) finely chopped semisweet chocolate and ¼ cup (60 mL) dried cranberries.

Plum Cake
with Crumble Topping

Makes 8 servings

HANNAH PAHUTA, chef: My Czech grandmother was probably the single greatest food influence in my life. She expressed her love through food and nurtured every member of our family regularly around her dinner table. I have made it a mission of mine to try to preserve her recipes, and thereby preserve her memory and what she believed in.

The link that food and memories have is magical. Bringing back an entire collage of happy memories is this plum cake (actually more like plum squares) that she made often. For me it is one of the most delicious desserts I have ever had, and just thinking about it takes me right back to her kitchen to sneak bits of crumble topping while it cools on her wooden table.

TOPPING

1 cup (250 mL) all-purpose flour
½ cup (125 mL) raw demerara sugar
⅓ cup (75 mL) cold unsalted butter,
  diced into small bits

CAKE

¾ cup (175 mL) unsalted butter, softened
¾ cup (175 mL) fine granulated sugar
1 tsp (5 mL) vanilla
3 large eggs
1 cup (250 mL) self-raising flour*

¼ cup (60 mL) all-purpose flour
½ cup (125 mL) plum juice**
30 plum halves** (approx)

*Self-raising flour is available in most supermarkets, but you can replace it with 1 cup (250 mL) all-purpose flour, 1 tsp (5 mL) baking powder and a generous pinch of salt.

**Jars of plum halves with juice are usually available in European delis.

TOPPING → Line a 9-inch (2.5 L) square cake pan with parchment paper. In a medium bowl, stir together the flour and sugar. Add the butter and blend with your fingers until it's like coarse bread crumbs. Set aside.

CAKE → In a large bowl, using a mixer or by hand, beat the butter and sugar until light and fluffy. Stir in the vanilla. Add the eggs, one at a time, beating well after each egg. Sift the self-raising and all-purpose flours together. Fold into the butter mixture alternately with the plum juice, making 3 additions of dry ingredients and 2 of liquid. Spread the batter over the bottom of the prepared pan. In a single layer, cover the batter with plum halves. Sprinkle with the crumble topping. Bake in the centre of a 350°F (180°C) oven until golden on top, 40 to 45 minutes. Cool on a rack before cutting.

Rum-Soaked Dark Fruitcake

Makes 6 fruitcake logs, about 2½ lb (1.35 kg) total

ELIZABETH: Forget all those nasty, slanderous jokes about fruitcake. I suspect those who utter them have never tasted a good fruitcake. For their conversion, I offer a chock-full-of-goodness fruitcake, slightly adapted from Rose's dark rum nut fruitcake, in her *Christmas Cookbook* published in 1979. This is the cake that I doubled and baked, at the request of the father of the bride and groom, for each of the Murray children's weddings. It's handy that the batter fits into a standard 13 -× 9-inch (3.5 L) metal cake pan because I like to cut this cake crosswise into 6 rectangular logs—perfect gifts for friends who hanker after a real home-baked taste of Christmas but don't bake. Store the wrapped logs in the refrigerator at-the-ready to slice and enjoy, a few fruity nuggets at a time, with a sherry, a good cup of tea or an espresso, or Mulled Cider (page 328) or wine.

FRUIT AND NUTS

3 cups (750 mL) chopped mixed
   candied peel
3 cups (750 mL) seeded Lexia or Muscat
   raisins (see Raisins, page 206)
2 cups (500 mL) currants, rinsed and
   patted dry
1½ cups (375 mL) halved candied cherries
1 cup (250 mL) slivered blanched almonds
1 cup (250 mL) pecan halves, chopped
1 cup (250 mL) dark rum
¼ cup (60 mL) all-purpose flour

BATTER

1 cup (250 mL) butter, softened
1¼ cups (300 mL) packed brown sugar
4 large eggs
2 tsp (10 mL) vanilla
1½ cups (375 mL) all-purpose flour
1 tsp (5 mL) each baking powder
   and cinnamon
½ tsp (2 mL) each salt, cloves and nutmeg

AGING

½ cup (125 mL) dark rum (approx)

FRUIT AND NUTS → Measure the peel, raisins, currants, cherries, almonds and pecans into a large bowl. Drizzle the rum over the fruit and nuts; toss. Cover and macerate (soak) at least 1 day or up to 3 days, stirring the mixture a few times a day, as time allows. Drain, reserving any liquid.

BATTER → Line 13-× 9-inch (3.5 L) metal cake pan with 2 layers of parchment paper; set aside. Arrange 2 racks in the oven, one in the centre of the oven for the cake and the other in the bottom position. Place a large wide pan on the bottom rack; pour in hot water to come halfway up the sides. In a very large bowl, using a mixer, beat the butter until light coloured. Beat in the brown sugar, beating until fluffy. Beat in the eggs, one at a time, beating well after each addition. Mix in the vanilla.

In a medium bowl, whisk together the flour, baking powder, cinnamon, salt, cloves and nutmeg. Stir a third of the flour mixture into the butter mixture, then the reserved soaking liquid, then the remaining dry ingredients in 2 additions to make a smooth batter.

Sprinkle the soaked fruit mixture with the ¼ cup (60 mL) flour; toss well. Scrape the batter over the fruit mixture and stir to distribute the batter evenly (although not generously) over the fruit mixture. Scoop into the prepared cake pan, pressing the fruit mixture firmly into the pan. Smooth the top.

Bake in the centre of a 300°F (150°C) oven until a tester inserted into the centre comes out clean, about 1½ hours. Let the cake cool in the pan on a rack. Remove the cake from the pan; peel off the parchment paper.

AGING → Place the cake on a rimmed baking sheet lined generously with plastic wrap. Cut a double thickness of cheesecloth big enough to enclose the cake. Wrap the cake with the cheesecloth and brush on enough rum to soak the cheesecloth. Wrap the cake in the plastic wrap and place in an airtight container. Store for at least 2 weeks, brushing the cheesecloth every few days with rum if time and budget allow, or until the cake is mellow and moist. The cake will keep for up to 1 year if refrigerated and doesn't need more than an occasional redrenching with rum (unless, of course, the cook needs to sample the cake to assess how well it's mellowing).

After the cake has aged, remove the plastic wrap and the cheesecloth. Cut the cake crosswise into 6 rectangular logs. Wrap the logs in plastic wrap and store in an airtight container until ready to serve.

> **NOTE**
> To serve, you can brush the top of the cake with liquid honey or corn syrup and cover the cakes with thinly rolled out marzipan or almond paste. On the other hand, you may enjoy the cake as is, letting the fruit and rum star in the pleasure.

Strawberry Shortcake, Two Ways

LONG BEFORE THE red and white maple leaf flapped at the top of flagpoles across the country, red and white strawberry shortcake was an all-Canadian summer tradition, perfectly timed for Canada Day. These two versions marry strawberries and cream, one over traditional tender scones (a.k.a. tea biscuits; recipe follows), the other over pavlovas (soft meringues). Take your pick. *Springridge Farm Strawberry Pavlovas pictured here.*

SPRINGRIDGE FARM STRAWBERRY PAVLOVAS
Makes 8 servings

THESE INDIVIDUAL PAVLOVAS are a stellar berry-cream-soft-meringue specialty of Springridge Farm, located on the Niagara Escarpment overlooking Milton, Ontario. And they're a scrumptious red and white variation on the strawberry shortcake theme. Springridge, a family entertainment farm run by third- and fourth-generation farmers, John and Laura Hughes and their family, bustles with activities—wagon rides and from-scratch baking of sweet and savoury pies—and features a café selling all kinds of preserves and already-picked berries for time-and-energy-pressed enthusiasts. Farmer John, as John Hughes is affectionately nicknamed, knows a thing or two about growing strawberries and making strawberry desserts, and this is his all-time best-loved recipe.

4 large egg whites at room temperature
1 cup (250 mL) granulated sugar, divided
1 tsp (5 mL) cornstarch
1 tsp (5 mL) white wine vinegar
½ tsp (2 mL) vanilla

3 cups (750 mL) whole strawberries, hulled and sliced
1 cup (250 mL) whipping cream
2 tbsp (30 mL) granulated sugar

LINE 2 RIMLESS baking sheets with parchment paper; set aside.

In a large bowl, using a mixer, beat the egg whites to soft peaks. Sprinkle in ¾ cup (175 mL) of the sugar; beat at medium-high speed until stiff and shiny. At low speed and just until blended, beat in the cornstarch, vinegar and vanilla.

Using a large serving spoon, scoop the meringue mixture into 8 slightly oval mounds, arranged 2 inches (5 cm) apart on the prepared baking sheets.

Place in the centre of a 350°F (180°C) oven; immediately turn the oven to 300°F (150°C). Bake for 30 minutes; turn off the heat, leaving the pavlovas in the oven for 20 minutes. Remove and let cool on the sheets on a rack.

Meanwhile, sprinkle the strawberries with ¼ cup (60 mL) of the remaining sugar. Let stand at room temperature until juicy, about 1 hour; stir.

Whip the cream with the 2 tbsp (30 mL) of sugar. Serve buffet style and let everyone assemble their own pavlovas.

OLD-FASHIONED STRAWBERRY SHORTCAKE
Makes 6 servings

ON JULY 1ST, Canada Day, Campbell House Museum close to city hall in downtown Toronto celebrates our national birthday with an event called Strawberries on the Lawn. Visitors can soak up the atmosphere of the early 19th-century home with period music and dancing, Canadiana Lemonade (page 327) and strawberry shortcake—all the while sitting on a shady lawn.

1½ cups (375 mL) hulled sliced strawberries
3 tbsp (45 mL) granulated sugar
6 warm Cream Tea Scones (page 192)
1 tbsp (15 mL) butter, softened (optional)

1 cup (250 mL) whipping cream, whipped
6 or more hulled and sliced strawberries
fresh mint leaves

IN A BOWL, combine the strawberries and sugar. Let stand for 1 hour at room temperature; stir.

Split the scones, buttering the cut bottom half of each scone, if desired. Place a bottom half on a dessert plate or in a shallow bowl; cover with a sixth of the juicy strawberry mixture (about ¼ cup/60 mL), then a scone top. Slather with whipped cream.

Repeat with the remaining scones, strawberries and cream. Garnish with the whole strawberries and mint leaves.

Chocolate Cheesecake

Makes 12 to 16 servings

. . . .

SHANNON FERRIER, home economist and cookbook author: For three generations, it's been a tradition in my family that the birthday person gets to choose his or her favourite cake. This one is my daughter Allison's and dates back a few years, to the time Allison, then a junior cook, first made it from a recipe in *Seventeen* magazine. Another family tradition is sharing our do-again-and-again recipes in a big three-ring binder. Only tried, true and beloved recipes like this cheesecake make it into the book.

. . . .

CRUMB CRUST
1 pkg (8 oz/250 g) chocolate wafers*
⅓ cup (75 mL) butter, melted
2 tbsp (30 mL) granulated sugar
¼ tsp (1 mL) nutmeg

FILLING
3 large eggs
1 cup (250 mL) granulated sugar
3 pkg (8 oz/250 g each) cream cheese,
    cubed and softened

2 cups (500 mL) chocolate chips,
    melted and cooled
1 tsp (5 mL) vanilla
pinch salt
1 cup (250 mL) sour cream
1 cup (250 mL) whipping cream

*Instead of chocolate wafers you
    could use 2 cups (500 mL) of chocolate
    baking crumbs.

CRUMB CRUST → Lightly grease a 9-inch (2.5 L) springform pan and wrap the bottom and sides in a large square of heavy-duty foil; set aside.

In a food processor, chop the chocolate wafers to fine crumbs. (Or place the wafers in a plastic bag and roll them into crumbs with a rolling pin. Transfer to a bowl.) Stir in the butter, sugar and nutmeg and toss to mix evenly. Press evenly over the bottom and up the sides to within ½ inch (1.25 cm) of the top rim of the prepared pan. Refrigerate while preparing the filling.

FILLING → In a large bowl, using a mixer, beat the eggs with the sugar until light. Beat in the cream cheese, a third at a time, until smooth. Beat in the melted chocolate chips, vanilla and salt, then the sour cream until smooth. Scrape into the crumb crust and place the pan in a broiler pan or shallow roasting pan. Place in the centre of a 350°F (180°C) oven and pour enough boiling water into the outer pan to come about 1 inch (2.5 cm) up the sides of the springform pan. Bake until the filling is just firm when the pan is gently jiggled, about 1 hour. Remove the broiler pan to a rack. Run a knife around the inside edge of the cake pan to help prevent cracking. Let stand until the water cools, about 30 minutes. Remove the pan from the water, discard the foil and place the pan on the rack to cool completely.

To serve, whip the cream and spread over the top of the cheesecake.

Pies and Tarts

Rhubarb Custard Pie

Makes 6 servings

....

ROSE: If my family knew they could have only one pie all year, this is the one they'd choose. But there are other reasons the pie is special. This was my mother's recipe, and it always reminds me of the long line of rhubarb that grew in our kitchen garden at the farm. As well, it was the very first thing I ever demonstrated on television almost 40 years ago. Wait for fresh, local rhubarb since wintertime forced rhubarb (grown inside) tends to be too juicy and may make the filling runny.

....

PIE

pastry for a 9-inch (23 cm) pie shell
  (see Reputation-Making Pastry, page 272)
3 cups (750 mL) coarsely chopped rhubarb
  (1 inch/2.5 cm pieces)
1 cup (250 mL) granulated sugar
3 tbsp (45 mL) all-purpose flour
2 tbsp (30 mL) butter, cubed
2 large egg yolks, beaten

MERINGUE

2 large egg whites
¼ tsp (1 mL) cream of tartar
¼ cup (60 mL) granulated sugar
2 tbsp (30 mL) water
½ tsp (2 mL) vanilla
¼ tsp (1 mL) salt

PIE → On a lightly floured work surface, roll out the pastry to a generous ⅛-inch (3 mm) thickness. Fit into a 9-inch (23 cm) pie plate. Trim to about ¾ inch (2 cm) from the rim; fold the overhang under and flute.

   In a large bowl, stir together the rhubarb, sugar, flour and butter; stir in the egg yolks. Spoon into the fluted pie shell. Bake in the bottom third of a 425°F (220°C) oven for 10 minutes; reduce the heat to 350°F (180°C) and bake until the filling is bubbling and the rhubarb is tender, about another 30 minutes. Remove the pie from the oven. Place on a rack and let cool to lukewarm.

MERINGUE → In a large bowl, using a mixer, beat the egg whites until foamy; add the cream of tartar and beat until stiff, moist peaks form, 3 to 5 minutes. Very gradually beat in the sugar. Add the water, vanilla and salt; beat until very stiff, shiny peaks form. Spread the meringue over the lukewarm pie, making sure the meringue touches the pastry edges all the way around. Swirl the meringue decoratively with a kitchen knife. Bake in a 375°F (190°C) oven for about 12 minutes or until the tips of the meringue are golden brown. Let the pie cool at room temperature.

"Schnitz" Pie

Makes 8 servings

ELIZABETH: Dutch apple pie may be a signature dish of Waterloo County, but my mother's version, which she called schnitz pie, comes from neighbouring Perth County. It's creamier than a standard Dutch apple pie and shifts the spotlight from a streusel topping to big pieces of fruit. Our family, my father especially, so loved schnitz pies that my mother made them through the seasons, starting with rhubarb in the spring, continuing with peaches in August and topping the year off with apples when Northern Spys hit the market.

pastry for a deep, 10-inch (25 cm) pie shell
  (see Reputation-Making Pastry, page 272)
5 medium-large apples, such as Northern
  Spy or Golden Delicious (about 2 lb/1 kg)
¼ cup (60 mL) whipping cream, divided

¾ cup (175 mL) packed light brown sugar
2 tbsp (30 mL) all-purpose flour
3 tbsp (45 mL) cold butter
½ tsp (2 mL) cinnamon or nutmeg

ON A LIGHTLY floured work surface, roll out the pastry to a scant ¼-inch (5 mm) thickness. Fit into a deep, 10-inch (25 cm) pie plate. Trim to about ¾ inch (2 cm) from the rim; fold the overhang under and flute.

Peel and halve the apples and cut each half into 3 wedges; remove the core from each wedge. Arrange the wedges snugly in a single layer in the pie shell, fudging a bit if necessary by trimming the pieces to make them all fit. Drizzle with half of the cream.

In a small bowl, combine the sugar and flour. Cut in the butter until crumbly; sprinkle over the apples. Drizzle with the remaining cream; dust with the cinnamon.

Bake in the bottom third of a 450°F (230°C) oven for 15 minutes; reduce the heat to 350°F (180°C) and bake until the apples are tender and the pastry is golden brown, about 40 minutes. Watch carefully and if the fluted edge of the pastry browns too quickly, shield the pastry with strips of foil. Let the pie cool on a rack. For divine results, enjoy the pie within 4 hours of the time it emerges from the oven.

Tarte au Sucre (Sugar Pie)

Makes 12 lovely long, thin wedges

ELIZABETH: In Quebec, everyone has a favourite *tarte au sucre*—usually the one they remember from their grandmother's table. Time does make taste memories more vivid! For all of us deficient in Quebec grandmothers' sugar pies, here's an excellent one, served at the popular Quebec City restaurant L'Échaudé, situated in historic Lower Town. Quebec City lawyer Roger Garneau, with whom I sampled L'Échaudé's *tarte au sucre*, was impressed, but later remarked that "while it was very good, it was not quite as good as my grandmother's." As if it ever could be!

While just fine plain, *tarte au sucre* can go beyond "grandma's version" and get just the right amount of "gussy" with lightly whipped cream and fresh berries on top.

PASTRY

1¾ cups (425 mL) all-purpose flour
¼ cup (60 mL) granulated sugar
pinch salt
½ cup (125 mL) cold unsalted butter, cubed
⅓ cup (75 mL) milk
1 large egg yolk

FILLING

1 cup (250 mL) packed brown sugar
2 tbsp (30 mL) all-purpose flour
1 large egg
1 large egg yolk
1 cup (250 mL) whipping cream

PASTRY → In a large bowl, whisk together the flour, sugar and salt. Using a pastry blender, cut in the butter until the mixture is crumbly. Measure the milk into a liquid measuring cup and whisk in the egg yolk. Drizzle over the crumbs, tossing to form a shaggy dough. Press into a disc. Wrap and refrigerate until firm, about 1 hour. (MAKE-AHEAD: Refrigerate for up to 1 day.) Let the dough soften at room temperature before rolling, at least a few minutes.

On a floured surface, roll out the dough to a 12-inch (30 cm) circle. Fit the dough into an 11-inch (28 cm) tart pan with a removable bottom, folding any excess inside, and pressing the layers to the side of the pan. Refrigerate until firm, about 30 minutes.

With a fork, prick the dough on the bottom of the pan at ½-inch (1.25 cm) intervals. Line with foil and fill with pie weights or dried beans. Bake in the bottom third of a 375°F (190°C) oven until light golden, about 15 to 20 minutes. Remove the foil and weights. Let cool on a rack. Reduce the heat to 350°F (180°C); move an oven rack to the centre of the oven.

FILLING → Combine the sugar and flour. Add the egg and egg yolk; whisk until smooth. In a saucepan, bring the cream to a boil. In a slow, steady stream, whisk the cream into the filling. Strain into the cooled pie shell.

Bake in the centre of the oven until the centre of the filling is just firm to the touch, about 30 minutes. Let cool in the pan on the rack. Serve within 4 hours.

Double-Crust Blueberry Pie

Makes 6 to 8 servings

....

ROSE: Every year in late summer, Steve Boothby and his wife, Bonnie Rollo, host an annual pickling day, complete with lunch, which once featured the best blueberry pie I had ever tasted—a masterpiece from Steve, who grew up in Muskoka, the source for the pie's wild blueberries. Steve says, "This recipe comes from my mom, Marion Boothby, of Bracebridge. At eighty-eight, she still can produce at least one of these pies a year."

Wild blueberries (or low-bush blueberries) grow in eastern, central and northern Canada, mainly in sandy, rocky soil or where there is a mowed or a burnt-over forest area. High-bush blueberries are grown commercially, extensively in British Columbia, but also in other parts of Canada. If you are using cultivated blueberries for the pie, add a squirt more lemon juice and ¼ tsp (1 mL) each cinnamon and nutmeg.

....

pastry for a deep, 2-crust 9-inch (23 cm) pie
   (see Reputation-Making Pastry, page 272)
4 cups (1 L) blueberries
⅔ cup (150 mL) granulated sugar
2 tbsp (30 mL) all-purpose flour

1 tbsp (15 mL) quick tapioca
¼ tsp (1 mL) salt
1 tbsp (15 mL) grated lemon zest
4 tsp (20 mL) fresh lemon juice
1½ tsp (7 mL) butter, in bits

LINE A 9-INCH (23 cm) pie plate with pastry; trim to the rim. Set aside.

Combine the blueberries, sugar, flour, tapioca and salt. Stir in the lemon zest and juice; let stand for 10 to 15 minutes.

Mix well and turn into the pastry-lined pie plate. Dot with the butter, wet the pastry around the rim, cover with the top pastry and press the two layers together gently along the rim. Trim the top pastry to about ¾ inch (2 cm) from the rim; fold the overhang under the bottom pastry. Flute both layers of the pastry together. Slash vent holes in the top pastry (a small circle in the middle and 4 or 5 slashes radiating from the middle). Bake in the bottom third of a 450°F (230°C) oven for 10 minutes; reduce the heat to 350°F (180°C) and bake until the blueberries gently bubble up through the slashed holes, about 30 to 40 minutes longer.

VARIATION: Canadian Apple Pie

If you want the apples to hold their shape, choose a variety such as Northern Spy, Crispin or Idared. Any of the McIntosh family, such as Cortland or Empire, turn into sauce when baked. Some people like to use a combination of apples to get an interesting flavour and texture.

Substitute the blueberry filling with 8 cups (2 L) peeled and cored apple slices, ¾ cup (175 mL) granulated sugar, 2 tbsp (30 mL) cornstarch, 1 tsp (5 mL) cinnamon and a pinch each nutmeg and salt. Proceed as in the main recipe, dotting the filling with 2 tbsp (30 mL) soft butter.

Lemon Meringue Pie

Makes 6 servings

ROSE: My brother, Allen Varty, has always had a great interest in food. He made me, his baby sister, a birthday cake one year when our mother was ill. He grows and preserves his own food and cooks for family gatherings, at which he always serves this renowned pie.

pastry for a 9-inch (23 cm) pie shell (see
    Reputation-Making pastry, page 272)

1 tbsp (15 mL) butter
2 tsp (10 mL) grated lemon zest
⅓ cup (75 mL) fresh lemon juice

FILLING
3 tbsp (45 mL) cornstarch
3 tbsp (45 mL) all-purpose flour
1 cup (250 mL) granulated sugar
¼ tsp (1 mL) salt
1½ cups (375 mL) water
3 large egg yolks

MERINGUE
1 tsp (5 mL) cornstarch
3 large egg whites
¼ tsp (1 mL) cream of tartar
3 tbsp (45 mL) granulated sugar

ON A LIGHTLY floured surface, roll out the pastry to a scant ¼-inch (5 mm) thickness. Fit into a 9-inch (23 cm) pie plate. Trim about ¾ inch (2 cm) from the rim; fold the overhang under and flute. With a fork, prick the shell at 1-inch (2.5 cm) intervals and refrigerate for 30 minutes.

Line the shell with foil; fill it with pie weights or dried beans. Bake in the bottom third of a 400°F (200°C) oven until the edge is light golden, about 20 minutes. Remove the foil and weights; continue baking until golden brown inside, another 10 minutes.

FILLING → In a heavy saucepan, stir together the cornstarch, flour, sugar and salt. Gradually stir in the water. Place over medium heat and, stirring constantly, bring to a boil; cook until thick and smooth, 2 to 3 minutes.

In a small bowl, beat the egg yolks. Whisk a small amount of the hot cornstarch mixture into the beaten egg yolks; whisk back into the saucepan and cook over medium heat, stirring constantly, for 2 minutes. Remove from the heat; stir in the butter, lemon zest and juice, blending well. Let cool about 3 minutes; stir until creamy, and then pour into the pie shell, smoothing the top.

MERINGUE → In a small bowl, dissolve the cornstarch in 2 tbsp (30 mL) water; set aside.

In a large bowl, using a mixer and clean beaters, beat the egg whites with the cream of tartar until soft peaks form. Gradually beat in the sugar until stiff peaks form. Beat in the cornstarch mixture 1 tbsp (15 mL) at a time. Spread over the lemon filling right to the edges and swirl into peaks with the back of a spoon. Bake in a 350°F (180°C) oven until the peaks are golden, about 20 minutes. Let cool on a rack for at least 2 hours and up to 6 hours.

Custard Pie with Maple Whipped Cream and Berries

Makes 6 servings

....

PAM COLLACOTT, cookbook author, food writer and broadcaster: The first recipe that always springs to my mind when I remember flavours from my childhood is my Grandma Searles' custard pie. In the 1950s she and my grandpa owned a fishing lodge on Rice Lake, in Ontario. In those days, Grandma cooked dinner every night for the fishermen staying in the 19 very rustic cabins, and every day (as I recall) there was a selection of homemade pies on the table. My favourite was her custard pie. It was very rich, quite firm, tasted sweet and delicious and felt lovely on my tongue! Through the years I asked her for the recipe many times, always to be put off until later. When she finally agreed to share it with me, after I was married, she was quite old and her vision was in decline. She died not many years later, so I'm glad I persevered in my nagging and can make this delicious pie occasionally for my own grandchildren. I like to serve it the day after it's made since the flavour of the filling seems richer on standing.

....

pastry for a deep 9-inch (23 cm) pie shell
   (see Reputation-Making pastry, page 272)
6 large eggs
1 cup (250 mL) granulated sugar
2 cups (500 mL) whole milk
1 tsp (5 mL) vanilla

nutmeg
1 cup (250 mL) whipping cream
3 tbsp (45 mL) maple syrup
2 cups (500 mL) assorted berries,
   such as raspberries, blackberries,
   blueberries, strawberries

LINE A DEEP 9-inch (23 cm) pie plate with pastry. Trim about ¾ inch (2 cm) from the rim; fold the overhang under and flute. Refrigerate.

In a large bowl, whisk together the eggs and sugar. Gradually whisk in the milk and vanilla until well combined. Pour through a fine sieve into the pie shell and grate or sprinkle nutmeg liberally overtop. Bake in the bottom third of a 450°F (230°C) oven for 15 minutes. Reduce the heat to 350°F (180°C) and bake until the filling is set (when a knife blade inserted into the filling comes out clean), 30 to 40 minutes. Cool completely on a rack before serving or refrigerating.

To serve, whip the cream with the maple syrup and pipe or spoon a dollop onto each serving. Arrange the berries alongside.

Traditional Mincemeat

Makes about 16 cups (4 L)

DOROTHY LONG, agri-food consultant: This recipe was my great-grandmother's—Ethel Mary Mann. In 1903, she travelled with her family from England with the Barr Colonists. As early settlers, the Barr Colonists faced many hardships but eventually settled in the area of Lloydminster, Saskatchewan. In 1904, Ethel married George Mann Jr. and together they raised four children.

I never met my Granny Mann, but family stories are of a strong, no-nonsense, hard-working, straight-laced woman who was respected by the community and her family. This is a recipe she made every Christmas, and the tradition was that each family member and any visiting guests any time during the flavour-developing stage would stir the mincemeat for luck. We continue this English tradition, with my mom making the mincemeat!

4 cups (1 L) peeled, cored and chopped
   apples (6 to 8 apples)
3 cups (750 mL) finely chopped beef suet*
2⅔ cups (650 mL) packed brown sugar
3 cups (750 mL) Lexia or Muscat raisins
   (see Raisins, page 206)
3 cups (750 mL) currants
2 cups (500 mL) mixed candied peel
1¾ cups (425 mL) sultana raisins

1½ tsp (7 mL) each cinnamon,
   mace and cloves
½ tsp (2 mL) nutmeg
½ cup (125 mL) brandy

*Suet is white kidney fat. Ask for it from a butcher or look for it already chopped and frozen in most supermarkets.

IN A LARGE bowl, stir together the apples, suet and brown sugar until the sugar dissolves. Stir in the raisins, currants, peel, sultana raisins, cinnamon, mace, cloves and nutmeg. Pour the brandy over everything and stir well to combine. Cover and refrigerate, to allow the flavours to blend, at least overnight or up to 1 week. (MAKE-AHEAD: Freeze in airtight containers for longer storage.)

DOUBLE-CRUST MINCEMEAT PIE

LINE A 9-INCH (23 cm) pie plate with a bottom layer of pastry. (See Reputation-Making Pastry, page 272.) Fill with 4 cups (1 L) Traditional Mincemeat. Cover with a top layer of pastry. Trim the edges and flute. Brush the top pastry with cream or milk and sprinkle with coarse granulated sugar. Slash steam vents in the top pastry and bake in the bottom third of a 425°F (220°C) oven for 15 minutes; reduce the heat to 350°F (180°C) and bake until the top is golden brown and the filling is bubbly, about another 30 minutes.

MINCEMEAT TARTS

FILL 12 TART shells with pastry cut to fit with a crinkle-edged cutter. Fill with 2 cups (500 mL) Traditional Mincemeat and cut out circles of pastry to fit over the mincemeat but not touch the edges. Brush the top pastry with cream or milk and sprinkle with coarse granulated sugar. Bake in the bottom third of a 425°F (220°C) oven for 10 minutes; reduce the heat to 350°F (180°C) and bake until the filling is bubbly and browned, about another 15 minutes.

Butter Tarts

Makes about 18 tarts

ELIZABETH: Lorna Harris of Victoria, British Columbia, is a major butter tart fan, willing to drive the whole Butter Tart Trail, which winds through the towns and villages of North Wellington County, Ontario. Her mission in life is to suss out the best butter tarts in Canada. In her honour, here is my favourite butter tart, its pastry crisp and golden and the filling not runny but moist and quivering, ready to spill out but able to control itself until the next bite.

½ cup (125 mL) currants (see Note)
¼ cup (60 mL) butter, softened
½ cup (125 mL) packed brown sugar
2 large eggs, at room temperature
1 cup (250 mL) corn syrup, or amber
 or dark maple syrup

1 tsp (5 mL) each fresh lemon juice
 and vanilla
pinch salt
half-batch Reputation-Making Pastry
 (page 272)

SET THE CURRANTS in a sieve over simmering water to steam for 5 minutes. Spread out on a towel and pat dry.

Meanwhile, in a medium bowl, beat together the butter and brown sugar until smooth. Whisk in the eggs, syrup, lemon juice, vanilla and salt; set aside.

Roll out the pastry, a third at a time, on a lightly floured pastry cloth or counter to a generous ⅛ inch (3 mm). Using a 4½-inch (7 cm) cookie cutter or clean, empty 28 oz (796 mL) can, cut out rounds and fit without stretching into muffin cups about 2¾ inches (7 cm) wide and 1¼ inches (3 cm) deep.

Into each tart shell sprinkle a small spoonful of currants; fill the shells two-thirds full with filling. (Too much filling and the tarts will overflow as they bake, creating havoc when it comes to getting the tarts out of the pans.) Bake the tarts in the bottom third of a 375°F (190°C) oven until the pastry is golden and the filling puffed and bubbling, 15 to 20 minutes.

Let cool on a rack for 1 minute. With an offset spatula (a tool with a rounded, blunt metal blade angled from the handle) or the rounded blade of a table knife, ease the tarts out of the muffin cups and let cool on the rack.

CONTINUED . . .

NOTE

Don't like currants? Try small sultanas (seedless raisins) or chopped walnut or pecan halves or chopped bittersweet chocolate or a combination of these. Some people even like coconut. None of these ingredients need to be soaked, like the currants, which relish a good plumping before use.

WHERE DID BUTTER TARTS COME FROM?

Good question. There are pastries with similar sweet fillings, such as Quebec's sugar pie, lassie tarts from Newfoundland, pecan pie of the southern United States. Was one of these the fore-tart of butter tarts? Culinary historian Mary Williamson, a serious collector of historic cookbooks and a butter tart sleuth, thinks not, and has revealed a very plausible link to border tarts of southern Scotland and northern England, the origin of many 19th-century immigrants. She has sourced the first written reference to this kind of tart in a 1900 cookbook compiled by the Women's Auxiliary of the Royal Victoria Hospital in Barrie, Ontario. The recipe was labelled simply "A filling for tarts." Just as some newborn babies appear before they have a name, "butter tarts" called as such were yet to come. But note how easy it is to change "border" into "butter" once time has passed. By the 1910s, butter tarts had caught on and recipes abounded. For example, butter tarts in the 1915 edition of the *Five Roses Cook Book*. The recipe reads:

> 1 egg, 1 cup brown sugar, 1 cup currants, Butter size of a walnut, Flavour to taste. Beat all until full of bubbles. Drop from teaspoon into lined patty tin, and bake in quick oven. One cup of dates may be added if desired.

Sound familiar? Only the addition of a 20th-century product, corn syrup, is missing.

Chocolate Peanut Butter Pie

Makes 12 servings

....

THIS IS THE pie that brings out those over-the-top adjectives—irresistible, luscious, decadent, fabulous—along with the usual line, "I really shouldn't." But this is one dessert where a small slice will satisfy. One pie easily serves a dozen people.

....

CRUST

1 cup (250 mL) graham cracker crumbs

2 oz (50 g) bittersweet or semisweet chocolate, chopped

¼ cup (60 mL) chopped dry-roasted peanuts

¼ cup (60 mL) granulated sugar

⅓ cup (75 mL) butter, melted

FILLING

1 pkg (8 oz/250 g) cream cheese, softened

1 cup (250 mL) smooth peanut butter

2 tbsp (30 mL) butter, softened

2 tsp (10 mL) vanilla

1 cup (250 mL) icing sugar

1 cup (250 mL) whipping cream

TOPPING

½ cup (125 mL) whipping cream

4 oz (125 g) bittersweet or semisweet chocolate, chopped

2 tsp (10 mL) corn syrup

½ cup (125 mL) coarsely chopped dry-roasted peanuts

CRUST → In a food processor, whirl the cracker crumbs, chocolate, peanuts and sugar until the mixture blends and looks crumbly. Drizzle the butter over the crumbs and pulse until they hold together when pressed. Press into the bottom and up the sides of a deep 9-inch (23 cm) tart pan with a removable bottom or pie plate. Bake in the centre of a 350°F (180°C) oven until firm to the touch, about 12 minutes. Let cool on a rack.

FILLING → In a large bowl, beat the cream cheese and peanut butter until smooth. Beat in the butter, vanilla and icing sugar until blended and smooth. In a separate bowl, beat the whipping cream to firm peaks. Stir a third of the cream into the peanut butter mixture; fold in the remaining cream to make a lovely smooth filling. Scrape into the shell; smooth its surface. Insert toothpicks discreetly in a half-dozen spots in the pie and cover with plastic wrap. Refrigerate until firm, at least 4 hours. (MAKE-AHEAD: Refrigerate for up to 1 day.)

TOPPING → Heat the cream just to boiling. Remove from the heat and stir in the chocolate, stirring until melted. Stir in the corn syrup. Let cool slightly; spoon evenly over the filling. Refrigerate for 1 hour to set the topping. Sprinkle the peanuts around the rim of the pie.

NOTE

When serving the pie, wipe the blade of the knife with a damp towel between each cut.

Hazelnut Tart

Makes 8 super-generous servings, 12 when people are being sensible

ELEANOR KANE, co-founder of Stratford Chefs School: When Marion Isherwood and I opened the Old Prune Restaurant in Stratford, Ontario, in 1976, this deep, shortbread-crust toasted hazelnut tart was the most popular dessert on the menu. In the early days of the restaurant, the head of wardrobe at the Stratford Shakespeare Festival, Bryan Walsh, was a regular, and was so enamoured with this tart that on one occasion he asked for a second serving, after which he asked for the remainder of the tart—and polished it off in good Falstaffian fashion.

CRUST
1 cup (250 mL) all-purpose flour
pinch salt
⅓ cup (75 mL) cold unsalted butter, cubed
⅔ cup (150 mL) seedless raspberry
  or black currant jam

TOPPING
1 cup (250 mL) hazelnuts (filberts)
6 large eggs, separated
pinch cream of tartar
1¼ cups (300 mL) granulated sugar, divided
3 tbsp (45 mL) unsalted butter, softened
icing sugar, whipped cream, raspberries

CRUST → In a large bowl, whisk together the flour and salt. Cut in the butter with a pastry blender, working until the mixture holds together when pressed. A handful at a time, press over the bottom of a greased 9-inch (2.5 L) springform pan. Bake in the centre of a 375°F (190°C) oven until lightly browned, about 10 minutes. Let cool on a rack. Spread the jam over the base.

TOPPING → Meanwhile, spread the nuts in a single layer on a rimmed baking sheet. Bake until the skins split, 6 to 8 minutes. Pour onto a clean tea towel and rub to remove most of the skins. Discard the skins; chop the nuts finely, leaving some the size of a grain of rice; set aside.

In a large bowl, beat the egg whites with the cream of tartar until soft peaks form. Gradually beat in ¼ cup (60 mL) of the sugar, beating until the peaks are firm and shiny.

In a separate large bowl, beat the butter and remaining sugar until combined. Beat in the egg yolks, one at a time. Beat until light and fluffy. Stir in the hazelnuts, then a third of the egg-white mixture. Fold in the remaining egg whites. Scrape over the jam, smoothing the top.

Bake in the centre of a 375°F (190°C) oven until no longer jiggly in the centre, about 35 to 40 minutes. Let cool on a rack for 10 minutes. Run a knife around the inside of the pan; remove the ring and let the tart finish cooling on the rack. (MAKE-AHEAD: Wrap in plastic wrap and store for up to 1 day at room temperature. To freeze, return the ring to the pan; wrap in plastic wrap and place in an airtight container. Freeze for up to 2 weeks.) Slide onto a flat cake plate. Dust the top with icing sugar and serve with whipped cream and raspberries.

Reputation-Making Pastry

Makes 6 single crusts or 3 double crusts

. . . .

ELIZABETH: In the early years of the Perfect Pie Contest in Warkworth, Ontario, I was fortunate enough to write about this immensely popular community event, and once to be a judge. (Sounds like a plum job until you're sampling your 60th pie.) No one could fail to notice the flakiness and tenderness of the crusts of the winning pies. The not-so-secret secret, according to one of the winners, was that the recipe for the pastry often came from the back of the box of a leading brand of lard. That particular recipe (adapted here) was not the only key to being a Perfect Pie winner, but it got competitors off to a good start. And can do the same for any pie maker.

. . . .

5½ cups (1.375 L) all-purpose flour
2 tsp (10 mL) salt
1 pkg (1 lb/454 g) cold lard, cubed

1 large egg
1 tbsp (15 mL) white vinegar
ice water

IN A LARGE bowl, whisk together the flour and salt. Add the lard; toss well. With a pastry blender or your fingers, work the lard into the dry ingredients until the mixture is crumbly, with a few larger pieces but most crumbs the size of long-grain rice.

In a liquid measuring cup, whisk together the egg, vinegar and enough ice water to reach the 1 cup (250 mL) mark. Drizzle over the crumbly mixture, tossing it with a fork as you drizzle around the bowl, and always aiming to moisten the dry spots at the bottom.

Gather into a ball that holds together well; divide into 6 portions. Form each portion into a disc. Wrap the discs individually and refrigerate until chilled, about 30 minutes. (MAKE-AHEAD: Refrigerate for up to 3 days or place in an airtight container and freeze for up to 1 month. Let pastry soften at room temperature before rolling.)

Roll out on a floured pastry cloth or counter using a floured rolling pin or one covered with a stockinet.

MEASURING DRY INGREDIENTS

When you are measuring all-purpose flour or granulated sugar (or large amounts of other ingredients such as cornstarch or rice flour), use only the nesting type of dry measuring cups, usually metal or plastic. Spoon the flour or granulated sugar into the cups (the cups should be dry) until heaping. Level off with a straight knife. For liquids, use glass liquid measuring cups with spouts.

PREBAKING (BAKING BLIND)

Some recipes call for baked or partially baked pie shells. Baking or partially baking a pie shell before filling it is called prebaking (baking blind).

› To prebake a pie shell, line the shell with foil and fill it with pie weights or dried beans. Bake in the bottom third of a 400°F (200°C) oven until the edge is light golden, about 20 minutes. Remove the foil and weights. Continue baking until golden brown in the middle, about 10 minutes. Let cool on a rack.

› To partially bake a pie shell, bake the lined and weighted shell until light golden, about 20 minutes. Remove the foil and weights. Let cool on a rack.

If you use beans rather than weights, you can reserve the beans for future pie shells that need prebaking. After each use of dried beans as weights, cool them completely, then place them in a jar clearly marked as "baking beans."

Heritage Oatmeal Cookies

Makes about 36 cookies

A TOTALLY UNSCIENTIFIC survey of the contents of Canadian lunchboxes reveals the presence of this very popular cookie. Oatmeal. Many years ago, this sweet treat was a pretty plain Jane, enhanced modestly with currants or raisins. Now, in the age of more-is-better, these cookies are subject to all kinds of baking hijinks, like coconut, chocolate, peanut butter and toffee chips, candy-coated chocolate, dried cranberries and more. We're taking them back to a delicious midpoint, with currants and walnuts and just a whisp of cinnamon.

¾ cup (175 mL) butter, softened
1 cup (250 mL) packed brown sugar
1 large egg
2 tsp (10 ml) vanilla
1¼ cups (300 mL) all-purpose flour
1 cup (250 mL) large-flake rolled oats
1 tsp (5 mL) cinnamon

½ tsp (2 mL) each baking soda
   and baking powder
¼ tsp (1 mL) salt
1 cup (250 mL) chopped walnut halves
1 cup (250 mL) currants or Thompson
   raisins
granulated sugar

LINE 2 RIMLESS baking sheets with parchment paper, or grease them.

In a large bowl, beat the butter and sugar until light. Beat in the egg, then the vanilla.

In a separate bowl, whisk together the flour, oats, cinnamon, baking soda, baking powder and salt. Stir half of the dry ingredients at a time into the butter mixture. Mix in the walnuts and currants.

Scoop up a well-rounded tablespoon (15 mL) of the dough; roll into a ball and place on a prepared sheet. Repeat with the remaining dough, placing the balls 2 inches (5 cm) apart. With a fork dipped in the sugar, gently press a criss-cross pattern onto the balls to flatten the dough. (MAKE-AHEAD: Freeze the dough on a baking sheet until hard; transfer to an airtight container and freeze for up to 1 month. Bake from frozen, adding a minute or two to the baking time.)

Bake in the centre of a 350°F (180°C) oven until golden underneath and just firm to the touch, about 12 to 14 minutes. Let cool on the baking sheets for 3 minutes. Transfer to racks to cool. Store in airtight containers for up to 1 week.

NOTE
If you like thicker, cake-ier oatmeal cookies, cover and refrigerate sheets of pressed dough until firm, up to 1 day, and bake from chilled.

Chocolate Chip Cookies, Two Ways

Makes about 48 cookies

ELIZABETH: Hands down, Canada's favourite. Here are two versions, a vanilla dough with semisweet chocolate chips, and a rich chocolate batter with white chocolate chips. What we like about these cookies is that the dough freezes like a dream. So if you hanker after fresh-from-the-oven CCCs, scoop and freeze a batch—that way you'll look good, able to whip up fresh cookies for an adoring, and always eager, audience in minutes, and without a mess.

CLASSIC CHOCOLATE CHIP COOKIES

1 cup (250 mL) butter, softened

¾ cup (175 mL) each granulated and packed
  brown sugar

2 large eggs

1 tbsp (15 mL) vanilla

2½ cups (625 mL) all-purpose flour

1 tsp (5 mL) baking soda

½ tsp (2 mL) salt

2 cups (500 mL) semisweet chocolate chips

1 cup (250 ml) chopped pecans or walnuts

LINE 2 RIMLESS baking sheets with parchment paper, or grease them.

In a large bowl, beat the butter with the granulated and brown sugars until fluffy. Beat in the eggs, one at a time, then the vanilla. In a separate bowl, whisk together the flour, baking soda and salt. Stir the dry ingredients into the butter mixture; stir in the chips and pecans. (MAKE-AHEAD: Scoop the dough, a rounded tbsp (15 mL) at a time; arrange, close but not touching, on prepared baking sheets. Cover and freeze until hard, about 4 hours. Layer with waxed paper in airtight containers. Return to the freezer for up to 1 month. Bake from frozen following the method given here, adding a few minutes to the baking time.)

Scoop the dough, a slightly rounded tbsp (15 mL) at a time, onto the prepared baking sheets, spacing the mounds 2 inches (5 cm) apart. Bake in the centre of a 350°F (180°C) oven until the cookies are lightly browned but still slightly soft in the centre, 10 to 14 minutes. Let the cookies firm up for 3 minutes on the baking sheets; transfer to racks to cool. Store in airtight containers for up to 1 week (if they last that long!).

VARIATION: Reverse Chocolate Chip Cookies
Replace ½ cup (125 ml) of the flour with unsweetened cocoa, sifting it with the remaining flour, soda and salt until no longer streaky. Replace the semisweet chocolate chips with white chocolate chips and replace the pecans with 1 cup (250 mL) slivered dried apricots, dried cherries or cranberries, chopped almonds, toasted hazelnuts or macadamia nuts.

Kids' Peanut Butter Cookies

Makes about 48 cookies

HEATHER HOWE, professional home economist and food writer: When it comes to cookies, peanut butter is right up there. A nice blend of crunchy and sweet, these cookies owe at least some of their popularity to kitchens having the ingredients on hand, especially that familiar jar of peanut butter in the cupboard. As well, easy-to-make peanut butter cookies are fun and inexpensive. I have been making these cookies with my two daughters, Rebecca and Olivia, ever since they had to stand on stools, forks in hands, ready to press the balls of dough into the characteristic criss-cross pattern. The girls are now very grown-up teenagers, keen soccer and hockey players and, not surprising, real fans of a good peanut butter cookie, or two.

1 cup (250 mL) butter, softened
¾ cup (175 mL) granulated sugar
¾ cup (175 mL) packed brown sugar
1 cup (250 mL) smooth peanut butter
1½ tsp (7 mL) vanilla
2 large eggs

2½ cups (625 mL) all-purpose flour
1 tsp (5 mL) baking powder
1 tsp (5 mL) baking soda
½ tsp (2 mL) salt
½ cup (125 mL) chopped peanuts (optional, but very nice if you like crunch)
2 tbsp (30 mL) granulated sugar

LINE 2 RIMLESS baking sheets with parchment paper, or grease them.

In a large bowl, beat the butter with the granulated and brown sugars until fluffy. Beat in the peanut butter and vanilla until smooth. Beat in the eggs, one at a time.

In a separate bowl, whisk together the flour, baking powder, soda and salt. Using a wooden spoon, mix half of the dry ingredients at a time into the peanut butter mixture. Stir in the chopped peanuts (if using).

Shape, by a slightly rounded tablespoon (15 mL) at a time, into balls; place, 2 inches (5 cm) apart, on the prepared baking sheets.

Place the sugar in a shallow bowl. Dip a table fork into the sugar and press a criss-cross pattern on the balls, flattening them to ½ inch (1.25 cm) thickness. Repeat the dipping and pressing. (MAKE-AHEAD: Freeze the flattened balls until hard; layer with waxed paper in an airtight container and store in the freezer for up to 1 month. Bake from frozen, adding a minute or two to the baking time.)

Bake in the centre of a 350°F (180°C) oven until the cookies are golden brown, about 10 to 12 minutes. Let cool on the baking sheets for about 2 minutes. Transfer to racks to cool completely. Store, layered with waxed paper, in airtight containers at room temperature for up to 5 days, in the freezer for up to 1 month.

Jam Jams

Makes 48 filled cookies

SISTER EDITH ELDER, in Whitehorse, Yukon: These have been my favourite cookies since I was a little girl. At age two and a half, I stayed at my maternal grandmother's house for several weeks. Whenever Grandma noticed that I was feeling homesick, she would take me to her kitchen cupboard. Stretching to reach the very top, she brought down her cookie jar. I clapped my hands with sheer anticipation. No one could bake cookies like my Gran.

COOKIES
1 cup (250 mL) butter, softened
1 cup (250 mL) packed brown sugar
2 large eggs
⅓ cup (75 mL) corn syrup
1 tsp (5 mL) vanilla
1 tsp (5 mL) baking soda
2 tbsp (30 mL) fancy molasses
5 cups (1.25 L) all-purpose flour

FILLING
1½ cups (375 mL) diced dates
¾ cup (175 mL) granulated sugar
¾ cup (175 mL) water
1 tbsp (15 mL) all-purpose flour

COOKIES → Line 2 rimless baking sheets with parchment paper, or grease them.

In a large bowl, beat together the butter and sugar until fluffy. Beat in the eggs, one at a time, then the syrup. Stir in the vanilla and baking soda, then the molasses. Gradually stir in the flour, 1 cup (250 mL) at a time, to make a smooth dough. Divide the dough into 4 quarters and flatten into discs; wrap each and refrigerate until firm, about 1 hour.

On a lightly floured surface, roll out each disc to a scant ¼-inch (5 mm) thickness. Using a floured 2½-inch (6 cm) round cookie cutter, cut out the cookies. Transfer to the prepared baking sheets, 1 inch (2.5 cm) apart. Reroll scraps. Bake in the centre of a 350°F (180°C) oven until golden, about 10 minutes. Transfer to racks to cool.

FILLING → Meanwhile, in a small saucepan, stir together the dates, granulated sugar, water and flour. Place over medium heat and bring to a simmer; cook until thickened, 6 to 8 minutes, stirring often. Let cool.

When the cookies and filling are both cool, sandwich cookies with filling, using about 2 tsp (10 mL) per sandwich. (MAKE-AHEAD: Store in an airtight container at room temperature for up to 10 days or freeze for up to 1 month.)

Historic Gingerbread Cookies

Makes about 45 cookies

BEFORE THERE WAS a Canada, there were gingerbread cookies. They made their written debut in Canada's first English-language cookbook, *The Cook Not Mad or Rational Cookery*, dated 1831, and published in Kingston in what was then called Upper Canada. This is a crowd-pleaser of a recipe, baked and offered to visitors to historic museums such as Fort York National Historic Site, where the cookies are cut into the shape of 19th-century soldiers. Cut out any shapes that appeal to you.

1 cup (250 mL) butter, softened
1 cup (250 mL) granulated sugar
1 cup (250 mL) fancy molasses
4 cups (1 L) all-purpose flour

2 tbsp (30 mL) ground ginger
1 tsp (5 mL) each baking soda, allspice,
    cinnamon and nutmeg
½ tsp (2 mL) each cloves and salt

LINE 2 RIMLESS baking sheets with parchment paper, or grease them.

In a large bowl, beat the butter and sugar until fluffy; beat in the molasses.

In a separate bowl, whisk together the flour, ginger, baking soda, allspice, cinnamon, nutmeg, cloves and salt. In three additions, stir the dry ingredients into the molasses mixture, stirring until the dough is smooth. Divide the dough into 2 discs; wrap and chill until firm, about 30 minutes. (MAKE-AHEAD: Refrigerate the discs in an airtight container for up to 5 days. Let warm to room temperature before rolling.)

On a well-floured work surface, roll the dough, 1 disc at a time, to ¼-inch (5 mm) thickness. Cut out shapes—rounds, gingerbread people, stars, teddy bears—and arrange a scant 1 inch (2.5 cm) apart on the prepared baking sheets. Reroll scraps.

Bake in the centre of a 350°F (180°C) oven until slightly darkened underneath and just firm to the touch, about 10 to 12 minutes. Let cool on the baking sheets for 3 minutes. Transfer to racks to cool. (MAKE-AHEAD: Store in an airtight container at room temperature for up to 10 days or freeze for up to 1 month.)

Fort York Shrewsbury Cakes

Makes about 48 cookies

....

ELIZABETH: I first tasted these crisp cookies at Fort York National Historic Site, where I am part of a group of volunteer historic cooks led by Bridget Wranick and Mya Sangster. There is always a historically appropriate treat for visitors touring the 1826 officers' mess kitchen, and very often it's a platter of these lovely caraway seed–flavoured small cakes (or, as we would call them now, cookies). Fort cooks are sticklers for accuracy and source all the recipes from 18th- and early 19th-century cookbooks—recipes that the mess's original cooks would have known and used.

Shrewsbury cakes come from *The London Art of Cookery* by John Farley (published in 1800), but there are also versions of these rolled sugar cookies in other cookbooks of the period, some flavoured with mace and cinnamon, others with sack (sherry) or orange-blossom water.

....

1 cup (250 mL) butter, softened
1 cup (250 mL) superfine sugar
1 medium egg

2 tsp (10 mL) caraway seeds
2½ cups (625 mL) all-purpose flour

LINE 2 RIMLESS baking sheets with parchment paper, or grease them.

In a large bowl, beat the butter and sugar until light. Beat in the egg, then the caraway seeds. Stir in the flour a third at a time to make a firm dough. Divide into quarters; flatten each into a disc. Wrap and refrigerate until firm, about 30 minutes.

On a lightly floured surface, roll out each disc to a scant ¼-inch (5 mm) thickness. With a cookie cutter, cut out rounds, each about 2 inches (5 cm) in diameter. Arrange on the prepared baking sheets about 1 inch (2.5 cm) apart. Reroll scraps.

Bake in the centre of a 350°F (180°C) oven until golden brown on the underside, about 8 to 12 minutes. Let cool on the baking sheets for 2 minutes; transfer to racks to cool. (MAKE AHEAD: Layer between waxed paper in an airtight container and store at room temperature for up to 5 days or freeze for up to 1 month.)

Nova Scotia Oatcakes

Makes about 48 oatcakes

....

A FAMILIAR PART of a bread basket in Nova Scotia is a wee stack of oatcakes. Not what would normally be called cake, but rather a crisp, oat-y cracker, oatcakes are something very delicious to hold in one hand while the other busies itself with spooning up a bowl of soup or trimming cheese to go on top of the oatcake. This recipe is an homage to all the Maritime oatcakes we have enjoyed, not forgetting the ones at Timmie's, consumed with pleasure in the company of Heather Mackenzie, former executive director of the association Taste of Nova Scotia and our guide to much of the province's best food and drink.

....

3 cups (750 mL) large-flake rolled oats
1½ cups (375 mL) all-purpose flour
½ cup (125 mL) packed brown sugar
½ tsp (2 mL) baking soda

½ tsp (2 mL) salt
1 cup (250 mL) cold butter, cubed
½ cup (125 mL) ice water

LINE 2 RIMLESS baking sheets with parchment paper, or grease them.

In a large bowl, whisk the oats, flour, sugar, baking soda and salt. Add the butter, tossing to coat the cubes with the dry ingredients. Using a pastry blender, work the butter into the oat mixture, pressing and blending until the butter is evenly distributed. (It takes more energy to incorporate the butter into the dry ingredients because of the rolled oats.)

While drizzling water over the oat mixture, toss the mixture with a fork until all the water has been used and it is possible to press the ragged mixture into a ball. Divide the ball in half and press each half into a flat rectangular shape.

Working with one rectangle of dough at a time, on a lightly floured surface, roll out the dough to a ¼-inch (5 mm) thickness and a 12- × 9-inch (30 × 23 cm) rectangular shape. With a pizza cutter, and using a ruler as a guide, cut the dough into 3-inch (8 cm) squares. Cut each square on a diagonal, into 2 triangles. Arrange on the prepared baking sheets, leaving a scant 1 inch (2.5 cm) between the triangles.

Bake in the centre of a 350°F (180°C) oven until firm to touch and golden brown on the bottom and the edges, about 15 minutes. Let cool on the baking sheets for about 2 minutes. Transfer to racks to cool completely. Store, layered with waxed paper, in an airtight container at room temperature for up to 5 days, in the freezer for up to 1 month.

NOTE
One of the blessings of these oatcakes is that you roll the dough only once. If, however, you are in love with round oatcakes, roll out the dough to the same thickness and cut out rounds. You will need to reroll the scraps, but the tally at the end will still be about 48 oatcakes, each about 2¼ inches (5.5 cm) in diameter.

Cookie-Press Short Shortbread

Makes about 5 dozen cookies, depending on size

EVER SINCE THE 19th century, when Scottish settlers started bringing us recipes for this rich butter cookie, shortbread has appeared on Canadian holiday trays of fancy cookies and little cakes. Always containing butter, sugar and flour, it has many variations. *Pictured (top) with Thimble Cookies (page 288).*

MARILYN SHORT: This recipe has been made by the women in our family (and now Asher, my son) every Christmas since 1920 and maybe even before that. I named it "short shortbread" as a bit of a play on words because my mother, Joyce Loudon Short, made it and because it is the shortest (most buttery, melt-in-your-mouth) shortbread I have ever eaten. Using a cookie press (see Note), it is also the easiest cookie anyone will ever make. Over the years, I added a little more butter to make this recipe even shorter.

2 cups (500 mL) salted butter
¾ cup (175 mL) icing sugar

½ cup (125 mL) cornstarch
2½ cups (625 mL) all-purpose flour

IN A LARGE bowl, using a wooden spoon, cream together the butter, icing sugar and cornstarch until light and fluffy. Gradually stir in the flour. Do not chill.

Using a cookie press, press the dough into festive shapes onto ungreased rimless baking sheets. Decorate with silver balls or coloured sugar.

Bake in the centre of a 300°F (150°C) oven until the bottoms are light golden, 20 minutes for small cookies and 25 for larger ones. (MAKE-AHEAD: Store in an airtight container for up to 1 week or freeze for up to 1 month.)

NOTE
A cookie press is a gadget into which you pack dough and press to extrude various shapes directly onto a baking sheet.

VARIATION: Rolled Shortbread Cookies
Increase the flour to 3½ cups (875 mL) and chill overnight. Roll to ¼-inch (5 m) thickness. With floured cookie cutters, cut into desired shapes and place on ungreased baking sheets. Decorate as desired, and place in the centre of a 325°F (160°C) oven. Immediately reduce the temperature to 275°F (140°C) and bake until firm and golden on the bottom, about 20 minutes.

Thimble Cookies

Makes about 24 cookies

. . . .

THIS RECIPE FOR thimble cookies (also called thumbprint cookies or Swedish tea rings) comes from Marilyn Short. "I still use this recipe for jam-filled cookies every Christmas, working from an old card written in my grandmother's script. We called my grandmother 'Lil' because she thought 'Grandma' sounded old and Chris, my sister, couldn't pronounce 'Hilda' when she was small. Love the old-fashioned feel—imagine having a thimble around the house—and the taste!" *Pictured on page 287.*

. . . .

½ cup (125 mL) butter, softened
¼ cup (60 mL) packed brown sugar
1 large egg, separated

1 cup (250 mL) sifted cake-and-pastry flour
¾ cup (175 mL) finely chopped walnuts
strawberry or raspberry jam

LINE 2 RIMLESS baking sheets with parchment paper or lightly grease them.

In a large bowl, cream the butter; add the sugar and beat until light and fluffy. Stir in the egg yolk and beat well. Gradually stir in the flour until the dough is smooth.

Shape into 1-inch (2.5 cm) balls.

In a small bowl, slightly beat the egg white. Roll each ball in the egg white, then in the walnuts; place on the prepared baking sheets, 2 inches (5 cm) apart. With a floured thimble or the end of a wooden spoon handle (or just your thumb), make a depression in the centre of each cookie.

Bake in the centre of a 325°F (160°C) oven for 5 minutes. Remove from the oven and make the depressions again; repair sides of the cookies if necessary. Bake until set, 10 to 12 minutes longer. Remove to a rack and fill each depression with some of the jam. (MAKE-AHEAD: Layer with waxed paper in an airtight container and store at room temperature for up to 1 week or freeze for up to 1 month.)

Mocha Shortbread Bars

Makes about 25 bars

....

CHRISTMAS WOULD NOT be Christmas for Monica Gray if there were no mocha shortbread bars in her cookie tin. This is one of the recipes Monica has baked for years, and it's handwritten into her keepsake recipes ledger. There's an elusive crunch to these bars; people are always surprised to find out the crunch is actually ground coffee—freshly ground, that is.

....

1 cup (250 mL) butter, softened
½ cup (125 mL) icing sugar
2 tsp (10 mL) each strong liquid coffee
  and vanilla extract
¼ tsp (1 mL) almond extract

2⅓ cups (575 mL) all-purpose flour
1 tbsp (15 mL) each unsweetened cocoa
  and ground coffee beans
¼ tsp (1 mL) salt
¼ cup (60 mL) granulated sugar

LINE 2 RIMLESS baking sheets with parchment paper, or grease them.

In a bowl, beat the butter with the sugar until fluffy. Beat in the liquid coffee, vanilla and almond extract.

In a separate bowl, whisk together the flour, cocoa, ground coffee and salt. Stir half of the dry ingredients at a time into the creamed mixture.

Divide the dough in half. On a sheet of waxed paper, shape each half into a long rectangle, 2 inches (5 cm) wide and 1 inch (2.5 cm) high. Wrap and chill until firm, about 1 hour. Cut into slices a scant ½ inch (1.25 cm) thick.

Arrange on the prepared baking sheets, about 1 inch (2.5 cm) apart. Bake in the centre of a 350°F (180°C) oven until firm and slightly darkened on the bottom, about 20 minutes.

Sprinkle the sugar into a shallow bowl. As soon as the bars are cool enough to handle, press them, one at a time, on all sides into the sugar. Let cool on a rack. (MAKE-AHEAD: Store in an airtight container at room temperature for about 1 week, or freeze for up to 1 month.)

Mocha-Hazelnut Nanaimo Bars

Makes 32 bars

THIS POPULAR LAYERED bar appeared suddenly in the 1950s not only in newspapers, but also in charity cookbooks such as the *Women's Auxiliary to the Nanaimo Hospital Cook Book* (1952), in which there were three such recipes, as well as the *British Columbia Women's Institute's Centennial of British Columbia Cookbook* (1958). Realizing how popular this cookie bar was, the test kitchens of several food companies developed various versions of it. After all, who can resist a bar that has a chewy chocolate base, a creamy flavourful centre and yet more chocolate in its luscious topping?

BASE

1½ cups (375 mL) graham cracker crumbs
1 cup (250 mL) flaked, unsweetened coconut
½ cup (125 mL) finely chopped toasted
  hazelnuts (filberts)*
⅔ cup (150 mL) butter
⅓ cup (75 mL) unsweetened cocoa
¼ cup (60 mL) granulated sugar
1 tbsp (15 mL) instant coffee granules
1 large egg, lightly beaten

FILLING

2 cups (500 mL) icing sugar, divided
¼ cup (60 mL) butter, softened
1 tbsp (15 mL) instant coffee granules

MOCHA TOPPING

2 tbsp (30 mL) butter
1 tbsp (15 mL) instant coffee granules
4 oz (125 g) semisweet chocolate,
  coarsely chopped

*To toast hazelnuts, spread them out on a baking sheet and place in a 350°F (180°C) oven until darkened slightly and fragrant, 5 to 8 minutes. Immediately enclose in a clean tea towel and rub the hot hazelnuts until most of the skins are removed.

BASE → Line an 8-inch (2 L) square cake pan with parchment paper, or grease it.
   In a large bowl, stir together the crumbs, coconut and hazelnuts; set aside.
   In a saucepan, heat together the butter, cocoa, sugar and coffee granules over low heat, stirring, until the butter is melted. Remove from the heat; whisk in the egg. Stir into the crumb mixture until well mixed. Press into the prepared pan; bake in the centre of a 350°F (180°C) oven for 10 minutes. Let cool on a rack.

FILLING → In a bowl, beat half of the icing sugar with the butter. Mix the coffee granules with 2 tbsp (60 mL) water until dissolved; beat into the butter mixture along with the remaining icing sugar. Spread over the cooled base.

CONTINUED . . .

MOCHA TOPPING → In a heatproof bowl over a saucepan of hot (not boiling) water, melt the butter with the coffee granules; add the chocolate and stir until melted and smooth. Spread over the filling. Refrigerate until the chocolate is firm, about 2 hours. Let stand at room temperature for 5 minutes to soften slightly before cutting into bars. (MAKE-AHEAD: Layer the bars between sheets of waxed paper in an airtight container and store in the refrigerator for 1 week or freeze for up to 1 month.)

NOTE
Always taste nuts before you use them to make sure they are fresh, and store them in the freezer to ensure they keep fresh.

VARIATION: In-the-Beginning Nanaimo Bars
Early Nanaimo bars contained custard powder in the filling and relied on only vanilla for flavouring. So for an original taste, omit the coffee throughout and substitute walnuts for the hazelnuts. For the filling, cream 2 tbsp (30 mL) custard powder and 1 tsp (5 mL) vanilla into the butter and half the icing sugar. Then gradually blend in 3 tbsp (45 mL) milk alternately with the remaining icing sugar.

VARIATION: Raspberry Nanaimo Bars
Substitute walnuts for the hazelnuts. Substitute 2 tbsp (30 mL) seedless raspberry jam for the coffee granules in the base, 2 tbsp (30 mL) raspberry liqueur for the coffee granules and water in the filling and 1 tbsp (15 mL) raspberry liqueur for the coffee granules in the topping.

Turtle Brownies

Makes 16 squares

ROSE: This recipe has been a favourite one and adapted by others ever since I created it for *Rose Murray's Comfortable Kitchen Cookbook.* A very easy brownie batter, when not fully baked, is covered with pecans and a quick caramel sauce (as Turtles candy is), baked a few minutes longer and sprinkled with chocolate chips for a decadent treat no one can resist.

BROWNIES

1 cup (250 mL) butter, in bits

4 oz (125 g) unsweetened chocolate, coarsely chopped

1¾ cups (425 mL) granulated sugar

4 large eggs, well beaten

1 tsp (5 mL) vanilla

1¼ cups (300 mL) all-purpose flour

½ tsp (2 mL) salt

TOPPING

½ cup (125 mL) whipping cream

½ cup (125 mL) packed brown sugar

¼ cup (60 mL) butter

1½ cups (375 mL) pecan halves

1 cup (250 mL) chocolate chips

BROWNIES → In the top of a double boiler or a large stainless steel bowl over hot (not boiling) water, melt the butter with the chocolate. Remove from the heat and stir in the sugar until well combined. Stir in the eggs and vanilla. Gradually add the flour and salt, stirring well after each addition.

Pour into a greased 13- × 9-inch (3.5 L) baking pan; bake in the centre of a 400°F (200°C) oven for 10 minutes. (The batter will not be totally cooked but should be set enough to add the topping.)

TOPPING → Meanwhile, in a small saucepan, combine the cream, sugar and butter; bring to a boil and boil for 2 minutes.

Sprinkle the partially baked base with the pecans; drizzle evenly with the caramel syrup. Bake until golden but not browned, 8 to 10 minutes.

Remove from the oven; sprinkle with the chocolate chips. Let them melt slightly for 1 to 2 minutes; swirl with a kitchen knife so that some caramel and nuts show through. Let cool on a rack. Cut into squares. (MAKE-AHEAD: Layer the squares between sheets of waxed paper in an airtight container and store in the refrigerator for 1 week or freeze for up to 1 month.)

Puckery Lemon Squares

Makes 32 squares

ELIZABETH: A couple of Decembers ago, Alison Fryer (manager of the Cookbook Store in Toronto), Dawn Woodward (creator of Evelyn's Crackers) and Liz Driver, Nettie Cronish, Rose and I (all cookbook authors and food writers) were pitted against each other for the best Canadian dessert in a contest organized by the Royal Ontario Museum.

The contest, to be judged by audience response, was in two parts. First, the pitch. We gave eloquent, impassioned pitches: Alison for lemon squares, Dawn for apple tarts with maple sugar in Red Fife pastry, Liz for carrot pudding, Nettie for cocoa oat bars, Rose for fruitcake and I for butter tarts. Second: the tasting, with all the dishes prepared by the chefs at the ROM according to our recipes.

Guess what won! The lemon squares. While nothing satisfies my sugar cravings more effectively than butter tarts, I'm going to heaven for an eternity of nibbling lemon squares.

Alison's recipe is adapted from one that was published decades ago, in the now out-of-print *Stars Desserts* cookbook. In Alison's words: "Whilst everyone pitched for desserts that included Canadian ingredients, I opted to go for a Canadian favourite when it comes to taste, lemon."

BASE
1½ cups (375 mL) all-purpose flour
½ cup (125 mL) icing sugar
¾ cup (175 mL) cold butter, cubed

FILLING
6 large eggs
2¾ cups (675 mL) granulated sugar
1 cup + 2 tbsp (250 mL + 30 mL)
    fresh lemon juice
½ cup (125 mL) all-purpose flour
3 tbsp (45 mL) icing sugar

BASE → Line a 13- × 9-inch (3.5 L) metal cake pan with parchment paper. In a large bowl, whisk together the flour and icing sugar; cut in the butter until the mixture is crumbly and holds together when pressed. Press evenly onto the bottom of the prepared pan.

Bake in the centre of a 325°F (160°C) oven until evenly golden and firm to the touch, about 25 minutes. Remove from the oven and reduce the heat to 300°F (150°C).

FILLING → Meanwhile, in a large bowl, whisk together the eggs and sugar until smooth. Whisk in the lemon juice, then the flour. Pour over the hot crust.

Bake until the filling is set and does not jiggle when the pan is gently wiggled, about 30 to 40 minutes. Let cool to room temperature; refrigerate until cold. (MAKE-AHEAD: Cover and store in the refrigerator for up to 3 days.) Cut into squares. Dust with the icing sugar.

Dream Bars

Makes 32 squares

....

WHETHER THESE SWEET treats are called bars, squares or slices, they are a delicious culinary tradition that blossomed in the 1950s and have remained popular ever since. This recipe, from Jean Morris, has its origins in community cookbooks.

....

BASE
1½ cups (375 mL) all-purpose flour
½ cup (125 mL) packed brown sugar
½ tsp (2 mL) salt
¾ cup (175 mL) butter

FILLING
2 large eggs
1½ cups (375 mL) packed brown sugar

2 tbsp (30 mL) all-purpose flour
½ tsp (2 mL) baking powder
1 tsp (5 mL) vanilla
1 cup (250 mL) chopped walnut
    or pecan halves
1 cup (250 mL) unsweetened
    shredded coconut
½ cup (125 mL) sliced candied cherries
icing sugar (optional)

BASE → Line a 13- × 9-inch (3.5 L) metal cake pan with parchment paper or grease it.

In a large bowl, whisk together the flour, sugar and salt. With a pastry blender, cut in the butter, working until the mixture is moist and crumbly. Press evenly into the bottom of the prepared cake pan. Bake in the centre of a 350°F (180°C) oven until pale gold, about 10 minutes.

FILLING → Meanwhile, in a large bowl using a mixer, beat the eggs until foamy; beat in the sugar, flour, baking powder and vanilla. Mix in the walnuts, coconut and cherries. Scrape onto the base. Bake until the top is golden brown, firm when gently touched and the filling has come away from the edges of the pan, about 25 to 30 minutes. Let cool on a rack. (MAKE-AHEAD: Cover and store in the refrigerator for up to 5 days or wrap in heavy-duty foil, place in an airtight container and freeze for up to 2 weeks.) Dust with icing sugar, if desired. Cut into squares or bars.

VARIATION: Ginger Macadamia Dream Bars
Use chopped macadamia nuts or slivered almonds instead of the walnuts and ¼ cup (60 mL) diced candied ginger instead of the cherries.

Date Squares

Makes about 24 squares

ALSO KNOWN AS matrimonial bars (so named, this is a guess, because dates lead to weddings), these crumble-bottom-and-top squares remain a top choice in coffee shops and bake sales. And that's something, given the tsunami of chocolate confections today. Perhaps date squares seem to be a healthier choice, what with all those flaky oats and fibre-rich dates. Or maybe dates—that inexpensive dried fruit—are something you can always keep on hand, hence use to make date squares more often. Truth is, date squares have earned their place in the panoply of Canadian treats because they taste good—just the right combo of chewy and smooth, tart and sweet. Do try them, warmed up, with a scoop of vanilla or *dulce de leche* ice cream.

FILLING

4 cups (1 L) chopped pitted dates
  (1 lb/500 g)
¾ cup (175 mL) granulated sugar
2 tsp (10 mL) grated lemon zest
¼ cup (60 mL) fresh lemon juice
2 cups (500 mL) water

CRUMBLE LAYERS

2½ cups (625 mL) large-flake rolled oats
1¼ cups (300 mL) all-purpose flour
1 cup (250 mL) packed brown sugar
1 tsp (5 mL) baking soda
1 tsp (5 mL) cinnamon
¼ tsp (1 mL) salt
1 cup (250 mL) butter, softened

FILLING → Line a 9-inch (2.5 L) metal cake pan with parchment paper or grease it.

In a medium saucepan, stir the dates with the sugar, lemon zest and juice and the water. Let stand for 30 minutes. Bring to a boil; reduce the heat and simmer, stirring often, until the dates soften and the filling thickens enough to mound firmly on a spoon, about 12 to 15 minutes. Set aside to cool.

CRUMBLE LAYERS → Meanwhile, in a large bowl, whisk together the oats, flour, sugar, baking soda, cinnamon and salt. Add the butter, and with a pastry blender, work the butter into the dry ingredients until the mixture is crumbly and moist. Press half of the crumbs into the bottom of the prepared pan, making an even layer. Spread the filling over the base, and crumble the remaining oats mixture over the top. Press lightly.

Bake in the centre of a 350°F (180°C) oven until the topping is golden, about 40 minutes. Let cool on a rack until the filling is firm, about 6 hours. (MAKE-AHEAD: Cover and store at room temperature for up to 4 days. Or divide into sections or squares, wrap with heavy-duty foil, place in an airtight container and freeze for up to 1 month.)

Preserves

Seville Orange Marmalade

Makes about 18 cups (4.5 L)

ELIZABETH: While the first marmalade recipes I tried were indeed good, it was with this recipe that marmalade reached its perfection, in simplicity of method, reliable results and the finest blend of strips of peel, clear jelly, bitter orange flavour and sweetness. My friend the artist Elizabeth Barry shared with me her recipe, one handed down by her marmalade-making father, then a retired major in the British army. Flash forward a decade or two: I recommend the recipe to friends Blandford and Marja Gates, who then, on a visit to a new friend, Elizabeth Barry, rave about the marmalade they have just made. "I must get that recipe," Elizabeth comments. "I love marmalade, but I haven't made any in years." Such pleasure I had in giving her back her very own recipe. (See Preserving Pointers, page 301.)

8 Seville oranges, unpeeled (4 lb/2 kg)   16 cups (4 L) water
2 lemons   15 cups (3.75 L) granulated sugar

SCRUB THE ORANGES and lemons in warm soapy water; rinse well. Trim the stem ends and any blemishes. Cut in half; squeeze the juice through a sieve set over a bowl.

Cut an 8-inch (20 cm) square of double-thickness cheesecloth. Pile the seeds and any membranes dislodged from the peel onto the cheesecloth; bring up the sides. Enclosing the seeds loosely, tie the pouch firmly at the top. Place in a large pot; pour in the juice.

On a board, cut the orange and lemon halves into thin strips. Add the strips to the pot. Add the water.

Bring to a simmer over medium heat. Simmer, stirring and pressing the seed bag often, until the peel is so tender it turns to mush when pressed, about 2½ to 3 hours. Remove the seed bag, and when cool enough to handle, press any juices back into the pot. Discard the bag. The mixture should measure 15 cups (3.75 mL). If more, continue simmering; if less, add water to make up the difference. Divide into 3 batches of 5 cups (1.25 L) each.

In a large preserving pan or Dutch oven, stir together one of the batches with 5 cups (1.25 L) of the sugar; bring to a boil, stirring. Boil hard, stirring constantly until the marmalade is thickening and bubbles noisily and the setting point has been reached.

Pour into hot preserving jars, leaving ¼-inch (5 mm) headspace. Seal with prepared discs and rings. Boil in a boiling-water canner for 10 minutes. Remove jars and let cool on rack. Repeat with remaining sugar and batches.

> **NOTE**
> Making marmalade can take up a whole day. A worthwhile day, but sometimes a marmalade maker just runs out of time. Try this. Once the peel and water has cooked down to 15 cups (2.75 L), divide into batches and refrigerate for up to 5 days.

PRESERVING POINTERS

Here's how to ensure that your jams, relishes, pickles and marmalade will keep safely for a year.

Preparing Jars and Equipment

We recommend using glass or stainless steel bowls and stainless steel pans with heavy bottoms when preserving.

Use proper preserving jars, the ones that are available in supermarkets and hardware stores. Check that any jars you're reusing are chip and crack free. Each time you use a jar, you require a new disc (lid). Jar rings or bands, if they are not bent or rusted, last a few trips through the canner. Have them handy. Before sealing the jars, warm the discs (lids) in a bowl of barely hot water.

Using a Boiling Water Canner

Heat the jars before filling them with preserves. Fill a boiling-water canner two-thirds full of hot water; add clean, empty jars upside down on the rack in the canner. Cover and bring to a simmer, timing this process so the jars are hot and ready to fill when the preserve is finished. With canning tongs, remove the jars, drain well and set them upright on a tray.

When you are filling the jars with preserves, use a funnel and small metal cup or ladle, and fill up to the headspace level recommended in each recipe. For chunky preserves, run a plastic knife down the inside of the jars to press out any air bubbles. Adjust the headspace level if necessary. Wipe the jar rim, if needed. Centre a disc on top of the jar and screw on a jar ring or band until you meet resistance, tightening without forcing (a.k.a. "fingertip tight").

Place the jars upright on the rack in the canner. Lower the rack; add more boiling water if needed, to come up 1 inch (2.5 cm) above the top of the jars. Cover the canner; bring to a boil, timing the processing time from this point.

Turn off the heat, remove the lid from the canner and let the boiling subside, about 5 minutes.

continued . . .

Preparing preserves for storage

Using canning tongs, transfer the jars to a rack or folded towel to cool, about 1 day. Check that the discs have snapped down, i.e., are well sealed. If, by chance, one of your jar discs did not seal (the disc will be curved up, not down), refrigerate the jar and use the contents within 3 weeks.

Wipe and label the jars. Remove the jar rings or bands if desired. Store in a cool, dry and dark place.

Testing for setting point

Before boiling up a jam or marmalade, chill two small plates in the freezer. As the preserve thickens, start testing for setting point. Remove the preserve from the heat. Drop a small spoonful onto a plate, tilt the plate slightly and let it cool. Press the blob with a finger. If the surface wrinkles, the preserve is set. If the preserve is still too liquid (doesn't wrinkle), return the preserve to the heat and the plate to the freezer.

Test every few minutes, using the coldest plate, until preserve sets.

Strawberry Jam

Makes about 8-cup (2 L)

WE VENTURE TO say that strawberry jam is Canada's most spread-on-toast preserve. But making jam is not an everyday sort of cooking—preserving has its own challenges to master. Take the set, for example. For a jam to set so it mounds on a spoon, the fruit needs to contain pectin. Alas, strawberries, while full of sheer strawberry-ness and vividly red, are weak in this gelling element. You can, nonetheless, make a soft-set jam by the traditional method of boiling fruit and sugar with a little lemon juice, but the fresh flavour of strawberries gets lost in the long boil needed for the jam to even thicken. One way to keep the very essence of strawberry without this long boil is to use commercial pectin made from citrus fruits. Light pectin crystals, available in supermarkets during harvest months, produce the brightest, clearest taste, a light set and a decidedly not-too-sweet preserve. Sublime on toast. (See Preserving Pointers, page 301.)

12 cups (3 L) whole in-season
   strawberries, hulled
1 pkg (49 g) light fruit pectin crystals

4½ cups (1.125 L) granulated sugar, divided
2 tbsp (30 mL) fresh lemon juice

POUR THE BERRIES, 4 cups (1 L) at a time, into a large wide and heavy-bottomed saucepan or Dutch oven. Crush with a potato masher. Repeat with 2 more layers of berries and mashing process. You should have 6 cups (1.5 L) crushed berries.

In a small bowl, combine the pectin crystals with ¼ cup (60 mL) of the sugar. With a long wooden spoon, stir into the berries.

Bring to a boil over high heat, stirring constantly. Stir in the remaining sugar. Bring back to a full rolling boil, one that foams and spurts and can't be stirred down. (Now you know why we specified a long wooden spoon.) Set the timer and boil hard for 1 minute. Remove from the heat. Stir in the lemon juice; let the jam settle. With a metal spoon, skim off any foam.

Pour into hot preserving jars, leaving ¼-inch (5 mm) headspace. Seal with prepared discs and rings. Boil in a boiling-water canner for 10 minutes. Remove jars and let cool on a rack.

> **VARIATION:** Vanilla Strawberry Jam
> Make as directed in the main recipe, replacing the lemon juice with 2 tsp
> (10 mL) vanilla extract. Add the extract just before filling the jars.

Ruby Port Cranberry Sauce

Makes about 3¾ cups (925 mL)

....

ELIZABETH: This chunky, almost whole-berry cranberry sauce is so good with freshly roasted turkey or any poultry, or spooned overtop cold turkey in day-after sandwiches. I like to make a few batches every Christmas, one for the Christmas Day Baird-and-Davis-families-with-friends dinner, one for gifts and a double batch for the Women's Auxiliary Bazaar (which supports research and care at the amazing SickKids Hospital), where the jars are snapped up at a premium price. (See Preserving Pointers, page 301.)

....

½ navel orange
1 cup (250 mL) water (approx)
1¾ cups (425 mL) granulated sugar

1 cup (250 mL) ruby port
4 cups (1 L) fresh or frozen cranberries

PARE OFF THE outer orange rind (the zest) from the half orange; cut into strips, each about the size of half a toothpick. Squeeze the juice from the orange; set aside. Simmer the zest in the water in a small covered saucepan until the zest is very tender, about 15 minutes. Pour into a large measuring cup. Add the reserved orange juice and enough water, if needed, to make 1 cup (250 ml).

Pour this orange-flavoured water into a large heavy-bottomed saucepan or Dutch oven. Stir in the sugar and port. Bring to a boil, reduce the heat slightly and boil for 3 minutes, stirring regularly. Add the cranberries; bring back to a boil. Reduce the heat to a slow simmer, stirring the sauce from time to time, and gently so as to keep as many of the berries whole as possible. Simmer until the sauce thickens, about 10 minutes.

Pour into hot preserving jars, leaving ¼-inch (5 mm) headspace. Seal with prepared discs and rings. Boil in a boiling-water canner for 10 minutes. Remove jars and let cool on a rack.

Peach and Apricot Chutney

Makes about 8 cups (2 L)

SWEET, TANGY AND pretty in a jar, this summer chutney is a fine complement to cheese and grilled or roasted pork and chicken. We recommend letting chutneys and relishes mellow for a few weeks before opening a jar. The flavours blend beautifully with a little time. (See Preserving Pointers, page 301.)

4 cups (1 L) sliced, peeled and pitted
   peaches
4 cups (1 L) sliced pitted apricots
2 cups (500 mL) diced onions
3 cups (750 mL) packed brown sugar
2 cups (500 mL) golden raisins
1½ tsp (7 mL) brown or yellow
   mustard seeds

1½ tsp (7 mL) coarse salt (sea, kosher
   or pickling)
½ tsp (2 mL) each ground cinnamon,
   coriander, cumin, and turmeric
½ tsp (2 mL) curry powder or paste,
   or additional cinnamon
¼ tsp (1 mL) ground cardamom
¼ tsp (1 ml) cayenne
2 cups (500 mL) real apple cider vinegar

COMBINE ALL THE ingredients in the order listed in a large Dutch oven or heavy-bottomed pot. Bring to a boil over medium heat, stirring often. Reduce the heat and simmer, uncovered, until no longer watery and a rich golden colour, about 1½ to 2 hours. Stir regularly, especially as the chutney thickens.

Pour into hot preserving jars, leaving ½-inch (1.25 cm) headspace. Seal with prepared discs and rings. Boil in a boiling-water canner for 10 minutes. Remove jars and let cool on a rack.

Fruit Chili Sauce

Makes about 8 cups (2 L)

....

JENNIFER GRANGE IS assistant manager of the Cookbook Store in Toronto. One of her family's favourite relishes is this chili sauce, with chunks of peaches and pears along with the anticipated tomatoes, celery and onions. (See Preserving Pointers, page 301.)

....

8 cups (2 L) peeled and chopped tomatoes

2 cups (500 mL) diced celery

2 cups (500 mL) peeled, pitted
   and diced peaches

2 cups (500 mL) peeled, cored
   and diced pears

2 cups (500 mL) chopped sweet red pepper

1 cup (250 mL) chopped sweet green pepper

1 cup (250 mL) diced onions

2 cups (500 mL) white vinegar

1 tbsp (15 mL) salt, pickling if desired

½ cup (125 mL) whole pickling spice

2 cups (500 mL) granulated sugar

IN A LARGE heavy-bottomed saucepan, stir together the tomatoes, celery, peaches, pears, red and green peppers and onions. Stir in the vinegar and salt. Tie the pickling spice in a loose pouch of double thickness cheesecloth. Submerge in the pan.

Bring to a boil, then reduce the heat to simmer. Cook at this gentle boil, uncovered, stirring often, until the tomatoes have broken down and the mixture has thickened, about 2 hours. Stir in the sugar; bring back to a gentle boil. Cook, stirring often, until the sauce thickens again, about 30 minutes. Remove the pickling spice, pressing any juices back into the sauce.

Pour into hot preserving jars, leaving ½-inch (1.25 cm) headspace. Seal with prepared discs and rings. Boil in a boiling-water canner for 20 minutes. Remove jars and let cool on a rack.

TOMATOES

RITA DEMONTIS, food editor of the *Toronto Sun:* Growing up in downtown Toronto meant summers wrapped around the Italian garden. My mother's garden brimmed with multi-hued roses, lilac bushes and lily-of-the-valley, but was also a place where one reached for sustenance. We had string beans, zucchini, onions, cucumber, rhubarb and tomatoes. Lots and lots of tomatoes.

Different types, the big, fat beefsteak, balls of bright orange for fresh salads and the slightly elongated romas, on which my mother kept a careful watch. Those babies were being groomed for that end-of-summer rite known as canning. If there weren't enough garden tomatoes—and there never were—

my parents would dutifully join other like-minded neighbours at the local Italian store and haggle for a couple of bushels to add to their stash.

To be honest, I loathed "tomato making" day—it meant we all had to get up super-early, spend hours scouring and boiling preserving jars and Italian "ginga-rella" bottles that were probably from the First World War and were used and reused throughout the seasons, and generally be on our best behaviour as our parents worked the complicated system of preparing the harvest.

Each tomato had to be scrutinized before being pulverized in this giant hand-cranked machine, and everyone was pressed into service—including the kids. If we didn't help in the garden, there was always a room to be dusted and vacuumed.

I hated the smell and sting of crushed tomatoes on my skin. But I loved the end of the day, when the prepared bottles and jars were placed in a large industrial-size drum, filled with old rags and water, a large fire merrily bringing the water to a boil for a good while before being extinguished and allowed to cool throughout the night, a large towel covering the precious cargo.

And I loved how a couple of pounds of the best of the tomatoes were set aside for dinner. My mother would drop them into boiling water and then plunge them into cold water in order to peel the skin quickly. Then she churned them with a hand press to separate the pulp from the seeds and put a large pot on the stove with a generous dollop of olive oil, a sweet onion, quartered, and several large leaves of fresh basil. Then she added the tomato pulp and simmered the whole thing with a bit of salt and freshly ground black pepper. At just the right moment, my mother would crack a good dozen fresh eggs into the mix, gently coddling them in the sauce, so that they poached to a smooth, buttery perfection. The idea was to keep the yolk a bit runny—and when it spilled into the savoury tomato sauce the taste was pure heaven. We hungrily sopped up the mixture with big chunks of crusty bread, using one last piece to clean the plate. It was the end of a most perfect day in my mother's garden.

Chunky Mustard Pickles

Makes 10 cups (2.5 L)

THIS IS A brilliant golden pickle, its sauce as puckery as its chunks of cauliflower and pearl onions. (See Preserving Pointers, page 301.)

PICKLE

1 small head cauliflower (about 1 lb/500 g)
2 cups (500 mL) peeled pearl pickling onions (about 10 oz/300 g)
12 small cucumbers (about 12 oz/375 g)
1 large sweet red pepper
½ cup (125 mL) coarse pickling salt
6 cups (1.5 L) hot water

SAUCE

3 cups (750 mL) granulated sugar
3 cups (750 mL) white or apple cider vinegar
1 tbsp (15 mL) each mustard seeds and celery seeds
½ cup (125 mL) all-purpose flour
¼ cup (60 mL) dry mustard
1½ tsp (7 mL) turmeric
¾ cup (175 mL) cold water

PICKLE → Trim the cauliflower and cut out its coarse core. Cut into bite-size florets. Place in a large bowl with the onions. Trim the ends off the cucumbers and cut into ¼-inch (5 mm) slices. Remove the stem and membranes and seeds from the pepper; cut into ½-inch (1.25 cm) squares. Add the cucumbers and pepper to the cauliflower and onions. All together there should be 12 cups (3 L) vegetables. A few more of one and a little less of another is not serious as long as they measure a full 12 cups (3 L).

In a large measuring cup or bowl, combine the salt and water, stirring until the salt dissolves. Let cool and pour over the vegetables. Place a plate over the vegetables to keep them submerged. Let soak at cool room temperature for 12 to 24 hours. Drain, rinse and soak again, this time covered with cold water, for 30 minutes. Drain and rinse thoroughly; set aside.

SAUCE → In a large saucepan, combine the sugar, vinegar, mustard seeds and celery seeds. In a bowl, whisk together the flour, dry mustard and turmeric. Whisk in the cold water to make a smooth paste. Whisk the paste into the vinegar mixture, whisking until the paste is completely dissolved. Bring to a boil over medium heat, whisking often, until the sauce is thick and smooth. Stir in the vegetables and bring back to the boil, stirring regularly; boil for 1 minute.

Pour into hot preserving jars, leaving ½-inch (1.25 cm) headspace. Seal with prepared discs and rings. Boil in a boiling-water canner for 10 minutes. Remove jars and let cool on a rack.

Must-Make Tomato Salsa

Makes about 8 cups (2 L)

ELIZABETH: This salsa uses ingredients available in most grocery stores in harvest season and adds just the right amount of zing to burgers, nachos, grilled cheese, and lots more. Feel free to add even more zing by including the seeds from the jalapeño peppers. I adapted this recipe years ago from a publication by Bernardin (the preserving equipment company) and it has won many devoted fans, who have made this salsa the "must-make" preserving item every fall. (See Preserving Pointers, page 301.)

8 cups (2 L) chopped peeled tomatoes
    (8 to 10 large, 4½ lb/2 kg)
4 cups (1 L) diced cubanelle* or sweet
    banana peppers
2 cups (500 mL) diced onions
1 cup (250 mL) each diced sweet red and
    yellow peppers
1 cup (250 mL) diced seeded jalapeño
    peppers (see Note)
4 large cloves garlic, minced
1 can (5½ oz/156 mL) tomato paste
2 tbsp (30 mL) granulated sugar

1 tbsp (15 mL) salt
2 tsp (10 mL) each sweet paprika
    and oregano
½ tsp (2 mL) ground cumin
2 cups (500 mL) cider vinegar
⅓ cup (75 mL) finely chopped fresh
    coriander (cilantro)

* Cubanelle peppers are long, sweet green
    peppers known for their flavour and lack
    of bitterness.

IN A LARGE Dutch oven or heavy-bottomed saucepan, stir together all the ingredients in the order listed. Bring to a boil over medium heat, stirring often.

Reduce the heat to low and simmer until the liquid thickens and the salsa mounds on a spoon, about 1 to 1½ hours.

Pour into hot preserving jars, leaving ½-inch (1.25 cm) headspace. Seal with prepared discs and rings. Boil in a boiling-water canner for 20 minutes. Remove jars and let cool on a rack.

NOTE
Be wary when handling hot peppers such as jalapeños. Wear rubber gloves when seeding and cutting the pepper and avoid touching yourself. A rub of the eyes will bring stinging and tears, and skin contact anywhere else an unpleasant burning sensation.

Tomato Butter

Makes about 8 cups (2 L)

....

ROSE: When I volunteered at the Tom Thomson Memorial Art Gallery in Owen Sound, I often found myself in the kitchen making food for fundraisers or gallery openings along with my good friend Ev Penny. When I asked Ev for a favourite recipe, her daughter, Barb Taylor, responded with this irresistible tomato butter—more like a savoury jam than a chili sauce—along with her own memories of the preserve. (See Preserving Pointers, page 301.)

....

BARB TAYLOR: Mom, now 94, asked me to help her answer your request for a treasured recipe. The enclosed one has been a constant in our family through all the years, and now we kids have picked up the habit. In the fall, the Penny house smelled lovely with the pickle simmering on the stove, and for most of those years growing up, the recipe was called "chili sauce." Then one day Mom announced that the proper name was "tomato butter," so we smartened up and that's what we call it now. We find it delicious with meat (especially beef), macaroni and cheese or cheese sandwiches.

....

20 cups (5 L) peeled and coarsely chopped ripe tomatoes (about 12 lb/6 kg)

2 cups (500 mL) white vinegar

4 cups (1 L) packed brown sugar

1 tsp (5 mL) each salt, cloves, cinnamon and allspice

¼ tsp (1 mL) cayenne

IN A LARGE heavy-bottomed saucepan, combine the tomatoes with the vinegar; cover and refrigerate overnight.

Reserving 2 cups (500 mL) of the juice, drain the tomatoes well. In the saucepan, stir together the reserved juice, the brown sugar, salt, cloves, cinnamon, allspice and cayenne. Bring to a boil and add the tomatoes. Simmer, uncovered, until thick and dark, about 3 hours, stirring often, especially near the end of the cooking.

Pour into hot preserving jars, leaving ½-inch (1.25 cm) headspace. Seal with prepared discs and rings. Boil in a boiling-water canner for 15 minutes. Remove jars and let cool on a rack.

Hot Dog Relish

Makes about 8 cups (2 L)

ELIZABETH: Many years ago, my friend Sandy Hall, a home economist, shared the recipe for this deliciously tangy and very colourful relish, which had come from her mother-in-law, Wynn Hall. This is the go-to condiment for hot dogs, burgers and frankly, any cold or cured meat that can do with a little relish. Thank you, Wynn Hall. You have added pep to many a meal, with many more to come. (See Preserving Pointers, page 301.)

9 cups (2.25 L) unpeeled finely chopped
zucchini (8 to 9 medium, 3 lb/1.5 kg)
3 onions, finely chopped
2 sweet red peppers, finely chopped
¼ cup (60 mL) coarse pickling salt
2½ cups (625 mL) granulated sugar
1½ cups (375 mL) cider or white vinegar

2 tsp (10 mL) dry mustard
1 tsp (5 mL) celery seeds
½ tsp (2 mL) freshly ground black pepper
½ tsp (2 mL) turmeric
1 tbsp (15 mL) cornstarch
1 tbsp (15 mL) water

IN A LARGE bowl, stir together the zucchini, onions, red peppers and salt. Let stand at room temperature for 1 hour, stirring occasionally. Drain in a large sieve. Rinse in a large bowl of cold water; drain again, pressing out the moisture.

In a large heavy-bottomed saucepan or Dutch oven, combine the sugar, vinegar, mustard, celery seeds, pepper and turmeric; bring to a boil. Add the drained vegetables; bring back to a boil, stirring often. Reduce the heat and simmer, stirring often, until the vegetables are tender and the liquid is slightly syrupy, about 15 minutes.

In a small bowl, stir together the cornstarch and water until the cornstarch is dissolved; stir into the relish. Simmer, stirring, until the liquid clears and thickens, about 5 minutes.

Pour into hot preserving jars, leaving ½-inch (1.25 cm) headspace. Seal with prepared discs and rings. Boil in a boiling-water canner for 15 minutes. Remove jars and let cool on a rack.

Crunchy Bread-and-Butter Pickles

Makes about 5 to 6 cups (1.25 to 1.5 L)

EVERYONE'S FAVOURITE PICKLE is an easy one to make and for decades, the winner to serve on sandwiches. (See Preserving Pointers, page 301.)

2 lb (1 kg) small cucumbers (about
   5 inches/11 cm long), unpeeled
1 cup (250 mL) thinly sliced white onion
3 tbsp (45 mL) pickling salt

1½ cups (375 mL) white vinegar
1¼ cups (300 mL) granulated sugar
1½ tsp (7 mL) mustard seeds
1 tsp (5 mL) celery seeds

WASH CUCUMBERS WELL, brushing them clean; then dry with a towel. Thinly slice (a scant ¼ inch/5 mm). You should have about 8 cups (2 L) slices.

In a large bowl, combine the cucumbers, onion and salt. Stir gently to help dissolve the salt. Cover with a thick layer of ice cubes. Cover the bowl and let it stand in a cool place for 4 hours. Drain in a colander and rinse well with cold running water.

In a large heavy saucepan, stir together the vinegar, sugar, mustard seeds and celery seeds. Bring to a boil over high heat, stirring to dissolve the sugar. Add the cucumber mixture and bring back to a boil.

Spoon the cucumber mixture into hot preserving jars and immediately ladle the simmering liquid overtop, leaving ½-inch (1.25 cm) headspace. Seal with prepared discs and rings. Boil in a boiling-water canner for 10 minutes. Remove jars and let cool on a rack.

NOTE
If desired, you can add strips of thinly sliced sweet peppers to the vegetable mixture. Also optional, ½ tsp (2 mL) turmeric added with the seeds will give a golden appearance to the pickles.

Pickled Baby Beets

Makes 5 to 6 cups (1.25 to 1.5 L)

ROSE: I still remember, growing up on a farm, what a joy it was to go down to the cellar and see the huge table that held all the preserved wealth from the garden. The colours alone were magic. Bright yellow peaches in clear syrup, green pickled cucumbers and beans, orange pickled carrots and brilliant jewel-coloured rosy beets—these were just a few of the many jars, or as we used to say, "sealers." Pickled beets were often considered one of the vegetables you could serve in the dead of winter when fresh vegetables were not abundant. I still use them this way—they're more of a main star than just a condiment. (See Preserving Pointers, page 301.)

3 lb (1.5 kg) small red beets
1 tsp (5 mL) black peppercorns
½ tsp (2 mL) whole cloves
1½ cups (375 mL) white or cider vinegar

¾ cup (175 mL) packed brown sugar
¾ cup (175 mL) water
1 tbsp (15 mL) pickling salt

IN A LARGE saucepan, cook the beets in boiling salted water until just tender when pierced with a fork, 20 to 30 minutes. (The time will depend on how long the beets have been harvested.) Drain well and when cool enough to handle, slip off the skins. (The fresher the beets are, the easier it is to peel them.) Halve or quarter any beets that are not tiny.

Divide the peppercorns and cloves among three hot 2-cup (500 mL) preserving jars. Tightly pack the cooked beets in the jars to within ¾ inches (2 cm) from the rim.

Meanwhile, in a saucepan, combine the vinegar, sugar, water and salt; bring to a boil. Boil for 2 or 3 minutes and pour over the beets in the jars, leaving ½-inch (1.25 cm) headspace. Using a plastic knife, press out any air bubbles and adjust the headspace if necessary. Seal with prepared discs and rings. Boil in a boiling-water canner for 30 minutes. Remove jars and let cool on a rack.

Candy and Drinks

Maple Walnut Fudge

Makes 36 pieces

....

ELIZABETH: It was Emily Richards who made this creamy, nutty fudge on *Canadian Living Cooks* on Food Network Canada. She says, and I agree, that beating it with a stand mixer is a good idea—a little lazy when you consider how many calories you will ingest from sampling—but still a good idea. On the other hand, beating fudge by hand is a long-standing Canadian tradition. After all, fudge was a Canadian favourite generations before stand mixers. Emily recommends a candy thermometer to monitor the boiling and cooling stages.

....

½ cup (125 mL) walnut halves

2 cups (500 mL) packed brown sugar

1 cup (250 mL) whipping cream

½ cup (125 mL) dark maple syrup

2 tbsp (30 mL) butter

pinch baking soda

2 tsp (10 mL) vanilla

LIGHTLY BUTTER THE sides and bottom of an 8-inch (2 L) metal cake pan, and the inside of a medium saucepan with a heavy bottom. Set the pan aside.

Toast the walnut halves on a small baking sheet in a 350°F (180°C) oven until darkened and fragrant, about 8 minutes. Let cool; chop coarsely.

Into the buttered saucepan, measure the sugar, whipping cream, maple syrup, butter and baking soda. Stirring constantly, cook over medium heat until the sugar has dissolved, the butter melted and the mixture has come to a boil. Continue boiling, without stirring, until a few drops of the syrup dropped into a glass of cold water forms a soft ball that can be removed and pressed flat, or until the candy thermometer registers the soft ball stage at 238°F (114°C), about 8 minutes. If beating the fudge with a stand mixer, pour the fudge mixture into the mixer's bowl; if beating by hand, pour into a wide heatproof bowl.

Meanwhile, fill the sink or a large heatproof bowl with cold water that comes up 2 inches (5 cm). Set the bowl of fudge right into the cold water and, without stirring, let the fudge mixture cool to lukewarm, about 100°F (38°C). Add the vanilla; beat until the fudge thickens and loses its gloss, about 8 minutes. Quickly stir in the nuts. Scrape into the buttered pan and smooth the top. Let cool until firm; cut into squares. (MAKE-AHEAD: Layer the fudge with waxed paper in an airtight container and store at room temperature for up to 2 weeks.)

Chocolate Praline Truffle Squares

Makes about 100 truffle squares

WHO HASN'T FALLEN in love with truffles? A crunchy praline gives a surprise contrast to this creamy, smooth truffle mixture that we've spread into a pan to cut into tiny squares. No need to keep your hands cold while you take on the tedious and messy task of rolling the mixture into little rounds. They are lovely served in tiny gold bonbon cups with after-dinner coffee and perhaps a cognac.

½ cup (125 mL) whole hazelnuts (filberts)
½ cup (125 mL) granulated sugar
3 tbsp (45 mL) water
½ cup (125 mL) whipping cream

12 oz (375 g) dark bittersweet chocolate, chopped
3 tbsp (45 mL) Frangelico liqueur, rum or brandy
unsweetened cocoa

TOAST THE HAZELNUTS on a rimmed baking sheet in a 350°F (180°C) oven until fragrant, about 5 minutes. Enclose and rub in a clean tea towel to remove most of the skins. Grease the sheet and return the nuts close together in a single layer.

In a small heavy saucepan, combine the sugar and water; cook over medium heat until the sugar dissolves. Increase the heat to medium-high; boil, without stirring, until a rich caramel colour, 5 to 8 minutes. Immediately pour over the hazelnuts; let cool completely and break into pieces. Finely chop the pieces in a food processor. (MAKE-AHEAD: Place in an airtight container and store at room temperature for up to 5 days.)

In a small saucepan, bring the cream to a boil; remove from the heat and whisk in the chocolate until melted completely. Whisk in the liqueur until smooth. Stir in the praline. Spread the mixture in a plastic wrap–lined 8-inch (2 L) square cake pan. Cover and refrigerate for at least 3 hours or overnight.

Holding the plastic wrap, carefully remove the chocolate mixture from the pan and place on a cutting board; peel off the wrap. With a long sharp knife, cut into squares about ¾ inch (2 cm). Sift the cocoa lightly overtop. (MAKE-AHEAD: Refrigerate in an airtight container for up to 2 weeks or freeze for longer storage.)

Rich Butter Toffee

Makes about 80 pieces

....

JUDY SHULTZ, author and former food editor of the *Edmonton Journal:* My father, Eugene Godin, made this rich butter toffee in a cast-iron frying pan, using a tin of Reindeer brand condensed milk plus half a pound (!) of butter. It was notably sticky, totally delicious and absolutely forbidden to kids with fillings in their teeth. The temptation was too much for me, and I probably lost more than one filling to my dad's toffee. The salt is my own addition, and it's optional. I like a flaky finishing salt, like Maldon, sprinkled lightly over the cooling toffee.

....

HERE'S EUGENE'S RECIPE, adapted by Ottawa chef Kathleen Stanier. Kathleen added whipping cream to compensate for the larger amount of condensed milk that was in a can of Reindeer brand condensed milk compared to what's in today's cans. We recommend using a deep saucepan you can clip a candy thermometer onto—something that Judy's father, with years of experience with his cast-iron frying pan, would never have needed.

....

1 can (300 mL) sweetened condensed milk
2 cups (500 mL) packed brown sugar
1 cup (250 mL) whipping cream
⅓ cup (75 mL) corn syrup

1 cup (250 mL) butter, cut into bits
1½ tsp (7 mL) crystal sea salt, such as
   Maldon (optional)

BUTTER THE INSIDE of a 9-inch (2.5 L) square baking pan; or line it with buttered parchment paper for easy removal.

In a deep medium saucepan, combine the condensed milk, sugar, cream and corn syrup. Bring to a boil over medium heat, stirring occasionally at first and more frequently as the mixture becomes hot. As soon as the mixture begins to boil, add the butter a few pieces at a time, stirring constantly. Continue stirring until the mixture reaches the firm ball stage, 250°F (120°C) on a candy thermometer, about 25 to 35 minutes. Immediately pour the mixture into the prepared pan. Sprinkle with sea salt if desired.

Allow to cool completely until very firm, about 3 hours. Remove from the pan and cut into small squares with a hot knife (run the knife under hot water; then dry completely). (MAKE-AHEAD: Layer with waxed paper in an airtight container and store at room temperature for up to 1 month.)

Caramel Corn

Makes about 10 cups (2.5 L)

....

FIONA MAYCOCK: Today we take for granted the availability of popcorn in specialty and grocery stores . . . something unheard of in the early Fifties in my Scottish family. My first experience enjoying the treat was on a visit to family friends, the McMichaels, who lived in Kleinburg at their home Tapawingo (later to become the McMichael Gallery). They had trimmed a huge Christmas tree with popcorn garlands and laid out bowls of the white nuggets for eating. My mother asked how it was made and soon after was trying to duplicate the recipe at home. It went well, except for the fact that no one had told her to put a lid on it! Popcorn was everywhere but in the pot! We had a good laugh over that incident. However, the next time the lid went on, and it was delicious. Many years later I found this wonderful recipe for caramel popcorn.

....

2 tbsp (30 mL) canola oil*
1 cup (250 mL) popping corn
3 cups (750 mL) whole almonds (with skins)
1 cup (250 mL) packed brown sugar
½ cup (125 mL) butter

½ cup (125 mL) corn syrup
1 tsp (5 mL) vanilla
¼ tsp (1 mL) baking soda

*If using a hot air popcorn popper, omit the oil.

IN A LARGE saucepan, heat the oil over medium heat. Add the popcorn and stir well to coat. Cover the pan and, shaking it often, cook until the corn stops popping, about 5 minutes. (You should have about 10 cups/2.5 L popped corn.) In a large roasting pan (a foil turkey roaster is excellent), combine the popped corn and the almonds.

Meanwhile, in a small, heavy-bottomed saucepan, combine the brown sugar, butter and corn syrup. Bring to a boil and boil gently for 3 minutes. Remove from the heat and stir in the vanilla and baking soda. Pour the hot mixture over the corn mixture and stir well to combine. Bake in a 250°F (120°C) oven for 1 hour, stirring every 15 minutes. Cool in the pan, stirring occasionally. (MAKE-AHEAD: Store for 5 minutes or until completely devoured! Seriously, store at room temperature in an airtight container for up to 2 days.)

Peanut Brittle

Makes about 2 lb (1 kg)

NUT AND DRIED fruit barks have come and gone, but peanut brittle has remained a favourite, especially when made with Canadian-grown fresh peanuts. Sturdy and long keeping, it's easily tucked into a gift package.

2 cups (500 mL) granulated sugar
1 cup (250 mL) corn syrup
1 cup (250 mL) water

2 cups (500 mL) peanuts
2 tbsp (30 mL) butter
¾ tsp (4 mL) baking soda

LIGHTLY OIL 2 rimmed baking sheets.

In a large heavy-bottomed saucepan, combine the sugar, corn syrup and water. Stirring constantly, heat until the sugar dissolves. Then, stirring frequently, cook to the soft ball stage (238°F/114°C). Continue cooking over medium-high heat, without stirring, until the mixture reaches the soft crack stage (280°F/137°C). Stir in the peanuts and butter. Continue cooking to the hard crack stage (300°F/150°C), stirring occasionally.

Remove from the heat; immediately stir in the baking soda and mix thoroughly. Quickly pour the candy onto the prepared baking sheets. As the candy cools, stretch it out by lifting and pulling the edges. Loosen from the sheets as soon as possible and turn the candy over. When it cools, break it into chunks. (MAKE-AHEAD: Layer with waxed paper in an airtight container and store at room temperature for up to 1 week.)

Canadiana Lemonade

Makes about 8 to 10 servings

....

LEMONADE — NOTHING COOLS so magically on a hot summer's day as a glass of the real elixir of summer. Frozen concentrates and powders are readily available in the 21st century, but Canadians still recognize the cooling benefits of real lemonade. Canadiana Lemonade was published in *The Canadian Housewife's Manual of Cookery* in 1861: "Cut in very thin slices, three lemons, put them in a basin, add half a pound of sugar, either white or brown; bruise all together well, add a gallon of cold water, and stir. It is then ready." Canadiana Lemonade is a signature summer drink served at Campbell House Museum, Toronto.

....

3 lemons

1 cup (250 mL) granulated sugar

6 to 8 cups (1.5 to 2 L) cold water

ice cubes

SLICE THE LEMONS thinly; remove any seeds. Place the slices in a large bowl. With a potato masher, broad wooden pestle or the bottom of a mug, press down on the lemon slices to release their juices. Add the sugar; continue mashing vigorously to extract the juice, release flavour from the peel and dissolve the sugar.

Pour in 6 cups (1.5 L) of the water and ice; stir well. Taste, adding water or ice if desired. Pour into glasses, including some lemon slices in each glass.

SPARKLING HONEY AND GINGER LEMONADE

Makes 10 servings

1 cup (250 mL) liquid honey

1 cup (250 mL) lemon juice (see Note)

1 tbsp (15 mL) finely grated fresh ginger

4 cups (1 L) water

1 lemon, thinly sliced

4 cups (1 L) chilled sparkling water,
soda water or water

ice cubes

IN AN AIRTIGHT container, stir together the honey, lemon juice, ginger and water. Refrigerate for at least 4 hours or overnight. Pour into a pitcher; stir in the lemon slices, sparkling water and ice cubes.

NOTE

Lemon juice should be freshly squeezed. Average to large lemons yield a good ¼ cup (60 ml) juice. Before squeezing, roll the lemons firmly on the counter to break down the membranes and yield each lemon's maximum juice.

Mulled Cider

Makes 6 servings

LOOK FOR FRESH apple cider at farmers' markets and roadside apple stands. There's no more flavourful way of warming up beside the fire on a cold, blustery day than with a mug of this spiced cider.

5 cups (1.25 L) apple cider
¼ cup (60 mL) fresh lemon juice
¼ cup (60 mL) packed brown sugar
4 whole cloves

1½-inch (4 cm) piece cinnamon stick
1½-inch (4 cm) piece dry ginger root
nutmeg
cinnamon sticks (optional)

IN A LARGE stainless steel pot, stir together the cider, lemon juice and sugar. Heat the mixture slowly over medium heat to the simmering point.

Meanwhile, tie the cloves, cinnamon stick piece and ginger root together in a piece of cheesecloth. Add the bag to the simmering liquid and heat over low heat for 15 minutes. Remove the spice bag. (MAKE-AHEAD: Prepare the mulled cider to this point up to 4 hours ahead and reheat slowly before serving.)

Serve hot with a sprinkling of nutmeg in each mug of cider and pop a cinnamon stick in each if desired.

VARIATION: Old Stone Fence
Add 3 tbsp (45 mL) rum to each mug of Mulled Cider.

Acknowledgements

THANKS TO—

All those people who were so giving of their recipes and stories. (Names in parentheses indicate the origin of the recipe.)

Julia Aitken
Julian Armstrong
Elizabeth Barry
Donna Bartolini
Neil Baxter
Catherine Betts
John Bishop
Steve Boothby
  (Marion Boothby)
Sharon Boyd
  (Stella Chomut)
Ted Boyd
Michael Bryne
Johanna Burkhard
Campbell House Museum
Rosa Carvalho
Wayson Choy (Mary Low)
Pam Collacott (Ann Searles)
Andrew Coppolino
Susan Cook-Scheerer
Rita DeMontis
Rollande DesBois
Nigel Didcock
  (Jeannine Dubois)
Liz Driver
Dorothy Duncan
Sister Edith Elder
Carol Ferguson
Shannon Ferrier
Rob Firing
Fort York National
  Historic Site

Margaret Fraser
  (Winnifred Fewster)
Alison Fryer
Marja Nevalainen Gates
  (Eila Nevalainen)
Michelle Gelinas
  (Elizabeth McCaffrey)
Jennifer Grange
Monica Gray
Jonathan Gushue
  (James Randel Gushue)
Sandy Hall (Wynn Hall)
Sandra Henderson
Heather Howe
Sharol Josephson
George Kapelos
  (Anna Kapelos)
Eleanor Kane
L'Échaudé Restaurant
Anne Lindsay
  (Marion Elliott)
Dorothy Long
  (Ethel Mary Mann)
James Lorimer
Lucille Lorie
  (Lenore Barrett)
Jennifer Mackenzie
Vince Marcoccio
Fiona Maycock
Dana McCauley
Mary Luz Mejia
Jean Morris
Marie Nightingale
Hannah Pahuta
  (Martha Danes)
Donna Paris (Rosa Altobello)
Eve Penny (Barb Taylor)
Colette Richard

Emily Richards
  (Ortenzia Fata)
Jane Rodmell
Monda Rosenberg
Judy Schultz (Eugene Godin
  and Kathleen Stanier,
  tester)
John Sewell and Liz Rykert
Adell Shneer (Sarah
  Taradash)
Marilyn Short (Hilda Shaw
  Loudon and Joyce Loudon
  Short)
Diane Slimmon
Springridge Farm (John
  and Laura Hughes)
Edna Staebler
Allen Varty
Daiene Vernile (Antonietta
  Caravaggio Vernile)
Daphna Rabinovitch Walters
Vanessa Yeung
  (Millie Yeung)

The creative team at Whitecap, including Theresa Best, Michelle Furbacher, Mark Gardiner, Tracey Kusiewicz, Mauve Pagé, Naomi Pauls, Nick Rundall and the hard-working sales staff.

Elizabeth's husband, George Baird, for 50 years of loving and generous support.

Rose's husband, Kent Murray, for his constant support and tireless proofreading, and her son, Allen Murray, for his computer assistance.

Index